OXFORD WORLD'S CLASSICS

AUTHORS IN CONTEXT

General Editor: PATRICIA INGHAM, University of Oxford
Historical Adviser: BOYD HILTON, University of Cambridge

GEOFFREY CHAUCER

AUTHORS IN CONTEXT examines the work of major writers in relation to their own time and to the present day. The series provides detailed coverage of the values and debates that colour the writing of particular authors and considers their novels, plays, and poetry against this background. Set in their social, cultural, and political contexts, classic books take on new meaning for modern readers. And since readers, like writers, have their own contexts, the series considers how critical interpretations have altered over time, and how films, sequels, and other popular adaptations relate to the new age in which they are produced.

PETER BROWN is Professor of Medieval English Literature at the University of Kent at Canterbury. He has taught at the Universities of Exeter, Connecticut, and California at Los Angeles, and at Virginia Polytechnic Institute and State University where he was a Fulbright Scholar. He has published widely on Chaucer and other aspects of medieval culture and has edited *A Companion to Chaucer* (2000) and *Companion to Medieval English Literature and Culture* c.*1350*–c.*1500* (2007).

AUTHORS IN CONTEXT

OXFORD WORLD'S CLASSICS

━━

PETER BROWN

Geoffrey Chaucer

━━

OXFORD
UNIVERSITY PRESS

Great Clarendon Street, Oxford OX2 6DP

Oxford University Press is a department of the University of Oxford.
It furthers the University's objective of excellence in research, scholarship,
and education by publishing worldwide in

Oxford New York

Auckland Cape Town Dar es Salaam Hong Kong Karachi
Kuala Lumpur Madrid Melbourne Mexico City Nairobi
New Delhi Shanghai Taipei Toronto

With offices in

Argentina Austria Brazil Chile Czech Republic France Greece
Guatemala Hungary Italy Japan Poland Portugal Singapore
South Korea Switzerland Thailand Turkey Ukraine Vietnam

Oxford is a registered trade mark of Oxford University Press
in the UK and in certain other countries

Published in the United States
by Oxford University Press Inc., New York

© Peter Brown 2011

The moral rights of the author have been asserted
Database right Oxford University Press (maker)

First published as an Oxford World's Classics paperback 2011

British Library Cataloguing in Publication Data

Data available

Library of Congress Cataloging in Publication Data

Data available

Typeset by Glyph International, Bangalore, India
Printed in Great Britain
on acid-free paper by
Clays Ltd, St Ives plc

ISBN 978-0-19-280429-7

1 3 5 7 9 10 8 6 4 2

ACKNOWLEDGEMENTS

My first thanks go to Andrew McNeillie, who invited me to write this book. Howard Bowman, Stefania Ciocia, Noi Connell, Kay Donaghay, Hugh Dyson, David Ellis, Angela Gallego-Sala, Marion Glasscoe, Angela Hurworth, Tom and Vone Meadley, Liz Rideal, Martin Rimmer, Paul Scott, Katie Sokolowska, and Gerlinde Wilberg all showed a continuing interest in its development, and provided help and support. A version of the first chapter benefited from discussions with postgraduate students and academic colleagues at the research seminar of the Canterbury Centre for Medieval and Early Modern Studies. MA students at the same Centre, taking a seminar on 'Chaucer and Gower', helped to sharpen some of my ideas. The School of English at the University of Kent generously provided me with a term of research leave in order to complete the first draft of *Geoffrey Chaucer*. It has been a pleasure to work with Judith Luna in preparing the book for publication, and Patricia Ingham as general editor has provided much valuable guidance and advice. Staff at the British Library in London, St Deiniol's Library in Hawarden, and the Templeman Library at the University of Kent have been unfailingly courteous and knowledgeable. To Michael Bennett go my thanks for reading the final draft and saving me from a number of blunders. Any errors that remain are entirely of my own making.

Canterbury

For Oliver and Louisa

CONTENTS

LIST OF ILLUSTRATIONS

A CHRONOLOGY OF GEOFFREY CHAUCER

Life and Works	*Historical and Cultural Background*
1321	Death of Dante
1327	Edward III crowned
*c.*1330	Gower born; Wyclif born
1335–41	Boccaccio, *Il Filostrato* and *Teseida*
1337	Beginning of Hundred Years War; birth of Froissart
*c.*1340 Birth	
1341	Petrarch made laureate at Rome
1346	Battle of Crécy
1347–9 Father (John) king's deputy butler at port of Southampton	
1348–9	Black Death
1351	Statute of Labourers
early 1350s	Boccaccio writes *Decameron*. Machaut, *Jugement dou roy de Navarre*
1356	Battle of Poitiers. King John of France taken and held in 'captivity' for four years at the English court
1357 Enters service of Countess of Ulster as a page	
1359–60 Chaucer a *valettus* in company of Prince Lionel; taken prisoner at Réthel, near Reims, and ransomed	
1360	Treaty of Brétigny with France
1360s–80s	Langland, *Piers Plowman*
1361	Second visitation of the plague. Froissart arrives in England to serve in Queen Philippa's household. Black Prince marries Joan of Kent
1362	Black Prince becomes Prince of Aquitaine
1363	Statute on Diet and Apparel
*c.*1365 Marries Philippa, a member of the queen's household and daughter of Paon de Roet	

Life and Works	Historical and Cultural Background
1366 Diplomatic mission to Navarre. Father dies. Mother remarries	
1367 Granted life annuity by Edward III as squire of king's household	Richard II born
*c.*1367 Birth of son, Thomas	
1368 Abroad on the king's service	Death of Blanche, Duchess of Lancaster. Oton de Grandson, Savoy poet, at the English court
1368–9	Hoccleve born
1369 In France on campaign with John of Gaunt	Death of Queen Philippa
1369–73	War renewed; French regain much of the territory ceded at Brétigny
1370 Letters of protection for going overseas on the king's service	Lydgate born
1371	John of Gaunt marries Constance of Castile
1371–3 Squire of the king's chamber before 1372 *Book of the Duchess*	
1372 Philippa Chaucer granted annuity from John of Gaunt for service in the household of Constance	
1372–3 Visits Genoa and Florence on the king's business	
1373	Boccaccio's lectures on Dante
1374 Appointed Controller of Customs; granted lifelong lease of a dwelling at Aldgate; granted a pitcher of wine a day for life by the king; given an annuity of £10 from John of Gaunt	Death of Petrarch
1375	Death of Boccaccio
1376 Payment for 'secret business of the king'	Good Parliament. Death of the Black Prince
1377 Various missions overseas	Death of Edward III and accession of Richard II. First poll tax. Death of Guillaume de Machaut
*c.*1378–80 *House of Fame*	
1378 Visits Lombardy on the king's business; appoints John Gower as his attorney	Beginning of papal schism
1379	Second poll tax

Life and Works	Historical and Cultural Background
1380 Released by Cecilia Chaumpaigne from the charge of *raptus*. Birth of son, Lewis	Third poll tax
*c.*1380–2	*Parliament of Fowls*
early 1380s	Gower, *Vox clamantis*
1380s	First version of Wycliffite translation of the Bible
1381 Mother (Agnes) dies	Peasants' revolt
1382 Appointed Controller of the Petty Custom in Port of London	Wyclif's teachings condemned at Blackfriars; Richard marries Anne of Bohemia
*c.*1382–6 *Boece* and *Troilus and Criseyde*	
1384	Death of Wyclif
*c.*1385	The first tribute to Chaucer's poetic powers, by Eustache Deschamps
1385–9 Justice of the Peace for Kent	
*c.*1385–7 *Legend of Good Women*	
1386 Appointed knight of the shire for Kent. Gives up Aldgate lease. Retires from controllership of customs. Wife admitted to the fraternity of Lincoln cathedral. Testifies in Scrope–Grosvenor trial.	Wonderful Parliament
1386–8	Appellant crisis
1387 Death of Philippa Chaucer	
*c.*1387 Begins *Canterbury Tales*	
1388 Surrenders his annuities	Merciless Parliament. Usk executed
1389	Richard II reaches his majority
1389–91 Clerk of the King's Works	
1390 Oversees constructions of the Smithfield tournament lists	
1390–3	Gower, *Confessio Amantis*
*c.*1391 *Treatise on the Astrolabe*	
1394 Annuity renewed by Richard II	Death of Anne of Bohemia
1394–5 Revises prologue to *Legend of Good Women*	
1395–6 Receives a gown of scarlet from Henry Bolingbroke	
1396	Truce with France. Richard marries Isabella of France. John of Gaunt marries Katherine Swynford, Chaucer's sister-in-law

	Life and Works	Historical and Cultural Background
1397	Granted a tun of wine a year by Richard	Richard's revenge on the Appellants. Second Wycliffite translation of the Bible
1398		Banishment of Henry Bolingbroke
1399	Takes lease on property in precincts of Westminster Abbey. Annuity supplement from Henry IV	John of Gaunt dies. Deposition of Richard. Bolingbroke succeeds as Henry IV
1400	Death. Buried in Westminster Abbey	Murder of Richard II

ABBREVIATIONS

A. CHAUCER'S WORKS

Astr	*A Treatise on the Astrolabe*	MLTE	Epilogue to the Man of Law's Tale
BD	The *Book of the Duchess*		
Bo	*Boece*	MLTI	Introduction to the Man of Law's Tale
ClP	The Clerk's Prologue		
ClT	The Clerk's Tale	NPT	The Nun's Priest's Tale
CYT	The Canon's Yeoman's Tale	PardP	The Pardoner's Prologue
		PardT	The Pardoner's Tale
FrankT	The Franklin's Tale	ParsP	The Parson's Prologue
GP	The General Prologue to the *Canterbury Tales*	ParsT	The Parson's Tale
		PF	The *Parliament of Fowls*
HF	The *House of Fame*	Ret	Chaucer's Retraction
KnT	The Knight's Tale	RT	The Reeve's Tale
LGW	The *Legend of Good Women*	SNT	The Second Nun's Tale
		SqT	The Squire's Tale
Mel	The Tale of Melibee	*TC*	*Troilus and Criseyde*
MerchP	The Merchant's Prologue	Th	The Tale of Sir Thopas
MerchT	The Merchant's Tale	ThP	Prologue to the Tale of Sir Thopas
MillP	The Miller's Prologue		
MillT	The Miller's Tale	WBP	The Wife of Bath's Prologue
MkT	The Monk's Tale		
MLT	The Man of Law's Tale	WBT	The Wife of Bath's Tale

B. JOURNALS AND SERIALS

ChauR	*Chaucer Review*	*PMLA*	*Publications of the Modern Language Association of America*
EETS	Early English Text Society		
NS	new series	*SAC*	*Studies in the Age of Chaucer*
OS	original series		

CHAPTER I

THE LIFE OF GEOFFREY CHAUCER

GEOFFREY CHAUCER came from a family of vintners. His great-grandfather was a taverner of Ipswich, his grandfather a London wine merchant, and his father a freeman of the city of London and sometime deputy to the king's chief butler. When Geoffrey was born *c.*1340 it was probably in that ward of the city of London known as the Vintry, close to the quays on the north side of the river Thames. It was where many wine merchants owned substantial houses equipped with capacious cellars for holding their stock. The Chaucer house was on the north side of Thames Street. Chaucer's mother, Agnes Copton, was a property owner in her own right, so her son entered a mercantile world that was relatively well-to-do.

The place or places of Chaucer's early education are not clear. He may have been a pupil at the nearby almonry school at St Paul's, where he would have learnt elementary Latin. There is an equally unproved hypothesis that he attended the Law Courts, which were beginning to function as a kind of unofficial London university. It is more likely that his education beyond elementary level derived from his activities in aristocratic households. The first reliable record, dated 1357, identifies Chaucer as a page (a very lowly position) in the household of Elizabeth, countess of Ulster, when he was in his mid to late teens. Chaucer was the recipient of a 'paltock' (a short, sleeved doublet), a pair of red and black hose, and a pair of shoes.[1]

The duchess's household soon merged with that of her husband and so Chaucer then entered the service of Lionel, earl of Ulster—the second son of the king, Edward III. In 1359–60 he accompanied Lionel in Edward III's great expedition to France (with which England was at war) as a *valettus* or yeoman. Lionel served in a division of the army led by his elder brother, Edward of Woodstock, known since Tudor times as the Black Prince. Chaucer was captured near Rheims, and was ransomed by the king for £16. This expedition was one of the earliest of Chaucer's many journeys overseas. In 1366 he made a diplomatic visit to Spain. In 1372 he travelled to Genoa and Florence, this time with the rank of esquire, as a member of a commercial mission. Its task was to arrange an English port for Genoese merchants, and perhaps to negotiate a loan for the bankrupt English court from an Italian finance house. Other visits to France and Italy, at the behest of the Crown, were variously concerned with marriage or peace negotiations.

In his early twenties, Chaucer had married Philippa Roet, a *domicella* in the queen's household and daughter of a knight of Hainault. Philippa's sister, Katherine Swynford, became John of Gaunt's mistress and eventually his third wife. From the time of their marriage both Chaucer and his wife received an annuity from the king, with the later addition of gifts, including a pitcher of wine daily to Geoffrey. In 1374 Chaucer was also granted a life annuity from Gaunt. Philippa died in 1387, but Chaucer kept the royal gifts flowing. As late as 1397, Richard II granted him a tun of wine yearly, a grant confirmed two years later by Richard's usurper, Henry IV. Chaucer was nothing if not a survivor.

During his thirties, Chaucer was resident in a property above Aldgate, one of the gates into the walled city of London. At this time he was a customs controller, collecting various export duties on wool and other commodities down at the wharves on the Thames riverbank between the Tower of London and London Bridge. It was a condition of Chaucer's appointment that he should perform his duties in person and keep the accounts in his own hand. In this decade (the 1370s) Chaucer was involved in a variety of other activities. He stood bail for a range of royal officials, wealthy merchants, and London citizens. He became the guardian of two Kentish heirs, responsibility for which may have brought him to Canterbury because one heir, Edmund Staplegate, owned property in the city. He was defendant in a plea of trespass and contempt, and two years later (1380) was released from further legal actions concerning the *raptus*—either rape or abduction—of one Cecilia Chaumpaigne.[2]

This eventful period culminated in Chaucer's appointment to two prestigious offices. For four years from 1385, when Chaucer was in his early forties, he was Justice of the Peace for Kent. As such, he was empowered with other commissioners to inquire into various kinds of crime, including trespass, ambush, profiteering, extortion, illegal use of liveries, false weights and measures, and offences of labourers against the labour laws. The sessions might be held at various towns within the shire, including Rochester, Sittingbourne, and Canterbury. Chaucer's fellow-commissioners were members of the gentry, wealthy landowners, knights, members of parliament, and sheriffs of Kent. Then, in 1386, Chaucer was elected by the sheriff of Kent as a knight of the shire to attend parliament. Parliament that year was dubbed the 'Wonderful Parliament' for its decisive actions to curb the authority of Richard II. It secured the dismissal of the lord chancellor, Michael de la Pole, and his impeachment for the misconduct of the war with France and the misuse of monies. Instead, parliament diverted resources towards defences on land and sea.

Between 1389 and 1391, when Chaucer was in his late forties, he enjoyed his most onerous and distinguished royal appointment, as clerk of the works. His responsibilities included the procurement, transport, and storage of building materials, tools, and other resources needed for construction and repair. Chaucer was responsible not just for the fabric but also for the workmen, as his job included finding and paying for the labour. He organized building work at St George's Chapel, Windsor, at the wharf by the Tower of London, at the palace of Westminster, and at Smithfield (where he erected scaffolds for a joust). His activities brought him into contact with the king's master mason, Henry Yeveley, whose wages he paid. Yeveley was the designer of the nave of Westminster Abbey and the nave of Canterbury cathedral. Chaucer's duties as a paymaster made him a target for robbers: within the space of four days in September 1390 he was robbed by highwaymen no fewer than three times, and twice at the same place in Hatcham, Surrey, appropriately named 'le fowle ok'.[3]

For the last two years of his life Chaucer leased a tenement (a small house) in the garden of the lady chapel at Westminster Abbey. It was taken over on his death by his son, Thomas, a wealthy landed gentleman with property in three counties and chief butler to four successive kings. Thomas's own heiress, his daughter, Alice, later became by marriage the duchess of Suffolk. Chaucer also had another son, Lewis, to whom he dedicated his treatise on the astrolabe. The traditional date of his death is 25 October 1400. He was buried in Westminster Abbey as a consequence of his work as a royal official. His supposed remains were exposed and measured in 1889. The coroner estimated that they belonged to a man about five feet six inches high. The tomb now visible, which became the nucleus of 'Poets' Corner', dates from the sixteenth century.

Chaucer's 'Autobiography'

The bulk of the evidence for this brief account of Chaucer's life, to be
elaborated in the chapters that follow, is taken from a compendious
volume of depositions, warrants, audits, and other documents found
in depositories such as the National Archives Office (formerly Public
Record Office) at Kew. They were assembled over many years by a
team of researchers and eventually published in 1966 under the editor-
ship of Martin M. Crow and Clair C. Olson as *Chaucer Life-Records*.
The materials this contains have formed the basis for all subsequent
lives of Geoffrey Chaucer. Occasionally, other documents have come
to light. Taken together, Chaucer's life records provide an exception-
ally vivid and circumstantial account of the working career of a court
official in the second half of the fourteenth century.

But in one major respect, the records are disappointing. They provide no direct information about Chaucer's career as a poet—the very
reason for being interested in his life history in the first place. The
official documents, however intriguing, are no substitute for the diaries and letters with which biographers of more recent writers can
hope to work. The absence of information on Chaucer's literary life is
to be expected: official records are not the place for personal musings;
he lived before the heyday of diaries and private correspondence;
and the role of poet was ancillary to his public activities. Thus, the
objective of the modern biographer, to achieve some kind of vicarious
intimacy with the subject, is not viable because of the nature of the
surviving evidence and because the preconceptions on which that
desire for intimacy is based are alien to the culture in which Chaucer
lived.

In these circumstances, the biographer turns to the second main
body of evidence, Chaucer's writings, in the hope that they will fill the
gap found in the official record. On first encounter they do seem to
provide a lifeline, for Chaucer periodically inserts a vignette, a self-
portrait, a reference to his identity as a poet, that seems to offer the
prospect of a personal history. By this route we learn something of
Chaucer's habits, appearance, and demeanour. The Host, who mas-
terminds the pilgrimage in which Chaucer acts as a reporter, invites
him to make a contribution. Harry Bailly, a 'large man' (GP 753),
observes that Chaucer is portly (at least in later life, when he was
working on the *Canterbury Tales*), for he 'in the waast is shape as wel

as I' (ThP 691–704).[4] He is also cuddly, a 'popet', or little doll, such as any woman would want to embrace. But closeness is balanced by distance, for his expression is 'elvyssh'—other-worldly, or abstracted, or mischievous. Chaucer's absentmindedness is a recurrent motif, as well as his difference and separation from the social group to which he ostensibly belongs. Here, the Host remarks that Chaucer rides looking down at the ground, as if he is searching for a hare, and does not associate himself with the other travellers ('unto no wight dooth he daliaunce [is not sociable]'), although the portraits of the General Prologue suggest plenty of interaction between him and his fellow pilgrims.

On another occasion, recorded in the *House of Fame*, written much earlier in Chaucer's career, his mute self-absorption is such that it produces a dazed expression. After he has finished work and made all his 'rekenynges', instead of seeking recreation he goes home and, 'domb as any stoon', sits with another book until he looks 'fuly das-wed [dazed]' (*HF* 641–60). The commentator here is a loquacious eagle, sent in dream by Jupiter, who has taken pity on Chaucer's attempts to write about love without any direct knowledge of it. So *distrait* does the poet's dedication to books make him that, as well as hearing no news ('tydynges') of love from distant places, he does not even hear the gossip ('neyther that ne this') on his own doorstep, 'of thy verray neyghebores | That duellen almost at thy dores'.

Here, other details of Chaucer's self-portrait begin to emerge. He is industrious and productive, to the point where the Man of Law, when called upon to tell his tale on the road to Canterbury, complains that Chaucer has retold in English so many of the old stories that there are barely any left (MLTI 45–76). If you don't find what Chaucer has said in one book, you will find it in another. Thus a sign of his productivity, and a prominent indicator of his identity, is authorship of books—books which may themselves have their own distinctive appearance. The 'Seintes Legende of Cupide', for example, now known as the *Legend of Good Women*, is to be found in Chaucer's 'large volume'. The text from which he culls material for the *Parliament of Fowls* is in an 'olde boke totorn' (*PF* 110). But Chaucer also presents his books in a kind of inventory, associating himself ever more closely with the act of authorship. The Man of Law mentions an early work, the *Book of the Duchess* ('In youthe he made of Ceys and Alcione'), and lists the contents of the *Legend* according to emblematic details,

as if recollecting manuscript illuminations of saints with their attri-
butes: the 'large woundes wyde | Of Lucresse', the 'swerd of Dido',
the 'teeris of Eleyne', and so on.

The G-prologue to the *Legend of Good Women*, written in Chaucer's
maturity, itself details many of Chaucer's other works, including his
version of the *Romance of the Rose*, *Troilus and Criseyde*, the *House of
Fame*, 'Deth of Blaunche the Duchesse', *Parliament of Fowls*, 'the love
of Palamon and Arcite' (now chiefly known through the Knight's
Tale), others unnamed except by genre—'many an ympne [hymn] . . .
balades, roundeles, vyrelayes'—and translations from Boethius, of
the life of St Cecilia (the Second Nun's Tale), as well as two now lost:
'Of the Wreched Engendrynge of Mankynde' by Pope Innocent III
and 'Orygenes upon the Maudeleyne' (*LGW* G405–20).[5] Chaucer
identifies himself with and by his oeuvre, and is virtually indistinguishable from it. Producing books *is* his life, his work—'he useth
bokes for to make' (G342)—and so much so that, in order to set his
life in order at the end of his days, or so he would have us believe, he
reneges on them. In his retraction to the *Canterbury Tales*, which follows the Parson's Tale—a treatise on sin and redemption—Chaucer
revokes his 'translacions and enditynges of worldly vanitees' (Ret
1084–7), a rubric that includes most of the works now considered to
be his major creations. He names and disowns his magnum opus,
Troilus and Criseyde, and also the *House of Fame*, 'the bok of the XXV.
Ladies', the *Book of the Duchess*, the *Parliament of Fowls*, the *Canterbury
Tales* (at least 'thilke that sownen into [encourage] synne'), a lost 'book
of the Leoun', and 'many another book' that he cannot bring to mind
as well as 'many a song and many a leccherous lay [lyric]'. Asking
Christ to forgive him the sins committed through the authorship of
these works, he now lays claim only to the translation of Boethius and
'othere bokes of legends of seintes, and omelies, and moralitee, and
devocioun'. This is not the Chaucer we have come to know.[6]

Before he penned the retraction, Chaucer's self-portrait is bookish
in a larger sense. It is not just that his own books enlarge his identity
and act as surrogates for it; his identity derives from books by others,
with which he surrounds himself and with which he works. The God
of Love, addressing the poet, declares 'God wot, sixty bokes olde and
newe | Hast thow thyself' (*LGW* G273–4)—a considerable library
for a private individual. They are books full of stories, some of which
Chaucer has overlooked, according to the god: one he recommends is

'a bok, lyth in thy cheste' (G498) which describes the great goodness of Alceste. What does Chaucer do with all these books? He reads them for pleasure—'On bokes for to rede I me delyte' (G30–9)—but he also reveres them in his heart and derives conviction from them through study, although sometimes the world outside is too distracting. 'The joly tyme of May', in particular, is a strong enough lure for him to abandon his books, and then 'Farwel my stodye'.

The contents of the books which so often claim his attention are many and various. The stories are Roman, Greek, Christian, the authors 'Valerye, Titus . . . Claudyan . . . Jerome', Ovid, or the thirteenth-century encyclopedist Vincent of Beauvais (*LGW* G280–310). Chaucer studies them not merely for the pleasures and benefits of reading but rather to undertake a process of assimilation, understanding, and retelling in his own right. It is essentially a process of translation, whether of the more literal variety, as in his fragmentary version of the French *Roman de la Rose*, or in the more general sense of transposition, as when Chaucer renders Boccaccio's tale of Troy, *Il Filostrato*, from the Italian for an English audience as *Troilus and Criseyde*, omitting large sections and introducing new material according to his own agenda.

The assumed role of translator allows Chaucer to sidestep some of the responsibilities of authorship. In the *Legend of Good Women*, the god of Love is angry with its author, seeing him as a 'worm' and 'mortal fo' who hinders his servants with a 'translacyoun' of the *Rose*, in which the pursuit of love is shown to be foolish (*LGW* G241–66). The book is 'an heresye ageyns my lawe' and Chaucer's culpability cannot be denied. The evidence is there 'in pleyn text'. Similarly, he has 'mad in Englysh' the book describing how Criseyde forsook Troilus, thereby drawing attention to the wickedness of women. Speaking in the poet's defence, Queen Alceste points out that Chaucer has not written 'Despit of love' out of his own malice, but rather as a by-product of what other authors, disparagingly called 'old clerkes', have written (G340–52). Such is his dedication to the process of authoring books, she says, that he probably takes little notice of the content of his sources: 'taketh non hede of what matere he take'. Thus the intention to be hostile to Love was not present. He wrote the *Rose* and *Troilus* 'Of innocence, and nyste [did not know] what he seyde'; or else the pieces were commissioned and he had no say—'Or hym was boden make thilke tweye | Of som persone, and dorste it not

withseye'—commissions indicating that he is already well known as
an author, for 'he hath write many a bok er this'.

The idea of Chaucer's sleepwalking his way through the 8,239 lines
of *Troilus*, or of writing them on automatic pilot at the behest of a
patron, is absurd. Chaucer's playfulness about his role as an author is
a significant feature of his self-portrait.[7] It frequently takes the form
of self-deprecation and artful clumsiness or insouciance when (we
suspect) the reverse was the case. The comedy can also turn more
clownish. The eagle in the *House of Fame*, carrying 'Geffrey' high in
the sky 'As lyghtly as I were a larke' (*HF* 546–74), finds that his charge
has become characteristically dazed, this time as a result of astonish-
ment and fear. The bird attempts to bring him to his senses with a
mannish 'Awak!' and 'Geffrey' does revive, but only to be told that his
companion finds him 'noyous for to carye'. There is buffoonery, too,
in the *Canterbury Tales*. Such is Chaucer's girth (no longer is he as
light as a lark, his waist the span of an eagle's talon) that the Host has
to urge the other pilgrims to make sufficient room for him: 'lat this
man have place! | He in the waast is shape as wel as I' (ThP 694–
700)—not that anyone knows who he might be. For the Host's mode
of address indicates that Chaucer as pilgrim, Chaucer the well-known
poet, has become anonymous. It is for the first time, even though the
pilgrimage is by now well under way, that the Host 'looked upon me',
the author of the great work that has given Harry Bailly his very life
and blood and presiding role. The failure of recognition is total:
'What man artow?' is all that the Host can muster. And Chaucer
remains unrecognized. When the Man of Law refers to the well-
known Chaucer he does not allude to the figure on the pilgrimage but
rather to an author outside its frame, someone who might be very
productive but who knows little about metre and 'ryming craftily'
(MLTI 48)—a criticism fully vindicated by the deliberately awful
'drasty rymyng' (Th 930) of pilgrim Chaucer's tale of Sir Thopas,
told at the Host's behest.

Concealed in the japery are some further contours of Chaucer's
profile, of his 'autobiography'. His representation of himself as an
author is not restricted to the private activities of reading, reflecting,
and writing. He also places himself in relation to more public and
social spheres, especially those of patronage and reception. As Queen
Alceste indicates, the behest of others more powerful can be the
impetus for the production of a particular text—a case well illustrated

by the prologue to the *Legend of Good Women* itself. Once the god of Love is somewhat appeased by Alceste, she suggests that the poet should make redress for his unwitting misdemeanours against women 'in the Rose or elles in Crisseyde' (*LGW* G421–76). The god of Love is persuaded by this proposed act of patronage, forgives Chaucer, and surrenders him to Alceste. He kneels to the queen, much as we see supplicant authors kneeling to a patron in the paintings that sometimes preface late medieval vernacular texts. Alceste commends as antidote to the *Rose* and *Troilus* 'a gloryous legende | Of goode women, maydenes and wyves, | That were trewe in lovynge al here lyves; | And telle of false men that hem betrayen'. She commissions, in effect, the *Legend* itself—an act that may well have had its counterpart in an act of patronage Chaucer experienced at the hands of Anne of Bohemia, Richard II's queen: 'And whan this book ys maad, yive it the quene, | On my byhalf, at Eltham or at Sheene' (F496–7).

The commission has arisen because of the ways in which certain of Chaucer's works have been read and understood. According to the god, they have made wise people withdraw from the pursuit of love by showing 'how that wemen han don mis' (*LGW* G266). That may be so, counters Alceste, but when Chaucer was younger he did maintain the god's 'estaat', or status, and the reception of his works was quite different (G400–64). His writings helped the ignorant, 'lewed folk', understand love and 'delyte | To serven yow, in preysynge of youre name'. Chaucer's own defence is that his intention has never wavered. However his works have been understood by his audience, he never thought to commit any infringement of love's laws: 'trewely I wende . . . | Naught have agilt, ne don to love trespas'. In the particular instances of the *Rose* and *Troilus*, he puts a distance between what the authors of his source material might have meant, and what he himself intended, which was to further and nurture truth in love, and warn against falseness and vice by good examples: 'what so myn auctour mente . . . this was my menynge'. The author's role, it seems, is to negotiate and persuade: negotiate meaning out of old books into new ones, and persuade an audience of one's best intentions. The process is volatile, and susceptible to misunderstanding.

At stake here is Chaucer's reputation. From his earliest poetry he represents himself as preoccupied by what his audience might think of him, and what the future might have in store for his fame as a writer. Chaucer is precocious among English poets in framing his identity, however playfully, through his function as an author. Only Thomas Hoccleve, of Chaucer's contemporaries, did anything similar, although self-promotion was a feature of works by French and Italian authors Chaucer knew. In the *House of Fame*, influenced by Dante, 'Geffrey' (*HF* 729) wonders aloud what it means for him to be carried skywards by a messenger from the gods. Is Jove intending to turn him into a star, to 'stellyfye' him (*HF* 583–92)? Thinking, as ever, of literary precedent, he knows that he is not Ganymede, 'That was ybore up, as men rede . . . And mad the goddys botiller'— although 'butler to the gods' might be a plausible outcome, given Chaucer's parentage. And at the very end of his life, in solemn mode, he calls on his listeners and readers, 'alle that herkne . . . or rede' (Ret 1081), in order to address them on his intentions for the *Canterbury Tales*—intentions he acknowledges to have been in large part sinful.

Retraction apart, what Chaucer's reputation is chiefly associated with is the topic of love. He represents himself as a poet dedicated to love, and that is one reason why the Retraction is so shocking. It is precisely his hard-won poetry of love that he abjures. Prior to the Retraction he exults in the role and is assiduous in cultivating it. In the *House of Fame*, the eagle has been sent by Jupiter to show some pity, precisely because 'Geffrey' has 'so longe trewely' served Cupid and Venus, and so attentively, but without reward (*HF* 605–40). In the *Legend*, with the help of Alceste, he has to mount a defence of himself as a poet of love before the god himself. According to the Man of Law, love is Chaucer's topic *par excellence*, so that he threatens to eclipse even his renowned classical forebear: 'For he hath toold of loveris up and doun | Mo than Ovide made of mencioun | In his Episteles, that been ful olde' (MLTI 53–5).

What credence should be given to Chaucer's self-portrait? Is it a purely fictional creation, or does it have some bearing on the identity of its creator? On the one hand it is important to be circumspect, and not confuse the two. Chaucer's poetic persona serves a turn: it is a useful and flexible conceit enabling the development of all sorts of literary strategies—not least that of engaging an audience's attention. On the other hand, a writer's self-portrait, even if found only within the frames of fiction, is evidence of a kind that can to some extent be tested from independent sources. For instance, Chaucer's authorship of the books to which his alter ego lays claim is not in serious doubt. He lists his works much as we now know them and even provides the titles of items now lost that the modern literary scholar would dearly like to find. Further, the differences between the inventories of his works, compiled at different times, allow us to plot the sequence of those compositions that define his poetic career. Thus, the Man of Law's list of Chaucer's works includes the 'Seintes Legend of Cupide', so it postdates the *Legend of Good Women*, which therefore probably precedes the *Canterbury Tales*.

Again, it is evident from what we know of Chaucer's sources that his reading was indeed wide-ranging and voracious, encompassing writings in French, Italian, and Latin as well as English. In addition to the narrative works by the pagan and Christian authors already mentioned, other works used in Latin include the Bible with its commentaries and glosses, Ovid's *Metamorphoses*, bishop Bradwardine on free will and predestination, and Messahalla's treatise on the astrolabe. French works with which he was familiar, other than the *Rose*, included writings by Guillaume de Machaut, Jean Froissart, Eustache Deschamps, and Oton de Grandson. Among the Italian works he read and used were Boccaccio's *Il Teseida* (as well as *Il Filostrato*) and Dante's *Divina commedia*. Bookish Chaucer certainly was, and a translator to boot, whether of Petrarch's Latin tale of Griselda and Boccaccio's Italian version, which became the Clerk's Tale; or of an Italian sonnet by Petrarch as found in *Troilus*; or of a Latin treatise on sin and penitence by Raymond de Pennaforte which he used as a basis for the Parson's Tale. Then again, as any reader of Chaucer's works will bear witness, he is indeed a poet of love. He covers many other themes as well, among which freedom, authority, and identity are important, but the topic of love is recurrent and predominant, whether focused on love between human beings or between God and his creatures. Love is the central issue of the dream visions, the glue that binds together many of the Canterbury stories and that connects them to each other, and the driving force of *Troilus and Criseyde*.

The Early Reception of Chaucer

To some extent, then, the Chaucer we access and verify through reading and studying his works is congruent with the self-portrait he creates. It also finds a measure of corroboration in the comments of his contemporaries and immediate successors.[8] For the French court poet Eustache Deschamps (*c*.1340–*c*.1410) he is indeed a love poet of

the first order, a great Ovid ('Ovides grans') and the god of earthly
love in Albion ('d'Amours mondains Dieux en Albie').[9] In *The
Testament of Love* by Thomas Usk, a writer beheaded for factional
intrigue in 1388, Love praises *Troilus* for its philosophical content
and the assiduous efforts of its author to promote Love's interests:
'evermore hym besyeth and travayleth right sore my name to
encrease'.[10] Venus speaks in a more earthy manner in the *Confessio
Amantis* (*c.*1390) by Chaucer's acquaintance, the lawyer John Gower
(*c.*1340–1408): Chaucer is 'mi disciple and mi poete', 'my owne clerk'
whose ditties and songs, made 'for mi sake', fill the land.[11] Chaucer's
renown as a poet of love has been helped, as Deschamps notes, by his
translation of the *Rose*—translation being, for him, the other dominant feature of Chaucer's poetic identity. As the refrain of Deschamps's
'Autre balade' of *c.*1385 puts it, he is 'Grand translateur, noble
Gieffroy Chaucier'.[12]

The themes of fame and translation are developed by Chaucer's
disciple, the prolific John Lydgate (*c.*1370–*c.*1451), a Benedictine
monk of Bury St Edmunds. Usk had attributed Chaucer's fame to his
excellence in speech, imagination, wit, and reason, in which 'he pas-
seth al other makers [poets]'. Lydgate agrees, adding that Chaucer
deserves the laurel as an English poet no less than Petrarch as an
Italian, and couching his great merits in terms of eloquence and
superior style. These have been achieved through a mode of translation that is a process of distillation.[13] Here we are beginning to see an
enlargement or appropriation of certain aspects of Chaucer's poetic
persona. Now his fame is being linked to specific features of his writing, and his excellence with national identity: he is 'Floure of Poetes
thorghout al breteyne'. More in keeping with, or closer in imitation
of, Chaucer's self-image is Lydgate's listing of Chaucer's works where
his identity is inextricably linked to the act of authorship. Lydgate
also notes Chaucer's success, along with that of Virgil, Dante, and
Petrarch, in securing aristocratic patronage: 'Support of princis fond
hem ther dispence'.[14]

The endorsement by other writers of Chaucer's self-image may
indicate little more than his success in promoting it: his disciples took
the cue. But if so his success was only partial. They do not seize on
the self-effacing, or insouciant, or retracting, or comic Chaucer but
rather those aspects of his persona that are more obviously meritorious, public, and praiseworthy, and which might redound to the credit

of a writer following in his tracks. Ostensibly overawed by his excellence, they reserve for their own use the traditional modesty *topos* of which disavowal of knowledge and competence is a variant. There is a strong element of self-interest here. If Chaucer is a poet to be reckoned with, he is also one to be used to good effect, in the service of his successors' own projects.

That process is particularly evident in a poem by Thomas Hoccleve (*c.*1368–1426), a clerk of the Privy Seal who claimed to know Chaucer personally. His *Regement of Princes* (1410–11) includes some adulatory lines along with one of the earliest portraits of the man Hoccleve called 'maister'. Chaucer's appearance, Hoccleve asserts, remains vivid in his memory a decade after his death: 'the resemblance | Of him hath in me so fressh lyflynesse'. He declares that he commissioned the portrait or 'liknesse' in order to remind the forgetful of the essential Chaucer: 'they that han of him lost thought and mynde | By this peynture may ageyn him fynde' (4997–8).[15] The image of Chaucer in the margin of the manuscript (London, British Library, MS Harley 4866, f. 88r) points at these very lines as if to underscore its authenticity (Fig. 1). Chaucer appears as he must have looked in the later years of his life, with grey hair and a forked beard. In build he is not unlike the plump 'popet' described by the Host on the pilgrimage to Canterbury, but there is no hint of playfulness here. This, once more, is the solemn and serious Chaucer, identified as a writer by the 'penner' or inkhorn around his neck and as pious by the rosary he holds in his left hand. The picture seems to endorse a number of features of Chaucer's poetic identity: Chaucer was who he said he was.

While the Hoccleve miniature may be the closest we will ever get to pictorial evidence of 'Chaucer the poet', it also prompts some scepticism: it is a memory image, not a portrait done from life; it is a reflection of Chaucer's own self-portrait; and, most important of all, it is part of a larger project with religious and political dimensions that have not much to do with Chaucer's ambitions but quite a lot to do with Hoccleve's. As the adjacent verses make clear, Hoccleve intends that the picture be used as if it were the image of a saint, both to memorialize Chaucer's life and to commit to memory and reflection the valuable qualities of his writings. Here, Hoccleve draws a particular contrast with the orthodox use of religious images, on which his recommendations are based, and the iconoclastic tendencies of the

Fig. 1. An early portrait of Chaucer (c.1411).

reformist movement known as Lollardy, then being persecuted for heresy. One of the Lollards' criticisms was levelled at the idolatrous adulation of religious images. So in the process of enshrining Chaucer Hoccleve categorically identifies himself as being on the conservative side of religious practice and belief—a point that would not have been lost on the prince to whom the *Regement* is addressed, Henry Monmouth, the future Henry V, who was in the process of framing his own policies for the suppression of Lollardy. Further, by associating himself so closely with Chaucer, Hoccleve was endeavouring to replicate the role of adviser to princes that his illustrious 'maister' had enjoyed with the prince's father, Henry IV. One element of that advice may have been to use Chaucer as an icon of national identity in order to help paper over the cracks in political and social unity generated by regime change: Henry IV had usurped the legitimate king, Richard II, in 1399.[16]

The extent to which Chaucer's persona could still be hijacked over a century later is illustrated by his profile in the revision of *Actes and Monumentes* (1570) by the Protestant reformer, John Foxe (1516–87). Although Chaucer belonged to the religion Foxe castigates, he thoroughly approves of Chaucer's anticlerical stance, calling him a 'right Wiclevian', that is a follower of John Wyclif (*c.*1325–84), the Oxford don whose reformist ideas fuelled Lollardy.[17] Thus, in Foxe's view, Chaucer belongs in the very opposite camp to the one where Hoccleve locates him. Foxe's views are derived in part from satirical works wrongly attributed to Chaucer, but nevertheless the *Canterbury Tales* would be sufficient to explain Foxe's admiration for Chaucer's revelations of 'the idle life of the priestes and clergy men'. So radical and subversive are Chaucer's views, in Foxe's opinion, that it is a wonder his books were not proscribed. That they were not is a tribute to his skills as a writer, enabling him to present truth 'under shadowes covertly' to hoodwink bishops but bring others to 'the true knowledge of Religion'.

Others before Foxe had seen Chaucer as a Protestant before his time, and it may be that he was making the case with special force in order to counteract a recent recapturing of Chaucer by the Catholic cause.[18] Chaucer's tomb, as now visible, was erected in Westminster Abbey in 1556, after the onset of the English Protestant Reformation, but during the brief reign of the Catholic monarch, Mary (1553–8). The tomb is of an altar design, with space at the side for a kneeling supplicant, archaic in the mid-sixteenth century, and of a kind found mainly in friars' churches of the late 1400s. The design was in vogue during the English Counter-Reformation as a means of asserting the resurgence of the older religion. Nicholas Brigham, who supervised the reburial of Chaucer, was an Exchequer official favoured by the queen. It seems likely that the installation of the tomb was a way of reclaiming Chaucer as a figure of national, Catholic, identity.[19]

For the appropriation of his poetic identity Chaucer himself must share the blame. His self-portrait is unusually prone to manipulation for, while seeking fame and authority, it also professes ignorance and incompetence. The effect is to open up a generous interpretative space in which a subsequent poet or religious partisan can easily recruit 'Chaucer' to the cause. The further consequence is that the sense of 'who Chaucer was' becomes ever more elusive and subject to perpetual redefinition. And if we return to the textual evidence for Chaucer's self-portrait, in the hope of finding firmer ground, we find that he has anticipated precisely those problems of interpretation and negotiation—as the Prologue to the *Legend of Good Women* makes clear. It is almost as if we have two Geoffrey Chaucers: one, the poet, whose identity is fluid and always in the process of becoming; the other, the court official, whose roles and functions seem relatively clear-cut.

Biographical Strategies

Bridging the gap between Chaucer the poet and Chaucer the king's servant, in order to ground his persona in historical evidence, has been the main task of recent biographers. The simplest strategy is that of finding matches between one body of evidence and the other. For instance, in the *House of Fame*, Chaucer mentions his 'rekenynges' as being part of his daily work and this is usually read as a reference to his employment as a customs controller when, the *Life-Records* tell us, he kept the accounts in his own hand. The years of his work at the wool quay (1374–86) coincide with the supposed date of composition of the *House of Fame*. More tenuous is the link between Chaucer's employment as Clerk of the King's Works (1389–91) and the Knight's Tale, although, again, the dates tally. In May and October of 1390 Chaucer was responsible for providing the scaffolds for joustings at Smithfield attended by the king and queen, among others. In Chaucer's Canterbury tale Theseus, the ruler of Athens, spends lavishly to have made some 'lystes roially' (KnT 1884), and the Knight describes the building in some detail. But these are fantasy lists in the style of a stone amphitheatre rather than the temporary timber constructions built in London. Such seemingly direct connections between life records and poetry are full of temptations to speculate. Did Chaucer draw on his knowledge of constructing buildings? It would seem odd if he had not done so. On the other hand, fantasy buildings of the sort he describes in the Knight's Tale can be explained by literary precedent, whether in the *Rose* or elsewhere.

In other cases the circumstantial evidence is quite compelling. As already mentioned, in 1372 Chaucer travelled to Italy as a member of a diplomatic mission, charged with negotiating a commercial treaty with the Genoese. As well as visiting Genoa Chaucer also travelled to Florence, probably in order to discuss financial matters with the Bardi banking house, which had already supplied Edward III with a large loan. Both Petrarch and Boccaccio were alive during Chaucer's visit, and accessible: Petrarch at Padua or Arqua, Boccaccio at Florence or Certaldo, while Dante (*c.*1265–1321) was celebrated in Florence through a series of annual lectures. There is no evidence that Chaucer met Petrarch or Boccaccio, or that he acquired on his trip books of their works that he was later to use. Nevertheless, it is from the early 1370s that the influence of Italian literature on Chaucer's writing begins in earnest.

Another way of bridging the gap between self-portrait and life record is by using the superstructure on which they each depend: the historical context. Here, the biographer attempts to bring social, political, or cultural factors into alignment with Chaucer's life and poetry. The triangulation can produce an urge to create a picture so complete or so compelling that it misrepresents the facts. For instance, in 1381 the peasants of Kent and Essex arose en masse, marched on London, and occupied it. For good measure, they beheaded the archbishop of Canterbury and sacked the Savoy, the London palace of Chaucer's patron, John of Gaunt. In that year, Chaucer was resident in London. Yet, throughout his writings, Chaucer makes only two passing references to this cataclysmic social upheaval—unlike his friend and contemporary, John Gower, who devoted an entire book to the revolution in his *Vox clamantis*. Chaucer's much more muted reaction is exasperating to the biographer hell-bent on integrating

Chaucer fully with his historical context, and the exasperation can lead to blatant invention. John Gardner imagines him observing the rebels through the window of his room: 'Chaucer, in his house over Aldgate, watched them come.'[20] A more extreme kind of wishful thinking stems not from gaps in the poetry, but in the life records. Since the records do not include any documents relating to Chaucer's death (no will, no inventory) Terry Jones smells a rat and constructs an elaborate theory of suspicious circumstances based on the wholly suppositional premise that Chaucer was murdered.[21]

To sensationalize Chaucer's life might draw attention to authentic conflicts and antipathies, but it encourages the pursuit of red herrings. On the other hand, a too safe approach, one that merely parallels an account of the poetry with a periodic update on events in Chaucer's life, avoids the key issue: in what ways was Chaucer's poetry a response to his 'moment'? Incorporating history as background is not the answer because it creates a mismatch between two very different kinds of material: the personalized stuff of fictional narrative and the generalized tendencies of factual overview. To break this impasse scholars have begun to change the emphasis of Chaucer's life history. Pearsall's magisterial work, *The Life of Geoffrey Chaucer*, focuses on the development of Chaucer's ideas, as manifest in his writings, as a response to his cultural situation. Paul Strohm has indicated the importance of exploring contiguous lives—those of the people who were Chaucer's immediate acquaintances, and who formed his first audience—in order to understand Chaucer's own. He has also urged a closer understanding of the various roles Chaucer assumed at different times in his career. What did it mean to be a squire? A knight of the shire?[22]

The implication is that the life records, rather than being a collection of inert documents with little of the vitality of Chaucer's poetry, raise questions that can open up new avenues of enquiry. For instance, they foreground London as the formative place of Chaucer's writing career; map his transition from mercantile origins to aristocratic milieu; give prominence to war and chivalry; provide evidence of Chaucer's encounters with other cultures; and so on. These reflections in turn suggest an approach, followed in the present book, that avoids the short-circuiting produced by too direct a connection between life records and poetry, as well as the tendency to fictionalize. It is to take a topic with roots in life records, Chaucer's poetry and historical writing alike, and present a conspectus. To do so prevents a reductive or fanciful interpretation of his life and work while at the same time showing how they are related to his society. One initial example will demonstrate the possibilities of this approach.

Finding a Voice

The prologue to the *Legend of Good Women* has already indicated that patronage was an important aspect of Chaucer's experience as a poet, and it was no less true of his experience as a royal official. The receipt of gifts, annuities, and commissions from those whose service he sought enabled him to live, to prosper, and to write. Patronage had an impact on Chaucer's poetry at a crucial, early stage of his writing career, bringing with it a complex set of power relations which in turn had a marked effect on his choice of language, genre, and persona.

Chaucer's first major composition was a dream vision known as the *Book of the Duchess* but originally titled 'the Deeth of Blaunche the Duchesse'. The duchess in question was the first wife of John of Gaunt, duke of Lancaster. She had died in 1368 and although he remarried twice, Gaunt continued to remember Blanche's death with an elaborate anniversary ceremony. It is possible that Chaucer's poem was commissioned for performance at one such ceremony, which may have taken place in St Paul's (where Blanche was buried) or more probably at the Savoy, Gaunt's London house.[23] The poem was probably completed before 1372 since it refers to Gaunt's earldom of Richmond, in Yorkshire, which ceased in that year. So at the time of composition Chaucer was about thirty years old.

The circumstances of the commission help to identify the nature of the poetic task that Chaucer faced.[24] We might reasonably assume that a certain sensitivity to the feelings of his commissioner, as well as an appropriate knowledge of his subject-matter, was the order of the day—in a word, due regard for decorum. Something of this is indicated by Chaucer's blend of genres: a dream vision, familiar to an aristocratic audience, which he incorporated with an elegy—that is, a work in praise of a person's distinctive qualities on the occasion of their death. Now the person commissioning the poem was none other than Chaucer's own patron, one on whom he partly depended for his livelihood and whom he had to satisfy. As a son of the reigning king, Gaunt exercised enormous influence and was an important international prince in his own right.[25] The poem had to reflect the splendour of his nobility, but also to offer a measure of consolation and reconciliation to the bereaved duke. Whereas that might not be an issue for a person of equal social standing, Chaucer was on a very different footing: not only was he in Gaunt's service, but he himself was not noble by birth. The differences in social status added a further complication to the task of creating a genuine and effective act of comfort. And although the purpose of the poem was to be intimate, personal, and to some extent private, it was nevertheless to be public property: an enactment of private, individualized sympathy by means of a performance before a gathering of powerful and influential people.

All of these problems might be summed up under the general heading of 'finding a voice', that is finding a mode of expression, as well as a genre, that would respond effectively to the complexity of the situation. And there was an added, complicating factor, less to do with social contingencies and more to do with Chaucer's own poetic development. He was right at the beginning of it. So 'finding a voice' also has implications for the discovery of his authorial identity. It means, in general terms, finding a way of responding to literary tradition, to the vast inheritance of poetry written in the main by French and Latin authors, in such a way as to make it his own.

The narrator of the *Book of the Duchess* introduces himself as an insomniac who tries to get to sleep by reading a tale from Ovid's *Metamorphoses*, the legend of Ceyx and Alcione. He discovers therein the existence of a god of sleep, Morpheus, to whom he offers an experimental prayer, only to find that his eyes do at last close. He dreams that his room is transformed into a palace of colour, light, pictures, and heavenly music. It is as if Chaucer has effected a transition from his life at home to his life at court. The sound of a hunt reaches his ears and without further ado he mounts a horse and gallops off to join in. The dreamer is not an effective hunter and soon he finds himself alone. A whelp fawns at his feet and he decides to follow it, moving as he does so through a paradisal landscape bursting with natural life. Suddenly, he notices a man, dressed in black, with his back to a huge oak tree. This isolated, melancholy figure declares that his name is Sorrow and he embarks on a lengthy account of the lady from whom he is separated and whose absence is causing him such excessive grief. The narrator listens attentively but fails to grasp the true situation until the closing lines of the poem:

'Sir,' quod I, 'where is she now?'	
'Now!' quod he, and stynte anoon.	*stopped*
Therwith he wax as ded as stoon	*became*
And seyde, 'Allas, that I was bore!	
That was the los, that here-before	
I tolde the that I hadde lorn.	*lost*
Bethenke how I seyde here-beforn,	
"Thow wost ful lytel what thow menest;	*know*
I have lost more than thou wenest."	*think*
God wot, allas! Ryght that was she!'	
'Allas, sir, how? What may that be?'	
'She ys ded!' 'Nay!' 'Yis, be my trouthe!'	
'Is that youre los? Be God, hyt ys routhe!'	*pity*
And with that word ryght anoon	
They gan to strake forth; al was doon,	*sound the horn*
For that tyme, the hert-huntyng.	
With that me thoghte that this kyng	
Gan homward for to ryde	
Unto a place, was ther besyde,	
Which was from us but a lyte—	
A long castel with walles white,	
Be Seynt Johan, on a ryche hil,	
As me mette . . .	*dreamed*

(*BD* 1298–1320)

If the poem is generally allusive and indirect, it is at the same time quite specific about the nature of the grieving man's predicament, his real identity, and that of the dead woman. She is referred to as 'White', that is Blanche, the dead duchess, and at the end of the poem Chaucer leaves his audience in no doubt about the true name of the man in black. He rides home to a 'long castel', a pun on 'Lancaster'; 'Be Seynt Johan', in the next line, includes the duke's first name; and the following words, 'on a ryche hil', refers to Richmond (rich mound) in Yorkshire, where Gaunt had a castle.

Coded references such as these offer the pleasures of a puzzle to an audience in the know. But they are also indicative of the levels of linguistic sophistication and subtlety of response that Chaucer expected from his readers and listeners. To give a further example from the passage cited: 'al was doon, | For that tyme, the hert-huntyng' is a statement describing the end of the hunting of harts and hinds. But it is also a covert allusion to the man in black's pursuit of Blanche, as well as to the process that has been enacted in the course of the dialogue between him and the dreamer—a process of therapeutic consolation, of getting down to the causes of his sorrow, of articulating them, in a hunting of the heart and its ailments.

Puns like this work at one remove, requiring the recipient to penetrate the surface meaning and identify a deeper one. Such word-play is symptomatic of the way in which the poem as a whole operates. It demands for its full realization a willingness to go beyond the apparent. A key instance is the case of the two speakers in the dialogue which occupies the central part of the poem. We know, as their medieval contemporaries knew, that the poem is a form of public address by Geoffrey Chaucer to John of Gaunt. But the poem does not opt for the direct speaking, man to man, that might reasonably be expected. Instead, the two take on individual personae: Chaucer the role of insouciant narrator and obtuse auditor of the man in black's lament; Gaunt the mantle of Sorrow. Thus the reality is to some extent depersonalized, objectified, given a public identity. And this very process of alienation helps to salve the grief because it effects a distancing, the introduction of a more dispassionate, external point of view, on otherwise highly subjective, internalized emotions.

The contrivance has other advantages. The audience is faced with two figures, the dreamer and Sorrow, known to represent Chaucer and Gaunt. But, by making them speak in part Chaucer can achieve what might not otherwise be possible. He relieves the dreamer ('himself') of the responsibility of uttering a eulogy of Blanche and credits it instead to Sorrow: Chaucer is Gaunt's scriptwriter. Here is an adroit, decorous manoeuvre, which praises Blanche in a way Gaunt might have liked but which Chaucer, if speaking in the voice of his ineffective persona, could never have achieved.

In other ways, too, the naïve role that Chaucer adopts complements and enhances Gaunt's, but the advantages are not all one way. On first encounter, the dreamer adopts a deferential manner, removing his hood and greeting him graciously, as best he knew, 'Debonayrly [courteously], and nothyng lowde' (518): son of a wine merchant meets international prince. But there is more than a twinkle of irony in the dreamer's eye. Self-effacing and self-deprecating though he may be through his bumbling alter ego, Chaucer uses it systematically to undermine the man in black's hauteur, and bring him down to earth. The grounding of the grieving man's emotional supercharge is linked with an attempt to socialize him, to reintegrate him with the community from which he has become isolated through his posturing as Sorrow.

The subversion of the man in black's self-dramatizing pose is effected by putting together two radically different kinds of diction, one appropriate to the naïve and literal-minded narrator, the other to the introverted nobleman. On the one hand the language of Sorrow is ornate, rhetorical, metaphorical, given to digression and the parading of familiar literary conventions. It is a language in which emotion lies hidden, a language utterly aristocratic in its sense of propriety and tradition. By contrast there is the language of the dreamer: demotic, colloquial, uncomplicated, brief, blunt to the point of insensitivity. It is a language thoroughly utilitarian and mercantile, implying that its speaker is a practical, no-nonsense, bluff individual. To juxtapose the two kinds of language, and the two worlds that they each suggest, is to identify the extent of the gap between man in black and dreamer. It is a gap of social as well as linguistic communication, which must be bridged if a real act of sympathy is to be achieved and Sorrow's sense of isolation ended.[26]

The two languages exist in a state of productive tension, as is clear from the opening exchange of the dreamer and the man in black. On perceiving that the knight is in a state of depression, the dreamer invites him to 'discure [reveal] me youre woo' (549) in the hope that he will be able to ease it. The man in black doubts that anyone can help and embarks on a one-hundred-and-fifty-line oration full of self-immolating oxymorons: 'my song is complaint, my laughter is weeping, my glad thoughts turn to heaviness . . . my good is harm . . . my wit is folly' and so on (598–619). Mention of Fortune then prompts a prolonged description of that goddess's attributes. Yet the dreamer, unlike the audience, fails to realize that the speaker's figurative language hints, however abstrusely, at some larger catastrophe and instead construes it at face value. He believes that the man in black is grieving because he has lost a game of chess with someone called Fortune. Understandably, he is perplexed at the extremity of Sorrow's reaction to the experience of losing, but nevertheless offers some misplaced consolation by citing the stoicism of Socrates and others in the face of much greater adversity. All of this is to no avail because the

dreamer has missed the point—or perhaps the point was too obscure
in the first place. With a note of exasperation in his voice that becomes
ever more pronounced as the dialogue proceeds, the man in black
declares that the dreamer doesn't really know what he's talking about
because he, Sorrow, has lost more than he, the dreamer, recognizes:
'Thow wost [know] ful lytel what thou menest; | I have lost more
than thow wenest' (743–4).

The dynamic process begins again, with the man in black trying to
explain the cause of his woe, the dreamer obtusely failing to understand. The lines just quoted occur as a refrain, and mark the divisions
or points of slow advance in this dialectic whereby Sorrow edges
nearer to speaking plainly and the dreamer edges nearer to enlighten-
ment. The refrain is heard for the last time in the closing lines cited
above. Having described at length the lady whom he has 'lost', the
dreamer asks the man in black, 'Where is she now?' He replies, 'That
is the loss I told you about before'. Then comes the refrain, a kind of
riddle long since solved by everyone except the dreamer: 'Thow wost
ful lytel what thou menest | I have lost more than thow wenest'. The
situation is becoming almost unbearable, and the audience by this
point must have been on the point of screaming at the dreamer what
he fails to see. Again, he is dimwitted: 'Allas, sir, how? What may that
be?' Then, at last, come the unambiguous words: 'She ys ded'.
A sudden, genuine flash of sympathy is now possible: 'Nay!' 'Yis, be
my trouthe!' 'Is that youre los? Be God, hyt ys routhe [pity]'. So at
last the two languages coalesce, social difference is levelled, the heart-
hunting (and soon the poem itself) ends, the mourning knight
renounces his isolation. These exceedingly spare, simple words carry
such a strong emotional charge precisely because of the verbosity and
circumlocution that precede them. They depend for their climactic
effectiveness on the dreamer's charade of naïveté and the knight's
extended, high-flown eulogy of Blanche.

The sudden simplicity of the closing phase of the dialogue is a
startling contrast to all that has gone before. The exchange is serious,
solemn, where those that preceded it were playful and comic—
comedy, like the use of personae, offering the possibility of distancing, and of relief from sorrow through laughter. But whatever else the
final point of synthesis and understanding may be, it is also a moment
of resolution in Chaucer's literary predicament. The two voices—of
the man in black and the dreamer—may be taken as articulations of

opposite kinds of literary creation of the sort accessible to Chaucer at this stage of his writing career. He was the inheritor of, and accomplished imitator of, a kind of literature—much of it written in French—which may loosely be called courtly. Its hallmarks were ornate, decorative, rhetorical effects, artificiality, remoteness. It was a literature intended for aristocratic consumption and it reflected aristocratic values. Its characteristic genres are romance and dream vision, its mode allegory. At the other extreme was a kind of language Chaucer knew from his own experience: colloquial, graphic, a working tool for men of affairs. Its characteristic genre is fabliau. In the *Book of the Duchess* he is experimenting with the two voices, one paying its dues to a certain kind of bookishness, the other cocking a snook at affectation in favour of plain speaking. Both have their limitations: if plain speaking emerges as dominant and more effective, it does so only after a prolonged engagement with authoritative, self-consciously 'literary', utterance.

It is this kind of enterprise—giving immediacy to inherited genres, narratives, and discourse—to which Chaucer devoted the rest of his writing. He did so not merely out of literary ambition, but in response also to social, political, and cultural issues. One way in which he addressed them was through his self-representation, as the *Book of the Duchess* makes clear. It was a highly effective instrument for mediating between poetry and society, patron and client, performance and audience, private emotion and its public expression. Chaucer's self-portrait, embodied in his poetic persona, did have an important historical identity and cultural function—even if it leaves open for speculation the question of 'what was Chaucer really like?'

CHAPTER 2

THE SOCIAL BODY

TODAY, the phrase 'fabric of society' is commonly used to describe the complexity of social relations. It is a turn of phrase that calls attention to the notion of fabrication, and suggests that society is an artificial concept, man-made. 'Fabric' in the sense of 'building' evokes a capacious structure of interdependent parts (in need of maintenance, prone to ruin) of which each section of society is a component. Alternatively, we might think of society as a woven fabric, each thread or social group contributing its sense and distinctive colour to the overall product, which is both ornamental and useful (though vulnerable to wear and tear). However, 'fabric of society' is not a figure of speech found in fourteenth-century England. Instead, a metaphor often used is that of the human body—and the difference is telling. Its implication is that human society is a natural state of affairs, something given by God, over which human agency has little control. The metaphor of the body also suggests that society is living, organic, a whole comprising interdependent parts which have no choice in their respective functions and no opportunity for change. It is also an explicitly hierarchical notion of social organization, with the 'head' controlling its 'members'.[1]

During Chaucer's lifetime, the social body—what in later centuries was called the body politic—underwent some severe shocks to the system. It was galvanized and exhilarated, then left wearied and despondent, by a protracted war with France. It suffered a severe haemorrhage when, in mid-century, plague killed between a third and a half of the population. Its mental and spiritual faculties were troubled by a swingeing critique of Church corruption launched by John Wyclif (c.1325–84). In 1381 its entire existence was threatened by open revolt. And in 1399 it underwent regime change when Henry of Bolingbroke usurped the legitimate king, Richard II.

When considering these events, it might seem either that, by 1400, the social body had proved remarkably resilient and was in rude good health; or, that it had undergone a cataclysm from which it would never recover and which would eventuate in civil war, the Reformation, and the alienation of labour. By any standards the events of the second half of the fourteenth century were unusually challenging. Yet Chaucer, who lived through them, sometimes at their epicentre, refers to them only in passing. In this respect he contrasts with other London writers, such as John Gower and William Langland, who both represent at length, and engage polemically with, significant upheavals—which they themselves regard as a kind of Armageddon. The absence in Chaucer's works of sustained accounts of social disasters might be taken to indicate that he was of the nail-paring school: untroubled by them because they were not fundamentally threatening. Closer consideration indicates that Chaucer's responses are no less embedded and passionate than those of his peers but, whether by dint of inclination or circumstance, they are more elliptical. He deals not with manifestations of disorder in the social body but with their underlying issues and causes. His stance is more reflective than agit-prop, inclined less to make ex cathedra pronouncements than to articulate the key terms of a debate. It avoids an authoritative voice in favour of locating responsibility for ethical decisions with the individual members of his audience.

Social Structures

In practice, there was no shortage of authorities able and willing to pronounce on the iniquities of the age. Thomas Brinton (*c.*1320–89) was a Benedictine monk who became bishop of Rochester in 1373. He believed in the importance of preaching, and delivered regular sermons to fellow clerics and to the courts of Edward III and Richard II—speaking in Latin or English, as occasion demanded. Using his influential position to inveigh against the abuses of power, Brinton made forthright comments on corruption at the papal court and oppressive taxation of the poor, among other topics. He appealed to the consciences of his listeners by referring them to fundamental Christian principles of poverty and probity. But, however reforming his voice might sound, his basic instincts were conservative rather than radical, as is evidenced also by his political activities: at court he allied himself to the Black Prince and took an active role in parliament; he opposed Wyclif and was present at the council at Blackfriars in 1382 which condemned his teachings; and he was a member of the commission that tried the peasant rebels of Kent.

Social revolt, and intimations of heresy, must have been repugnant
to a man of Brinton's position and persuasion. In October of 1373 he
preached at St Paul's on the proper ordering of society. Brinton represents the Church as the fount of truth, with ramifications for all
social groups. Just as the sun is a single light but capable of producing
many rays, so the Church has its congregation of the faithful who
constitute its many members. They are, quoting Corinthians 1 10: 17,
'being many . . . one body'. The whole of society is a 'mystical body'
with each part functioning for the benefit of the others under the
aegis of God. It is a classic statement of the theory:

. . . the heads are kings, princes, and prelates; the eyes are wise judges and
true counsellors; the ears are clerics; the tongue, good learned men; the
right hand, soldiers ready to mount a defence; the left hand, merchants and
faithful artisans; the heart, citizens and burghers placed as if in the centre;
the feet are farmers and labourers as if firmly supporting the entire body.[2]

The idea of the social body was not new. It occurs, for example, in the
twelfth-century *Policraticus* of John of Salisbury. Its antiquity helped
to provide an aura of authenticity, but the concept was far from ossi-
fied. Brinton adapted it to changing circumstances by including mid-
dling social groups of merchants, artisans, citizens, and burghers.[3]

Another old but still widespread theory divided the population
into a hierarchy of three orders: those who pray, those who fight, and
those who work—clergy, knighthood, and peasantry.[4] The structure
underlies Gower's conception of the way in which society should
function but, in his view, the world is upside-down. In *Vox clamantis*
(the voice of one crying), first completed before 1381, he writes:

In former times the prelate carried on only the work of divinity; now, he
cannot possess God because of the world. In former times the curate was
devoted to his cure, and now he wanders about outside it, making the
rounds of the whole population. In former times priests were chaste, and
now they are lecherous. The leisure which they seek fosters the greatest
harm. In former times scholars zealously taught good morals, but now, on
the other hand, learning is corrupt. Indivisible Love bound monks together
like a passion; now Envy strives to rule their cloisters. In former times
Austerity used to subdue the friars in the flesh, but now their easy rule
spares them. And in former times knighthood was prompt in service, but
now their service is slow in coming, since their life is evil. In former times
the merchant asked a fair profit for himself, and now he tries to get his
profits dishonestly. Guileless simplicity of mind used to be associated with

the peasant; now his untamed heart makes him savage. The law, which the power of money has everywhere subjected to itself, used to be just and propitious, sparing no one. Equal rank is now attained through inequitable doings, and every traveler goes beyond the bounds of his path.[5]

The rhetorical mechanisms at work here—harking back to a golden age 'in former times', formulaic inversions—have a long ancestry, but it does not follow that Gower's satire is merely conventional. Like Brinton, he extends his account of moral torpor to include groups, such as lawyers— the group to which Gower himself belonged and which he elsewhere describes as entrapping hapless litigants as if they were flies caught in a spider's web—and merchants, who do not obviously belong in the strict categories of praying, fighting, and manual labour.[6]

Gower's analysis is conducted in terms that are idealistic and ethical and which derive from traditional satire. Nevertheless, it is directed at his own, immediate society, which is represented as dysfunctional. Groups that should be interdependent, working for the common good, have become atomized. Instead of co-operating they compete out of self-interest and jostle for supremacy. Worse, they aspire to adopt each other's traits: 'Servants are now masters and masters are servants, and one who has learned nothing thinks he knows everything. The peasant pretends to imitate the ways of the freeman, and gives the appearance of him in his clothes. And the gentleman changes himself into this base fellow and wants to enjoy his churlish vice.'[7]

According to Brinton and Gower, theories of social structure are more honoured in the breach than in the upholding. Their need to reiterate the theories, as well as their subject-matter, itself indicates a sense of threat to the status quo. But it also suggests that the theories themselves may have become inadequate to account for the situations in which they found themselves. Accommodating though Brinton and Gower are towards those groups not traditionally included in either the social body or the three orders model, neither theory is well equipped to capture the complexity of late fourteenth-century English society. And complex it certainly was, to the point of being radically different from those models traditionally used to describe it. So much is evident from a Statute on Diet and Apparel of 1363 which attempted to regulate the food and clothing appropriate to different social groups.[8] The attempt must have warmed Gower's heart, yet his favoured scheme of the three orders is too general, and too rigid, to have much practical application here. 'Those who work' are regarded as being of the 'estate of a groom', a category also covering carters, ploughmen, and herders of sheep, oxen, cows, and swine and others whose goods and chattels do not exceed forty shillings in value. They must not wear anything but coarse cloth ('blanket' and russet) and secure their clothing with girdles made of linen. Grooms are also classed with servants, whether of lords at one end of the social spectrum, or craftsmen at the other, for the statute intends to prevent the insubordination of servants as a group by setting limits to what they can eat or wear. They must not eat fish or flesh more than once a day, or wear anything of gold or silk, embroidered or enamelled. Yeomen and craftsmen are given a little more latitude. The material from which their clothes are made can be worth up to forty shillings, but they are forbidden accessories made of precious materials and fur except that of lamb, rabbit, cat, or fox (furs themselves having their own hierarchy). The restrictions ease further as the social level advances. While squires and others of *gentil* status below the rank of knight, with land or rent worth less than £100 a year, might not wear any kind of fur, those worth 200 marks (£132) or more might wear silk and silver and their wives fur of miniver (squirrel). The wives of knights poorer than this are forbidden miniver or precious stones. As the social groups diversify, so the criteria for defining them also multiply. Working and fighting may still be applicable categories, but questions of income and property ownership have become pressing. Thus, merchants, citizens, and burghers who possess goods and chattels worth £500 may attire themselves in the same way as squires with land or rent worth £100. While such an edict might seem to conflate social distinction, and make a merchant to all intents and purposes look like a squire, in practice some key differences remain: land ownership counts for more than ownership of property and possessions; and squires and knights have access to that mysterious quality, gentility, that is denied to merchants. Further up the social scale, the privileges granted seem to enter the realm of romance: the ladies of knights with incomes between 400 marks and £1,000 may wear almost anything they please, bar ermine.

Although the sumptuary legislation of 1363 was withdrawn the following year it nevertheless opens a window on to a hierarchical society deeply self-conscious about status and its outward trappings. Social rank is not a matter for organic co-operation in the manner of the social body as advocated by a Brinton, but instead an occasion for competition, display, and jealous guarding, and something increasingly difficult to discern from visible signs. At the same time, the underlying bases on which rested differences in status and social identity were themselves changing. These impressions are confirmed by legislation of 1379, specifying the poll tax due from each social group, where there is an even more discernible criss-crossing of traditional social boundaries.[9] Although there are distinct categories of nobility and clergy, each splinters into many subdivisions, while there is an intermediate band not only of lawyers and merchants but also of aldermen, mayors, franklins, and hostlers (among others). The diversity and abundance of groups is fascinating. Here are dukes; knights 'able to spend as much as a baron'; widows of squires 'of a lesser estate'; squires 'not in possession of lands, rents or castles'; apprentices who follow the law; the mayor of London and mayors of other 'great towns'; each alderman of London (to pay like a baron); great, sufficient, and lesser merchants; farmers of manors and parsonages; pardoners and summoners who are married; married laymen; single men and women; abbots; prioresses; deans; provosts; treasurers; curates; monks; canons; and ladies of religious houses. The status of each is determined by their worth for taxation purposes and some intriguing equalities emerge. The rate levied on a widowed baroness (forty shillings) is the same as that levied on a prior holding a benefice valued between £200 and 500 marks (£330); a squire of lesser estate and a franklin are both taxed at 6s 8d; a 'great merchant' and a knight at twenty shillings.

Chaucer has been dubbed 'the glory of the age and its epitome' by one historian, May McKisack, and certainly his own life history confirms that the crossing of social boundaries, and advancing through the hierarchy, were indeed possible.[10] His mother, Agnes Copton, was a property owner in her own right, so the mercantile family into which Chaucer was born was already of considerable status—equivalent, perhaps, in poll tax terms, to that of a lesser knight. And it was into the social circles of knights and the nobility that Chaucer moved when, in his mid-teens, he became a page in the household of Elizabeth, Countess of Ulster, c.1357. Yet within ten years the documents refer to Chaucer as an esquire. The meaning of the appellation had changed considerably during the first half of the fourteenth century and was no longer restricted to those of aristocratic birth.

More, it had become a means whereby those of lower social groups
might achieve a measure of gentility.[11] The rank of squire is precisely
the vehicle that conveyed Chaucer from merchant's son to *gentil* rank.
A deposition made in 1386 by 'Geffray Chaucere esquier' states that
he had then borne arms for twenty-seven years—a further sign of his
gentil status. Newly arrived, by dint of personal merit, in a world of
largely inherited status, 'Geoffrey Chaucer, squire' is still, in Lee
Patterson's words, a somewhat in-between figure: 'the son of a rich
merchant, but one educated in noble households; a king's squire, but
one who fulfilled the duties of clerical administrator; a modest servant of the Crown, but one who numbered among his friends some of
the king's closest associates'.[12]

Marginality, being in the group but not of it, participating but
detached, is what comes across in Chaucer's literary persona, and
nowhere more so than in his self-portrait in the *Canterbury Tales*, when
the Host does not recognize him for what he is as he rides alone from
the main company of pilgrims, staring at the ground 'as thou woldest
fynde an hare' (ThP 696). At the beginning of his composition, Chaucer
represents those pilgrims in a series of twenty-nine portraits that have
been taken as an accurate cross-section of his own society. 'God's
plenty', as John Dryden called them, may have been the illusion
Chaucer was trying to create, but if so he used decidedly selective principles. Set alongside the poll tax categories of 1379 the portraits look
decidedly unrepresentative (one entire group, the nobility, is absent;
there are only two women; and so on). Nor do they sit easily with the
notion of the three estates: although there are idealized portraits of a
knight, a plowman, and a parson, it would be difficult to allocate the rest
of the pilgrims according to the categories of fighters, workers, and
prayers.[13] Chaucer may have been guided by a less prescriptive, more
flexible notion of society's strata. While that does not explain his select-
ivity, it could explain the inclusion of a pilgrim such as the Franklin,
whose social group is notoriously difficult to define.[14] It might also be
reasonable to conclude that what guided Chaucer was the teeming life
around him, which, from his liminal position, he was ideally placed to
observe either at court, or at the wool quay, or in the streets of London.
No doubt there is an element of first-hand reportage in the descriptions—a strong element, his pilgrim persona would have us think—
but in point of fact a dominant influence on this most bookish of
writers is the literary one of estates satire.[15]

With its origins in classical antiquity, estates satire is a means of characterizing society according to the types who inhabit it (the grasping lawyer, the wolfish priest, the much-married woman). Many of the details of Chaucer's portraits that strike a modern reader as done from the life are entirely conventional, as in the case of the monk out of his cloister. For all that, Chaucer gives his inherited material a decidedly new spin and here it is worth comparing his approach with that of Gower, whose *Vox clamantis* has one foot in the same tradition. Gower stays with the generalities—castigating monks as a group and at a distance through sustained, high-flown rhetoric.[16] Chaucer individualizes the stereotype, placing 'the Monk' in a particular narrative framework where he interacts with other members of society and, through his appearance, revealing something of his mindset.[17] Not least among the indicators is his 'array', or clothing, which includes sleeves lined with that eloquent marker of social aspiration, fur: in this case the expensive squirrel variety and at that 'the fyneste of a lond' (GP 194). And the Monk engages with 'Chaucer the pilgrim', who, far from condemning him, appears to accept him for what he is, even to the point of condoning his policy of absenteeism from the cloister: 'I seyde his opinion was good' (GP 183). Thus the diction is low-key, accessible, direct. The outcome is irony, not satire; ethical ambiguity, not moral clarity; a personal vantage-point, not an authoritative podium; and, by virtue of these strategies, a recognition on Chaucer's part that his audience's responses are likely to be comparably varied and personalized. To say as much might seem to depoliticize Chaucer, to place him apart from the direct involvement with contemporary issues and events that is such a hallmark of other writers such as Gower and Langland. Yet the 'voice' that Chaucer develops from his earliest long poem, the *Book of the Duchess*, to his late masterwork, the *Canterbury Tales*, is in its own way quite radical. For it locates the task of interpretation and the construction of meaning not within an institution, such as the Church, or within a particular social group, but with the individual—inadequate, absent-minded, and laughable though that person might be.

Religion and Piety

Chaucer's emphasis on the individual as the locus of moral judgement parallels a strong growth in forms of lay piety that sought to intensify the Christian experience through personal agency rather than through the more traditional routes of liturgy and priest. One practitioner is Chaucer's Plowman (GP 529–41).[18] He is faithful to his estate as a 'trewe swynkere [worker]'; lives in peace and 'parfit charitee', working for the poor without pay; observes the two key commandments to love God and neighbour as himself; and is punctilious in paying his tithes. So he respects the precepts and duties of the Church, but pious practice is embodied in him rather than in the institution itself, even though he is not of a religious calling. Those of a similar inclination, if literate, had access to a considerable range of written guides in English designed to instruct them in the elements of the faith and the arts of virtuous living. One example is the *Pricke of Conscience*, which exists in more copies than the *Canterbury Tales*; another is the Parson's Tale itself, which derives chiefly from two manuals on sin and salvation, by Raymond de Pennaforte and William Peraldus. More recherché practices, also of interest to the laity as models of private devotion, were described by the so-called mystics of the period: Richard Rolle, Julian of Norwich, the unknown author of the *Cloud of Unknowing*, and Walter Hilton. Between them, they mapped a terrain that located religious experience within the psyche of the individual responding directly to the example set by Christ. Within gentry circles, where the opportunities for reading and reflection were circumscribed by the practical demands of everyday life, there developed a distinctive variety of lay piety designed to balance active and contemplative urges.

To what extent is the worldliness of Chaucer's Monk an indicator of more general failings? As already suggested, the portrait is an example of traditional anticlerical satire that can be matched in the contemporaneous writings of a Gower or a Langland. But the sheer volume of criticism, however routine, is itself instructive. That the corruption of the Church was a serious issue, and of immediate concern, is clear from the writings of John Wyclif, and is further evidenced by the reaction of insiders such as bishop Brinton who campaigned for reform on their own account. They were facing an uphill task. The Church was inextricably embedded in politics (archbishops of Canterbury were customarily chancellors of England), sharply conscious of its own power, and keen to protect hard-won rights and privileges. It was also extremely wealthy: the priory of Christ Church Canterbury, for instance, was a major landowner and administered extensive estates across the south of England. In these circumstances the spiritual mission of the Church was all too easily compromised. Nor did the papal schism (1378–1418) do much to enhance the Church's spiritual authority since two popes, one resident in Rome and the other in Avignon, each claimed the prerogative over the other. Then there was the sheer multiplicity of office-holders, each with his or her own supposedly authentic and sometimes competing claim over the soul of the individual. Chaucer describes six members of the ecclesiastical establishment, only one of whom (the Parson) has any claim to integrity. The Prioress's compassion is directed at the suffering of small animals rather than those of human beings; the Monk's priorities are hunting and good living; the Friar is a Don Juan and the father of numerous offspring; the Summoner, who quarrels with the Friar, is an inveterate lecher; and the Pardoner is enveloped in a self-destructive cycle of exploitation and greed. Satirical portraits perhaps, but also topical.

The proliferation of its office-holders was only one symptom of the Church's pervasiveness. Its buildings—abbeys, cathedrals, parish churches—were everywhere apparent in town and country. Outside and within, ceremony, sculpture, wall painting, stained glass reiterated the central narratives. Religious drama performed outside the Church, whether in the form of individual pageants, saints' plays, or elaborate civic cycles describing the whole sweep of Christian myth from Creation to Doomsday (as at York and Chester), reinforced the message in more accessible ways. The association of particular saints with a church, a town, a guild, a name-day, made religious practice and ideas meaningful at group, community, and individual levels. Even the ordering of time followed a religious structure. Great liturgical feasts, such as those of Christmas and Easter, divided up the year; individual days were dedicated to particular saints; and the progress of day and night was measured by the canonical hours, marked by the chiming of bells. Religion did not merely determine much of the social routine, it was dominant also in the ways people experienced and thought about their lives. The supreme university discipline was theology: there, Christian dogma was taught and debated as the bread and butter of intellectual activity. Christian ideas were promulgated more widely through preaching, both in Latin and the vernacular, as occasion demanded. The many surviving sermons in English show that they could be vivid, arresting expositions peppered with moralized stories or illustrations known as *exempla*.

The moral compass of the individual was further conditioned through instruction within the parish on the nature of sin and by the practice of confession and penance.

The Miller's Tale, Chaucer's evocation of fourteenth-century Oxford, illustrates some of the ways in which the Church as an institution, Christian practice, narrative, and thought patterns saturated civic life. Old John, a carpenter, routinely works for the abbey at Oseney. His student lodger, well versed in theology but more attracted to astrology, hatches a plan to seduce his landlord's young wife, Alisoun. He feigns a religious trance, John is taken in by the ruse, and calls on a local saint, St Frideswide, to protect them. He readily believes Nicholas's supposed vision of a second Flood, and is particularly exercised by the thought of losing Alisoun. What persuades him to accept Nicholas's suggestion that, like a latter-day Noah, he should save them by using three 'boats' or tubs, not one, is Nicholas's reminder of the trouble Noah had with his wife in persuading her to come on board his single ark. This is not a biblical detail, but one familiar from the mystery play, customarily staged by carpenters' guilds, in which Mrs Noah is a notorious scold who would rather drink and gossip than fall in with her husband's plans. John is presumably familiar with such plays by virtue of his profession. Absolon, Alisoun's second lover, certainly is, because to show off his versatility and skill he sometimes plays the demented Herod 'on a scaffold high' (MillT 3384). He is a parish clerk who carries the censer, takes up the offertory, and mixes in words from the Song of Songs in his wooing of Alisoun. Some of that wooing takes place at the parish church, which Alisoun attends on 'halydayes', holidays or saints' days, when she takes particular trouble with her appearance.

The interpenetration of religious and secular practices, ideas, and attitudes is part and parcel of the culture Chaucer describes. Once Alisoun and Nicholas have spent a happy night together in 'revel' and 'melodye' in the carpenter's bed while he sleeps, exhausted with his labours, in a tub lashed to the roof-beams, Chaucer evokes the onset of a new day: 'the belle of laudes gan to rynge, | And freres in the chauncel gonne synge' (MillT 3652–6). There is no suggestion here that the juxtaposition of sexual and sacred is intended to cast a detrimental light on the lovers as adulterers. This is a fabliau, and its moral priorities lie elsewhere: John has got what he deserved because he is an old man and should not have married a young and attractive woman. Indeed, the lauds bell and the friars' singing seem more like an act of post-coital praise and celebration for the 'myrthe' and 'solas' of the night. Chaucer depends on his audience's ability to recognize the co-existence of religious and secular spheres without any necessary imperative to use one as a means of judging the other. The whole story is framed as a Noah-play; Nicholas's abrupt avowal of love to Alisoun, when he grabs her by the crotch, alludes to Gabriel's Annunciation to Mary; and the retaliatory behaviour of the once effete Absolon, once he has been outwitted by Alisoun and Nicholas at the infamous shot-window, recalls the Harrowing of Hell by Christ: he takes his soul to 'Sathanas' (in fact the local smithy, a place of furnaces, flames, and hot metal) and then tortures Nicholas by thrusting a searing plough-blade into his arse in a way reminiscent of the punishment reserved for sodomites in the afterlife. Such allusions can strike a modern reader, used to more strict divisions between the secular and the religious, as shockingly blasphemous. They were probably regarded at the time as uproariously funny. Being able to think of the religious in terms of the secular, or the secular in terms of the religious, was second nature to Chaucer and his audience—the product of a culture that, whatever its religious shortcomings and defects, was profoundly and securely Christian.

It would require a good deal of special pleading to argue that the Miller's Tale endorses Christian values as distinct from Christian forms of expression. The adulterers get away scot-free and the pious John is ridiculed and regarded henceforth as mad for his Noah fantasy. Nevertheless there is a strong case to be made for Chaucer as a *religious* writer and not merely one who was unavoidably steeped in Christian culture. When he employs a mode of scholastic debate on theological ideas, as he does in the Wife of Bath's Prologue, the results are hilarious but they also raise profound issues about the status of the Bible as an authoritative text, and about the male bias of its interpreters. Or, when he uses a sermon as the Pardoner's preferred discourse, the exemplum of three dissolute gamblers, who find their own death through inveterate avarice, packs a powerful punch even though, and also because, the narrator himself is caught up in the same cycle of sinfulness. Other writings are more direct and uncompromising explorations of, and meditations on, the religious life. Chaucer's *ABC* is a lengthy and devout prayer to the Virgin Mary, each stanza beginning with a different letter of the alphabet. The Parson's Tale, already mentioned, is a no-nonsense treatise on sin and penance that

occupies a strategic position at the end of the *Canterbury Tales*. The
Second Nun's Tale tells the early Christian story of St Cecilia among
the pagans of Rome; the Prioress's Tale that of St Hugh of Lincoln;
the Man of Law's Tale the arrival of Christianity in Northumberland
through the agency of Custance. Chaucer's lyric, 'Truth', states in so
many words that the search for truth is coterminous with the pursuit
of the Christian faith, seen as a kind of pilgrimage:

> Forth, pilgrim, forth! Forth, beste, out of thy stal!
> Know thy contree, look up, thank God of al;
> Hold the heye wey and lat thy gost thee lede,   *spirit*
> And trouthe thee shal delivere, it is no drede.   *fear*
>
> (Truth, 18–21)

There is a similar, if more controversial, tone of heartfelt piety in
Chaucer's Retraction to the *Canterbury Tales*, and in the invocation at the
end of *Troilus and Criseyde* when the narrator urges his audience to recognize Christ as the only true exemplar of fidelity, love, and suffering.

An acknowledgement of Chaucer' religious proclivities—the
extent to which the tenets of the Christian faith mattered to him—
adds to the force of his anticlerical satire. Like all true satire, it lampoons abuses in order to magnify the need for reform. There is a
particularly instructive example in the Reeve's Tale, one that targets
not just the venality of a church official but also his and, by extension,
the Church's complicity in a wider social disorder. Its central figure is
a miller of Trumpington, near Cambridge. Symkyn wishes to 'saven
his estaat of yomanrye', that is, to preserve the free status of the social
estate in which he, a yeoman, finds himself (RT 3921–82).[19] To that
end he has sought an advantageous marriage to the bastard daughter
of the local parson. She has come 'of noble kyn', which could allude
to the social status of her mother as much as her father, and has been
well brought up. In order that Symkyn should form an alliance with
her, the parson bestows a handsome dowry, 'ful many a panne of bras'.
Subsequently, husband and wife enjoy many 'halydayes' parading in
their matching red finery. Others, in fear of Symkyn, treat his wife
deferentially and call her 'dame'. She responds with appropriate dis-
dain and aloofness, 'What for her kynrede [lineage] and hir nortelrie
[upbringing]' which, the Reeve contemptuously adds, 'she hadde
lerned in a nonnerie'. They have a daughter of twenty years, whom
the parson wishes to make his heir 'Both of his catel [possessions]

and his mesuage [property]'. He is making her marriage a difficult business because he wishes to match her with someone from the nobility and so accelerate his own and Symkyn's social standing: 'bistowe hire hye | Into some worthy blood of auncetrye [ancestry]'. Then follow some biting lines that go beyond the mordant tone adopted by the Reeve, who, as an oldish carpenter, has taken personal umbrage at the Miller's Tale. Instead of using his goods charitably, by caring for his parishioners, the 'blood' of the Church, the lecherous parson is instead misappropriating Church wealth for the personal gain of his own 'blood' and thereby creating a travesty of what the Church should be:

> For hooly chirches good moot been despended
> On hooly chirches blood, that is descended.
> Therefore he wolde his hooly blood honoure,
> Though that he hooly chirche sholde devoure.
>
> (3983–6)

The contrast with the pilgrim Parson, who seeks to protect his parishioners or sheep from the devouring 'wolf', only makes more heinous the activities of the Trumpington parson. And alongside that other member of his estate, the Plowman, who is a 'trewe swynkere', Symkyn's social ambitions look even more absurd and inappropriate. Fabliau logic dictates that, by the end of the story, the illegitimate nature of his social pretensions, and with them those of his father-in-law, will be thoroughly discredited and revealed for what they are.

The Black Death

Chaucer lived through, and benefited from, a period of unusual social mobility—one that contradicted and challenged traditional views about the structure of society and its underlying beliefs. What brought about this state of affairs? The causes are complex, and are rooted in population decline and famine in the early decades of the fourteenth century. However, a major contributory factor was the impact of a disease that struck with particular ferocity in mid-century, and which recurred in 1361, 1368–9, 1374–9, and 1390–3. Referred to at the time as 'the pestilence' or 'the great mortality', but known since the nineteenth century as the 'Black Death', it comprised two varieties of plague: bubonic and pneumonic.[20] Bubonic plague is a disease of rodents—usually rats—that can be transmitted to humans by fleas. Once established in the human population it becomes infectious (i.e. transmutes into pneumonic plague) and is transferred by water droplets such as those that occur in coughing and sneezing. The symptoms of plague are sudden and alarming: a bubonic infection manifested as large swellings (buboes) in the groin, armpits, and other lymph nodes; blotchy discoloration of the skin caused by subcutaneous haemorrhages; blistering; and discharges of blood in the urine and faeces. Pneumonic plague targets the lungs and causes coughing, shortness of breath, and the frequent production of blood-stained sputum. Death follows from lack of oxygen. Both diseases kill their victims quickly: bubonic plague within six to twelve days, pneumonic within four or five.

The Black Death originated in Asia and was brought to Europe by merchants trading out of Genoa. Having raged through France, it soon crossed the Channel—probably from Gascony. The first reported outbreaks were in the summer of 1348 at the ports of Melcombe Regis (now part of Weymouth), Bristol, and Southampton. Within eighteen months, between one third and one half of the population was dead. Thomas Walsingham, a monk of St Alban's abbey, recorded in his chronicle that 'Towns once packed with people were emptied of their inhabitants, and the plague spread so thickly that the living were hardly able to bury the dead'.[21] Survivors believed, as well they might, that they were witnessing the onset of the Last Judgement. Its cause, according to Christian commentators, was human sinfulness. They saw extravagant tournaments, of the sort held the year before the plague struck, as symptomatic of the degeneracy of the age. In a sermon preached on the eve of a later outbreak, Brinton pinpointed wearers of costly clothes, slanderers, and false merchants as examples of the spiritually slothful—a disorder typical of the nation at large. Being unstable in faith, dishonourable, and false, the English are not loved by God, and

It is undoubtedly for that reason that there exists in the kingdom of England so marked a diminution of fruitfulness, so cruel a pestilence, so much injustice, so many illegitimate children—for there is on every side so much lechery and adultery that few men are contented with their own wives, but each man lusts after the wife of his neighbour, or keeps a stinking concubine in addition to his wife, however beautiful and honest she might be; behaviour which merits a horrible and wretched death.[22]

The recommended remedies were contrition and penance, and some heeded the call. The treasurer's accounts at Canterbury cathedral for

1350 show a surge in donations at the shrine of St Thomas, indicating an unusually large influx of pilgrims. Bishops and archbishops had instigated orders for penance and intercessory processions and recommended prayer, notably to Mary. One prayer, later translated from the Latin by Chaucer's disciple, John Lydgate (*c*.1370–1450), appeals to her to be 'our shield from stroke of pestilence'.[23] The idea of plague as a sword-blow or arrow-strike from God is recurrent and links to one of the symptoms of the disease—a tingling 'pins and needles' sensation, as if the sufferer were being pricked by the points of arrows—and to St Sebastian, a martyr killed by arrows, who was frequently invoked for protection.[24]

Other explanations for plague, and other remedies, were not in short supply. The medical faculty at the Sorbonne were commissioned by the French king, Philip VI, to set out the causes of the disease, and ways of avoiding it. By October of 1348 they had completed an impeccably argued document proving that the first cause of the pestilence was a configuration of Saturn, Jupiter, and Mars in Aquarius in 1345 'one hour after noon on 20 March'.[25] This had produced noxious vapours on earth which had in turn infected humans. Therefore, as other medical authorities confirmed, it was necessary to avoid corrupt air, contact with the infected, and even their gaze. Filling one's immediate air with sweet scents, say by burning juniper, or by using a nosegay, was recommended, as was flight. Other explanatory frameworks were more sinister. A widespread, popular belief attributed the plague to well-poisoning by the Jews. The remedy, across Europe, was their persecution, torture, and slaughter.

Once the tide of death had receded, the consequences for the living were mixed. Walsingham remarked: 'Rents dwindled and land was left untilled for want of tenants (who were nowhere to be found).'[26] The chronicler of the cathedral priory at Rochester lamented the shortage of 'servants, craftsmen, and workmen, and of agricultural workers and labourers', while those that remained demanded 'triple wages', practised 'idleness', and were not prepared to take orders.[27] Priests, for their part, forsook their benefices for more lucrative activities, such as singing private masses for the dead, while unqualified men stepped into the vacancies.[28] Having lost so much of their workforce, Church and secular landowners attempted to impose labour services. Modern historians have verified these tendencies, which were exacerbated by the repeated return of pestilence.[29] Land values fell, the price of labour increased, and while food prices initially rose they fell from the mid-1370s, thus further increasing the real value of wages. The population, at roughly six million in 1348 before plague struck, did not recover that level until the end of the fifteenth century. If plague acted as a catalyst, and eased pressure on over-stretched resources, it was also instrumental in changing labour relations, creating wealth (through sudden inheritance as well as through labour), and opening up opportunities for personal advancement.

What impact did plague have on Chaucer, other than by creating the general conditions that helped his social progress? He was a child of about six when the first, fearful outbreak struck. The family was then living in Southampton, where, since 1347, his father John had been deputy to the king's chief butler. As such, it was his responsibility to oversee the arrival of wine from Bordeaux for use at court. Although Southampton was one of the first places to be hit by plague, it did not suffer as badly as other towns and Chaucer's immediate family escaped scot-free. But in London a number of close relatives died in the course of 1349: John Chaucer's stepfather, Richard; his half-brother, Thomas; Agnes Chaucer's uncle, the moneylender Hamo Copton; and Hamo's son, Richard. The Chaucers were considerably enriched by the resulting acquisition of money and property. They returned to London in October 1349, when the worst of the pestilence was over, to take up residence in Hamo Copton's house. Some twenty years later, plague gave Geoffrey Chaucer a second lucky break. His first major commission, the *Book of the Duchess*, was occasioned by the death of Blanche, duchess of Lancaster. It is generally thought that she had fallen victim to the epidemic of 1368–9.

From his reading Chaucer was aware, in general terms, of a tradition that gave literature a therapeutic value in avoiding psychological illness, such as melancholy, or physical affliction, such as the plague.[30] The idea is explicit in Giovanni Boccaccio's *Decameron* (*c*.1350–3), which Chaucer probably knew. Boccaccio begins by describing the onset of plague in Florence in 1348, and produces a vivid account of familiar themes: its causes, symptoms, contagiousness, the lack of a cure, and responses both pious and hedonistic. The abiding impression is of social desolation. Individuals, and even children, are abandoned by their families to die alone; makeshift fraternities of gravediggers profit from the glut of corpses; the smell of rotting flesh fills the air; humans are given no more respect than 'dead goats'; and there are mass, depersonalized burials in large trenches, where the bodies are 'stowed tier upon tier like ships' cargo'.[31] To escape these depressing circumstances, and secure their own survival, a group of seven young women and three young men, all of good birth, leave the city with such servants as they can muster to take up temporary residence on a country estate. There, in the sweet air and natural surroundings, they pursue amusements designed to distract: dances, songs, delicious meals, and, above all, telling stories: one hundred of them over the fourteen days of their residence.

Chaucer also knew a poem by the French musician and court poet, Guillaume de Machaut (*c*.1300–77), the *Jugement dou roy de Navarre*, which again uses plague as a pretext.[32] In this instance, the narrator recalls that, in November of 1349, at a time normally dedicated to harvest and social activity, the air was dark and hazy and, being filled with a deep melancholy, he decided to stay indoors. The world seems as if it has been turned upside-down by greed and hatred, and the consequence is an eclipse of the sun and moon that presages divine retribution. The air turns 'Horrible and fetid, putrefied and infected' (315) as the dreaded symptoms of plague affect the populace. God releases death, 'gluttonous and famished' from his cage, the cemeteries overflow, the fields are left unploughed. The narrator stays resolutely within his own house until, one day, he hears the sound of music, celebrating the end of the epidemic. Filled with joy, he goes outside into the sweet air and mounts his horse in order to hunt some hares. When Chaucer wrote the *Book of the Duchess*, he turned to Machaut's poem. Although plague is not part of his subject-matter, the poem is an appropriate model in view of the supposed circumstances of Blanche's death. What Chaucer found directly useful was Machaut's treatment of melancholy (which afflicts both Chaucer's narrator and the man in black), the contrasting use of darkness and light, monochrome and colour; the opposition of personal isolation and social integration; and the use of a hunt to break the cycle of inwardness and enclosure.

Unlike Boccaccio and Machaut, Chaucer does not represent plague as a cataclysmic event.[33] He was too young to grasp as it happened the enormity of the 'great mortality' of 1349, and subsequent outbreaks, horrendous though they were, produced less *Angst*—presumably because they were more of a known quantity. Chaucer notes in passing the opportunities for enrichment that the plague provided: his thrifty Doctour of Physik, much in demand when the disease struck (however ineffectual his remedies), 'kepte that he wan in pestilence' (GP 442). Plague is even an occasion for humour in Chaucer's lyric to Henry Scogan, tutor to the sons of the future Henry IV, written during the outbreak of 1390–3. He accuses his friend of being responsible for the present 'diluge of pestilence' (Scogan 14) because he has offended the gods, and especially Venus, by abandoning his mistress. The link between planets and plague is taken more seriously in the Knight's Tale, where Saturn states that his very glance is sufficient to cause an epidemic: 'My lookyng is the fader of pestilence' (KnT 2469). In this poem of two heroes, Arcite is momentarily successful in winning Emelye from his rival, Palamon, but suffers a fatal accident on Saturn's orders and endures a disgusting, plague-like death from a toxic implosion of internal organs. No medical treatment avails him, 'Ne may the venym voyden ne expelle', his muscles being 'shent with venym and corrupcioun' (2751–4).

In the Pardoner's Tale, plague is the backdrop to a story of moral degeneracy. Sin, especially avarice, is the cause of death, and the menace of pestilence helps to create a mood of impending judgement from on high. The three 'rioters' who meet their destiny are, much like some of the inhabitants of Boccaccio's Florence, of the devil-may-care persuasion, enjoying debauchery even as a shadowy death creeps ever nearer. Hearing from their tavern the sound of a bell being rung at the head of a funeral procession, they discover it tolls for a friend of theirs 'sodeynly . . . yslayn to-nyght | Fordronke, as he sat on his bench upright' (PardT 673–88). He is the victim of a sinister figure using plague as his instrument: 'Ther cam a privee theef men clepeth Deeth . . . He hath a thousand sleyn this pestilence.' The taverner confirms that, in a 'greet village' a mile or so distant, 'man and womman, child, and hyne [farm worker], and page' are all dead. Undeterred, and in a drunken rage, the rioters set off for the village to avenge their friend by killing Death—black comedy indeed. On the way they verbally abuse an old man, who courteously guides them to the gold that is to cause their destruction. In a frenzy of greed the so-called friends kill each other, all moral norms—as well as social ones—decisively abandoned.

The Wars of Edward III

Violent death came in other forms, too. England was at war throughout Chaucer's lifetime, and although there were pauses for truces and negotiations (and plague), and the sporadic outbreaks of peace could last for several years, war kept breaking out. Waging war, with all its political, logistical, and financial implications, was a dominant activity of the society Chaucer knew. As its progress ebbed and flowed war brought in its wake euphoria and despondency; it enriched some individuals but led to unsustainable levels of taxation and virtually bankrupted the English crown; it was by turns a source of social unity and social division; it made international heroes of Edward III and the Black Prince, but they died having lost most of what they had gained. By virtue of his close involvement in the daily life of the court, Chaucer was well placed to observe the fortunes of war. More, he was actively involved in one military campaign in the course of which he was captured and ransomed; and he was a participant in some peace negotiations. In his writings, he represents and reflects on various aspects of warfare, and discusses the advantages of peacemaking.

The main enemy was France—a France made up of regions each ruled by a powerful lord with allegiance to the king.[34] Since the twelfth century, the English monarch had been one such powerful lord, holding large swathes of land including Aquitaine or Gascony, east of Bordeaux, over which the French crown also claimed sovereignty. France's claim was of particular moment once Edward III became king of England: he was related through his mother to the French king, Philip VI, and was the closest male heir to Philip's predecessor, Charles IV.[35] Matters came to a head when Philip confiscated Gascony in 1337, prompting Edward to pursue his rival claim to the French throne. Edward publicly proclaimed himself king of France, at Ghent in 1340, and quartered the arms of France (featuring the fleur-de-lis) with his own.[36]

The war thus begun just before Chaucer's birth endured until 1453, a half-century or more after his death—hence its customary designation as the Hundred Years War. Thanks to the territorial and dynastic issues that lay at its root, the alliances to which it gave rise, and its social and financial impact, it was a conflict fully European in scope. It absorbed English energies and resources from Scotland through Flanders to Spain, and especially in France. Even within Chaucer's lifetime, when neither he nor anyone else knew of the long haul ahead, the hostilities passed through many phases. If Edward III's emphasis was on the proactive waging of war, Richard II was more interested in exploring the possibilities for peace. But Edward himself found that maintaining the initiative was not always possible. During his reign the war falls into two main periods. Until the Treaty of Brétigny in 1360 the English achieved some notable successes. Thereafter, until the death of Edward in 1377, the French began to redress the balance.

By 1357, England was in a dominant position. King Jean was a prisoner in the Tower of London, where he had joined his ally, David II of Scotland, whose army had been defeated at Neville's Cross, near Durham, in 1346. Edward had also made considerable territorial gains. By the Treaty of Brétigny he secured sovereignty over Calais; the northern counties of Ponthieu, Montreuil, and Guines; and an expanded Aquitaine now covering roughly one third of France. The agreed ransom for Jean was a vast 3,000,000 crowns—one hundred times more than the exchequer's annual revenue at the start of hostilities. Edward's reputation across Europe as a valiant warrior, and that of his son, was never greater. Their achievements were based on daring and surprise, effective weaponry, and superior strategy and tactics: the English longbow, used to such devastating effect at Crécy, was also critical in securing victory at Sluys and Poitiers; the *chevau-chée*, or war ride, whereby armies would move rapidly across enemy territory, burning, looting, and sacking, had proved highly effective in cowing opposition and instilling terror.

Chaucer saw action in the campaign of 1359–60, when English fortunes were on the cusp between final victory and a protracted war of attrition. Spurred on by the successes of Crécy, Calais, and Poitiers, and with Jean II in captivity, Edward had set his sights on Rheims. His objective was to have himself anointed king of France in the very town where the ceremony was traditionally performed. He was confident enough of success to carry a gold crown in his luggage. Chaucer, then in his late teens, was probably one of the many *valetti* (yeomen), paid 6*d* a day, who served in the small company of seventy men led by his patron Lionel, earl of Ulster. Lionel's followers included a banneret (a knight with vassals, serving under his own banner), five knights, twenty-three esquires, and forty archers on horseback. The company was part of a division led by his elder brother, the Black Prince. Many years later, in 1386, at a trial to settle a dispute between Sir Richard Scrope and Sir Robert Grosvenor over the right to bear certain arms, Chaucer recalled seeing the arms borne by Richard and Henry Scrope 'en Fraunce devaunt la ville de Retters'.[37] Retters, or

Réthel, north-east of Rheims, lay on the Black Prince's route from Calais: in late November 1359 the Prince attempted to cross the river Aisne there, but was unable to do so because of enemy action.[38] Chaucer went on to attest of the Scropes: 'il lez vist armer par tout le dit viage tanque le dit Geffrey estoit pris' (he saw them armed for the entire journey in the course of which the said Geoffrey was captured).[39] No known record identifies the place of capture, but Chaucer was deemed valuable enough to be ransomed by the king on 1 March 1360 for £16—the going rate for a *valettus* serving a royal household. The record of payment says vaguely he was taken 'in partibus Francie'—in parts of France. A truce was made nine days later, Edward having failed to take Rheims.

Chaucer returned to Calais in October for the ratification of the Treaty of Brétigny, again in the service of Lionel, who, at the king's command, and along with the Black Prince and other nobles, attended the formal ceremonies on 24 October. Thanks to a financial statement of expenses made by another member of Lionel's household, Andrew de Budeston, we know that Chaucer probably returned to London ahead of his master, since he was paid 9s as a messenger for carrying letters from Calais. Chaucer soon became a trusted envoy in his own right. There are several records of his journeys to France and Flanders (no fewer than nine in 1376–7), now ranked as an esquire, 'on the king's secret business'.[40] Froissart records one such mission to Montreuil in 1377 when Chaucer accompanied Sir Guichard d'Angle and Sir Richard Stury. They met with their French counterparts to discuss the possibility of a marriage between Richard, son of the Black Prince and now heir to the English throne, and Marie, the king of France's daughter.[41]

France at this time was in a parlous condition, its towns devastated and its countryside ravaged. After Poitiers, roaming bands of English soldiers and mercenaries, known as 'Free Companies', supported themselves by extortion, plunder, and ransom. The absence of a king led to feuding at court, and social unrest to a peasant uprising, the Jacquerie.[42] But the French were learning from their mistakes, English derring-do was faltering, its luck running out. When hostilities resumed in 1369, French forces avoided open battle and instead kept to their walled towns, occasionally resorting to highly effective guerrilla tactics by harassing the long tail of English soldiers and supply trains as they advanced cross-country. Edward III was no longer in his

prime but approaching sixty and facing growing opposition to the
length and cost of the war. Growing disaffection also characterized
Aquitaine, ruled by the Black Prince since 1362. His Gascon subjects
were restive at the application of an English style of government and
taxation. Worse, the prince had contracted an incapacitating disease—perhaps dysentery—while on campaign in Spain. He appeared
at the siege of Limoges (1370) in a litter. The heir to the throne and
England's hero was dead within six years and his father, already senile,
died a year later, in 1377. Their enemies had not been slow in exploit-
ing the weakness of leadership, and by the truce of Bruges (1375) that
concluded the second phase of the war the French won back much of
the territory previously lost. The size of English-ruled Aquitaine was
reduced to a narrow coastal strip around Bordeaux, and although
England retained Calais it lost its other acquisitions.

Chaucer represents war as both glorious and cruel.[43] His pilgrim
Knight is not a warrior from the battlefields of France but rather a
crusading hero with a taste for exotic adventure who had 'foughten
for oure feith at Tramyssene [Tlemcen, north Algeria] | In lystes
thries, and ay slayn his foo' (GP 62–3). It is his son, the Squire who,
for all his courtly accomplishments, has ridden with the cavalry
against neighbouring enemy forces: 'he hadde ben somtyme in chyv-
achie [*chevauchée*] | In Flaundres, in Artoys, and Pycardie' (85–6)—
precisely those parts of the Low Countries and France where the
fighting had been frequent and fierce. But it is their silent companion,
the Yeoman, who is in service to the Knight, whose portrait speaks
most evocatively about the war with France. He is a master of the
weapon that proved so decisive and deadly at Sluys, Crécy, and
Poitiers:

> A sheef of pecok arwes, bright and kene,
> Under his belt he bar ful thriftily   *bore very properly*
> (Wel koude he dresse his takel yemanly;   *knew; take care of*
> His arwes drouped noght with fetheres lowe),
> And in his hand he baar a mighty bowe.
>
> (104–8)

The Knight's Tale, like its teller and his retinue, celebrates the lure
and idealism of warfare while recognizing its more gruesome effects.
An early scene shows duke Theseus of Athens preparing to set off on
a high-minded campaign to defeat Creon the tyrant of Thebes, by

besieging his city. He turns it into a ruin, having demolished the buildings (he 'rente adoun bothe walle and sparre and rafter') and destroyed its defences, leaving it with 'waste walles wyde' (KnT 990, 1331). Theseus has been persuaded to go by the mourning widows of knights slain by Creon—not because of their deaths as such, but because the men's bodies have been dishonoured. Creon has not allowed the Athenian knights burial, but has instead left their corpses all in a heap for the dogs to eat. A shiver of excitement at Theseus's decisive resolve to right a wrong is caught in the effect of his banner, which bears an emblem of the god of war and is so dazzling that 'alle the feeldes [background] glyteren up and doun' (977). The same glamorous Mars is devastating in his effects on humankind and on nature more generally. His temple, described in detail later in the poem, includes a wall painting of a wasteland reminiscent of modern conflicts as well as medieval ones. There is a forest, devoid of man or beast, 'With knotty, knarry [gnarled], bareyne trees olde, | Of stubbes [stumps] sharpe and hidouse to biholde' (1977–8). The painting also includes images of burning, murder, destruction, and slaughter of plague-like proportions all too familiar from the chronicle accounts of the war with France:

> The shepne brennynge with the blake smoke;   *stable*
> The tresoun of the mordrynge in the bedde;
> The open werre, with woundes al bibledde . . .
> The careyne in the busk, with throte ycorve;   *corpse; woods*
> A thousand sleyn, and nat of qualm ystorve;   *killed by plague*
> The tiraunt, with the pray by force yraft;   *taken away*
> The toun destroyed, ther was no thing laft,
> Yet saugh I brent the shippes hoppesteres . . .   *dancing on the sea*
>
> (KnT 2000–17)

Some of the details Chaucer uses may be traced to the traditional iconography of Mars as a planet-god with influence over certain 'children' (such as Arcite in the Knight's Tale) and the violence and conflict they endure. On other occasions, Chaucer drew more directly on his first-hand knowledge of war. One of the stories told by the Monk to illustrate the tragic end of famous men features Pedro the Cruel, supported by the Black Prince but ousted from his throne by his bastard half-brother, Henry of Trastamara, and then betrayed and murdered by Henry in 1369:

>   . . . at a seege, by subtiltee,
> Thou were bitraysed and lad unto his tente,   *betrayed*
> Where as he with his owene hand slow thee,
> Succedynge in thy regne and in thy rente.   *tribute*
>
>   (MkT 2379–82)

Chaucer was reasonably close to the event and probably received some verbal account of it. John of Gaunt married Pedro's daughter, Constance, in 1371 and Chaucer's wife, Philippa, was for a time a member of her London household. Chaucer himself had travelled to Spain with a safe-conduct from the king of Navarre in 1366, but the exact purpose of his journey is unknown.[44]

Revolt

The devastating plague of 1348–9 and its subsequent outbreaks led to severe shortages of labour, falling prices, and rising wages. Parliament, which represented landowners, responded by endeavouring to control the labour market. The Statute of Labourers (1351) set wages and prices at pre-plague levels and imposed penalties, including fines and imprisonment, for those found in breach of the regulations. Commissioners, including justices of the peace, enforced the Statute at county level.[45] War and political crisis exacerbated the already fraught relations between landowners and labourers. By the mid-1370s the southern counties of England were experiencing the war at first hand: in 1377, the French landed on the Isle of Wight and soldiers looted and started fires before ransoming the island for one thousand marks. French ships also made successful raids on Winchester, Hastings, and Rye. The seigneurial class seemed to have lost the ability to defend the country, to beat the enemy, or to govern: John of Gaunt's attempted siege of St Malo in the summer of 1378 was a failure; the king, Richard II, was a boy; and his advisers were prone to factional in-fighting. To add insult to injury, in 1377 parliament introduced a poll tax to raise yet more finance for the war. The second poll tax of 1379, described earlier, calculated tax liability across the social spectrum, but it bore particularly hard on poorer people and local communities. The third poll tax of 1380 imposed a levy of three groats or one shilling on all adults over fifteen—roughly the equivalent of three days' wages. There was widespread evasion and tax commissioners were appointed to investigate non-payment, enforce compliance, and mete out punishment. One chronicler, Henry Knighton, reports that girls were subjected to vaginal examination in order to determine if they were 'adult' or not.[46]

The insurrection that followed, in a mood of popular outrage, is widely known as the 'Peasants' Revolt' but the term is misleading if taken to mean an undifferentiated mass of impoverished agricultural workers. The largest group paid rent for the land they worked, but some were very substantial peasants and the leaders of village communities. Others were servants, and a significant minority were craftsmen, artisans, and traders of the sort found in village society: weavers, carpenters, cobblers, pedlars, tailors, fullers, glovers, tilers, dyers, millers, inn-keepers, hosiers, skinners, bakers, butchers, spinsters, cooks. Most were self-employed and some were relatively wealthy. And while the revolt was one of 'those who work' there were occasional alliances with those who did not: members of the gentry who either sympathized with the rebels or who had local scores to settle; and poor priests—some of whom, like John Wrawe in Suffolk, took leading roles.[47] The rebels also attracted considerable support from urban centres. Although local conditions, levels of mutual trust, and motivations, varied, the riots in such places as Maidstone, Canterbury, St Albans, Cambridge, and, above all, London, were the result of rebels and townsmen making common cause.

The rising began during May 1381 near Brentwood in Essex when Chief Justice Robert Bealknap attempted to indict certain villagers in Fobbing, Corringham, and Stanford-le-Hope for resisting payment of their poll taxes. In response, according to the *Anonimalle Chronicle*, the villagers confronted him en masse, turned the tables, and 'made him swear on the Bible that never again would he hold such sessions nor act as a justice in such inquests. And they forced him to tell them the names of all the jurors. They captured all of these jurors that they could, beheaded them and threw their houses to the ground.'[48] The rebellion spread quickly to other villages and towns across a swathe of eastern and south-eastern England and caused isolated disturbances as far away as Bridgwater, Chester, and York.[49] The targets of the rebels' wrath were anyone and anything to do with officialdom, and especially with the imposition of the Statute of Labourers and the poll taxes. Thus justices of the peace, jurors, lawyers, and royal servants received short shrift. The rebels also made a point of burning court rolls and muniments so that, according to the chronicler

Thomas Walsingham, 'once the memory of ancient customs had been wiped out their lords would be completely unable to vindicate their rights over them'.[50] As their actions gathered momentum, leaders emerged who commanded widespread loyalty, notably Wat Tyler and Jack Straw or Rackstraw—shadowy figures who nevertheless exerted real authority. Ideological leadership came from the likes of John Ball, a 'chaplain of evil disposition' according to the *Anonimalle Chronicle* whom the Kent rebels released from Maidstone gaol on their march to London.[51] His doctrine of radical Christianity, though not unusual for the time, made some observers believe that he drew inspiration from John Wyclif, and therefore represented a combustible amalgam of political and religious sedition.[52]

The rebels' demands are filtered through the words of more or less hostile chroniclers who nevertheless agree that what the rebels wanted, above all, was freedom. By freedom they meant an end to serfdom (servile status) whereby 'bondmen' paid labour dues to lords.[53] Their rationale was that all are equal in the eyes of God or, in the words of a dictum popularized by John Ball, 'When Adam delved and Eve span | Who was then the gentilman?' It followed that any contractual arrangement should be a matter of choice, not birthright. Those responsible for reinforcing servility and inequality, notably lawyers, were to be killed—legal matters thereafter to be determined 'by the decrees of the common people'.[54] Just as the secular hierarchy was to be levelled, so was the ecclesiastical. Ball envisaged an end of archbishops, bishops, abbots, and priors, the redistribution of the Church's wealth among the laity, and the non-payment of tithes except to priests poorer than the giver.[55] Yet the rebels remained loyal to the king, whom they saw as their natural lord in a people's monarchy, however much they hated his advisers or wanted a reform of lordship in general.

Driven by a heady mixture of grievance and hope, many thousands of rebels converged on Blackheath, near Greenwich, on 12 June 1381.[56] Many thousands more from Essex and other eastern counties assembled on the opposite bank of the river Thames. The rebels marched on London the following day, the feast of Corpus Christi (a traditional time of revelry and carnival). Their two points of entry into the city were north-east of the river, at Aldgate; and south of the river at London Bridge, where they encountered little resistance: the townspeople lowered the bridge, in defiance of the mayor. Once inside the city, the rebels found that disaffected inhabitants had begun their work for them. John of Gaunt's palace, the Savoy (on the site of the present Savoy Hotel in the Strand), was already in flames, its charters, records, and contents soon destroyed (the rebels prohibited looting). Thomas Walsingham's description is enough to make a museum curator weep:

> . . . they broke the gold and silver vessels, of which there were many at the Savoy, into pieces with their axes and threw them into the Thames or the sewers. They tore the golden cloths and silk hangings to pieces and crushed them underfoot; they ground up rings and other jewels inlaid with precious stones in small mortars, so that they could never be used again. And so it was done. Finally, and in order not to pass by any opportunity for shaming the duke completely, they seized one of his most precious vestments, which we call a 'jakke', and placed it on a lance to be used as a target for their arrows.[57]

The rebels hated John of Gaunt with particular venom: the wealthiest and most powerful landowner bar none, he was also blamed for the introduction of the poll tax, military defeat, and reversing the work of the Good Parliament of 1376 which had exposed and impeached war profiteers and corrupt advisers. Gaunt had the good sense to be in Scotland at the time of the revolt, on a diplomatic mission. Others were not so fortunate. Lawyers and royal officials were vulnerable, and immigrants were slaughtered—especially Flemings, who were noted for their weaving; and Lombards, involved in money-lending.

The king, along with his chief officials and some soldiers, had withdrawn to the Tower of London, but on the morning of 14 June Richard emerged to meet the rebels at Mile End, attended by his mother and a company of knights and squires. The rebels presented their demands for an end to serfdom and Richard 'had it proclaimed before them that he would confirm and grant that they should be free, and generally should have their will'.[58] He agreed to issue letters patent to that effect, sealed with the royal seal, on condition that the rebels should disperse—as some then did. Either at the same time as the Mile End conference, or afterwards (the chronology is unclear), the rebels entered the Tower of London and seized those they regarded as traitors to the king: Simon Sudbury, chancellor of England and archbishop of Canterbury; the royal treasurer, Robert Hales; William Appleton, an influential Franciscan friar; and others. These they executed on Tower Hill, parading their heads through the streets on stakes before displaying them on London Bridge. The archbishop's head was placed in the centre, and higher than the others, with a red mitre fixed to it with a nail.

Negotiations continued the next day, when the king with a retinue of about 200 people, including the mayor, William Walworth, met Wat Tyler and the rebels at Smithfield. Tyler reiterated their demands, urging the speedy completion of the promised letters patent. Richard complied but something in the rebel leader's manner, which the chroniclers variously describe as menacing, disrespectful, arrogant, or just plain churlish, provoked an altercation with a squire. Walworth intervened, drew his sword, and wounded Tyler, who was soon finished off in the resulting fracas. The rebels grew restive at the sudden death of their champion, but a cool-headed Richard rode forward and placated them by announcing that he was their new leader. Reinforcements arrived, having now found the courage to confront the invaders. The rebels were surrounded and persuaded to leave the city and return home. Richard knighted Walworth on the spot, along with two former mayors, Nicholas Brembre and John Philipot, and another alderman, Robert Launde. The head of Tyler, later joined by those of Jack Straw and John Ball, soon took the place of Sudbury's on London Bridge. More general retribution followed. Richard rescinded his letters patent or 'charter of freedom' and set up two royal commissions to root out the rebels in London and elsewhere. Walworth, Brembre, Philipot, and Launde were leading members. Some one hundred rebels were executed but in general terms restraint, not vindictive persecution, was the order of the day. The parliament that met in November and December of 1381 recognized that the corruption of royal officials had been a major cause of the revolt and issued a general pardon (which excluded those known to be guilty of particular crimes). The poll tax itself was abandoned.

The heroes of the hour had been the king and Walworth—the latter in his sudden assumption of gentility a striking example of how rapidly social boundaries could be crossed. As a number of contemporary commentators pointed out, it was the merchant mayor who acted in a true, knightly fashion while the so-called knights, faced only with rustics, had remained supine throughout the emergency. To an upholder of the three estates model, such as Gower, who witnessed the revolt, it was especially irksome to find that, when it came to the crunch, 'those who fight' didn't. Immediately afterwards, he penned a new, prefatory book to his prophetic magnum opus, *Vox clamantis*. It provides a first-hand account of the rebellion in the form of a nightmare vision full of biblical and classical allusions. For Gower, the whole idea of the revolt is anathema, the worst possible outcome of the ills the rest of his work describes, for revolt overturns and transgresses the rightful, hierarchical boundaries between the orders of society. In their rage the peasants, whether young or old, bear arms, no matter that their weapons are improper to their estate and ludicrous: a stake, pole, distaff, axe, sickle, pitchfork, or quiver carried upside-down. By performing such an outrageous inversion of their social position, they lose their humanity. Their leader from Kent is a rapacious boar breathing flames from its chest, setting houses and cities on fire, attacking with its huge teeth while 'hot foam mixed with human blood flecked its shoulders'.[59] The rabble that follows him are a huge pack of dogs, roaming free—their howling a music that Satan rejoices to hear. Yet 'those who fight' fail to mount a defence, being too timorous, confused, or ineffectual. It is a catastrophic and shaming failure: 'neither the shield nor the lance of the nobles, with which their age-old honor should have been defended, offered any opposition then'.[60]

Gower the lawyer had good reason to feel queasy at the actions of the rebels. Other writers were more attuned to their cause. William Langland was a London poor priest of the sort that became active in the revolt: an unbeneficed member of the clergy who probably made his living as a chantry priest, that is, by saying masses for the dead in return for payment (something of a growth industry in post-plague years). In the second version, or B-text, of his great visionary poem, *Piers Plowman*, written in the 1370s, he creates an allegorical episode critical of the predatory ways of a 'fat cat', generally taken to be John of Gaunt. In other respects Langland is a traditionalist. He is wary of landless labourers and describes the knight's familiar role as protector of those who work and those who pray. Yet there are some telling comments about the proper relations between a knight and his tenants. He should not harass them with legal proceedings; should administer taxes with mercy and meekness; refuse bribes; and treat bondmen with respect, for while inferior on earth they may be superior in heaven. Langland underlines his point with a *memento mori*. In a charnel-house it is impossible to tell a churl from his bones for in death social difference is negated: 'At churche in the charnel cherles aren evele to knowe [difficult to tell apart] | Or a knyhte from a knave or a quene [servant] fram a queene' (C-text VIII. 45–6).[61] Bones are bones.

These words are spoken by Piers Plowman himself, who has appeared suddenly to offer help to some lost pilgrims in their quest for truth. His guidance is spiritual (they must follow the Ten Commandments) as well as practical (they should work conscientiously according to their allotted roles). By making a ploughman the authoritative voice of his poem (at one level of interpretation Piers is none other than Christ himself) Langland was adapting precedent but also positioning himself outside of 'authority' as generally conceived. Piers knows the way to truth not by rote or through orthodox routes of instruction but intuitively, through his own natural wit. He is an empowered and empowering figure. Although he was pivotal to the poem since its inception in the 1360s A-text, from a post-revolt perspective Piers looks unusually challenging since ploughmen, central to peasant society, had been among those taking an active part in the rebellion. If Langland is no rabble-rouser for the rebels' cause, he nevertheless seems to understand their predicament, and Piers Plowman became one of their mascots. In the letters of John Ball, circulating in 1381, they are urged to 'stondeth togidre, in Godes name, and biddeth Peres Ploughman go to his werk'.[62] 'Peres Ploughman', like 'Hobbe the Robere', is a popular collocation and not necessarily a direct reference to Langland's work. Even so, it is indicative of shared concerns that both priests should have chosen the same hero.

Chaucer's response to the events of 1381 was more muted, even though some of the events were uncomfortably close to home—quite literally so. His own living quarters at the time of the revolt were at Aldgate, a property he held on condition that he should keep it ready for garrisoning in time of emergency. It was through this gate that one main cohort of rebels entered the city. Then there was the ferocity of their attack on the palace of their *bête noire*, Chaucer's patron, John of Gaunt. Again, Richard Lyons, castigated by the Good Parliament and imprisoned for profiteering from the war, then butchered by the rebels, was an associate of John Chaucer, Chaucer's father, and from 1374 to 1376 Chaucer's own 'line manager' as collector of customs while Chaucer was a customs controller at the wool quay. Or again, the gruesome massacre of Flemings at St Martin's church in the Vintry, the area in London where Chaucer grew up, happened in Thames Street, where John Chaucer owned a tenement just a few doors away. But it would be wrong to suggest that Geoffrey was directly in the line of fire even though he was the sort of person the rebels targeted: a royal official, and someone shortly to become a justice of the peace, charged among other duties with enforcing the labour laws.

If Chaucer felt the heat of the rebellion, it is not immediately apparent in his writings. He is neither enraged like a Gower nor engaged like a Langland. Instead he mentions the revolt only in passing and in comments refracted through two pilgrim narrators. The Knight provides Saturn with a speech in which he describes, among other baleful consequences of his planetary influence, 'the cherles rebellyng' (KnT 2459). Rebellion is a traditional effect of Saturn's rule so the phrase need not of itself mean 'the Peasants' Revolt', but Chaucer's audience would inevitably have made a connection to the events of 1381. The Nun's Priest, in his own voice, makes a much more specific allusion. His tale is a rural fable, freighted with rhetoric in a mock-heroic style, about the adventures of a cock and a hen, Chauntecleer and Pertelote, who belong to a poor widow. Chauntecleer is tricked by a fox, seized, and carried off to the woods. There is uproar in the henyard. In the adjacent cottage the widow and her two daughters jump up, rush outside, and give chase:

> And cryden 'Out! Harrow and weilaway!   *Alas!*
> Ha, ha! The fox!' and after him they ran,
> And eek with staves many another man.
> Ran Colle oure dogge, and Talbot and Gerland,
> And Malkyn with a dystaf in hir hand;
> Ran cow and calf, and eek the verray hogges,   *also*
> So fered for the berkyng of the dogges,   *frightened by*
> And shoutynge of the men and wommen eeke,   *also*
> They ronne so hem thoughte hir herte breeke.
> They yolleden as feendes doon in helle;
> The dokes cryden as men wolde hem quelle;   *kill*
> The gees for feere flowen over the trees;
> Out of the hyve cam the swarm of bees.
> So hidous was the noyse—a, benedicitee!—   *God save us!*
> Certes he, Jakke Straw and his meynee   *followers*
> Ne made nevere shoutes half so shrille,
> Whan that they wolden any Flemyng kille,
> As thilke day was maad upon the fox.   *that*

(NPT 3380–97)

Chaucer's description is a comic pastiche of details found in chronicle descriptions of the revolt: impulsive action; violent emotion; an atmosphere of fear and fright; frenzied activity; chaos; the sense of a world turned upside-down by sudden cataclysm; a confusion of people and animals, with pigs running rampant, geese and bees breaking bounds; a wry treatment of the peasants and what they carry (staves, a distaff); and above all the hideous noise, whether of shouts or barks or (in later lines) trumpets and horns, which is hellish in its intensity—worse even than the shrill shouting of Jack Straw and his followers as they hunted down and butchered Flemings.[63]

The comparison strikes a modern reader as a joke in bad taste, trivializing one of the most barbaric, animalistic moments of the rebels' London carnival. But it may be that Chaucer's referent is not the revolt as such, but the Technicolor version of it in *Vox clamantis*. In other words, he might be cocking a sardonic snook at the way in which his friend, 'moral' Gower, portrayed the rebellion, showing how even a henyard catastrophe can outclass it. Or it may be that Chaucer's studied nonchalance is an entirely appropriate and authentic response to the events of 1381. They were horrendous while they lasted, but were soon over and negligible in their long-term effects. The revolt was readily assimilated to existing explanatory frameworks such as the reign of Saturn, and soon found a relatively comfortable place in the collective memory. Such interpretations imply that Chaucer was merely a child of his estate, reacting as a royal official might to an unprecedented episode that threatened to tear apart the fabric of society. Yet, as we have seen, Chaucer was both an insider and an outsider and in this case too there is evidence of his ability to think 'outside the box'.

The first of the Canterbury tales is told by a representative of the seigneurial class, the Knight. Its hero, Theseus, encounters a number of challenges to his rule, some of which threaten the very core of his chivalric ethos. Yet he emerges triumphant as the upholder of a social hierarchy validated by cosmic order. In a summing-up speech designed to reconcile his citizens to their lot he refers to the predetermined 'bounds' of life and nature. Those who question or challenge the status quo are characterized as wilful rebels against God himself: 'rebel is to him that al may gye [guide]' (KnT 3046). Generally speaking, the other pilgrims are impressed by the Knight's 'noble storye', and it is particularly well received by those who share his social status, or aspire to it, 'namely the gentils everichon' (MillP 3113).

The Host now turns to the Monk and invites him to provide the next tale. So it would seem that Harry Bailly, the landlord of the Tabard Inn at Southwark, is proceeding decorously according to the received model of the three estates, whereby a prominent representative of 'those who pray' takes his turn after a prominent representative of 'those who fight'. But a member of the third estate, 'those who work', has rather different ideas. The drunken Miller is not at all enamoured of the story he has just heard and insists on telling one of his own in order to *quite*, or pay back, the Knight. The Miller is described in the General Prologue much as we have come to expect 'peasants' to be: inebriated, animalistic, repellent, grotesque, licentious.[64] He is 'big . . . of brawn . . . of bones', brutish in wrestling and breaking down doors, with red, sow-like hair in his beard and a tuft of hairs sprouting from a wart on his nose 'Reed as the brustles of a sowes erys [ears]' (GP 545–56). The bagpipes with which he pipes the pilgrims along are a traditional image of phallic excess. Comic and menacing, the Miller is also described by Chaucer the pilgrim narrator as a *cherl* (MillP 3182) and he muscles in to stage in narrative terms a veritable 'cherles rebelling' of his own, subverting a romance with a fabliau. Ribald and scatological, the Miller's Tale is also a sophisticated critique of the world described by the Knight, in which any use of ideology to guide or justify social practice is held up for ridicule.[65]

The Reign of Richard II

Richard was ten years old when he came to the throne in 1377, four-teen when he faced down the rebels at Smithfield. It was hardly an auspicious start to his reign. He was never meant to be king, for that role was intended for his father, the Black Prince, a war hero. The early years of Richard's reign were marred by in-fighting as his advisers and particularly his uncle, John of Gaunt, jockeyed for position in the general councils that managed the governance of the realm during Richard's minority. Then there was the social upheaval of 1381. The revolt, however, provided Richard with some 'bounce': he was never the object of the rebels' ire; dealt with the crisis decisively when his chief allies had already been killed; and was humane in the aftermath—however much men such as Sir Robert Tresilian, the chief justice, pursued a policy of repression. Thereafter, Richard's reign fluctuated between periods when he successfully advanced the interests of his friends and favourites and periods when their opponents, using parliament as an instrument of justice, curbed their power.

A major crisis, with implications for the rest of Richard's reign, occurred in 1387 when five lords (the duke of Gloucester and the earls of Arundel, Derby, Nottingham, and Warwick) formed an alliance to appeal to Richard against what they perceived as the malign influence and traitorous conduct of Richard's close advisers. The 'Appellants' had five main targets: Sir Robert de Vere, ninth earl of Oxford, whom Richard had showered with land, property, and extraordinary marks of favour, including the titles marquis of Dublin and duke of Ireland; Michael de la Pole, a former chancellor impeached for embezzlement the previous year but still a member of the king's inner circle; chief justice Tresilian, mentioned above; Sir Nicholas Brembre, a former mayor who had been knighted by Richard at Smithfield and who had since furnished Richard with a number of large loans; and Alexander Neville, archbishop of York. De Vere went so far as to raise an army to defend his privileges but it was routed by the Appellants at Radcot Bridge, near Oxford. The king took refuge in the Tower of London. Negotiations with the Appellants led to his humiliation. The objects of their attack were put on trial at Westminster by the so-called Merciless Parliament of 1388. De Vere, Tresilian, and de la Pole had their lands confiscated and were condemned to death. Brembre was tried and sent for execution, Neville forfeited his lands. A further four chamber knights were tried and one, Sir Simon Burley, an influential former tutor to the king, was beheaded. A hollow kind of reconciliation followed: at a mass in Westminster Abbey the lords reaffirmed their homage to the king and he renewed his coronation oath. Richard never forgot the deep affront to his dignity and authority and continued to harbour resentment. Two years later, when he was of age and had strengthened his position in political terms, he crushed the Appellants and installed a new coterie of favoured advisers.

The nature of the king's counsel was therefore an enduring controversy. In the process of his struggle with the magnates and with parliament Richard became increasingly distant, cultivating a mystique about his royal person through extravagant display, exalted terms of address, and the production of monumental art designed to promote his authority as king (Fig. 2).[66] But there were more positive aspects to his reign. Inclined more to the arts of peace than those of war, Richard concluded a treaty with the French, encouraged the production of

Fig. 2. Portrait of Richard II holding the orb and sceptre,
symbols of royal authority (c.1395).

painting, sculpture, and architecture and, with his marriage to Anne of Bohemia early in 1381, acquired for his court a cosmopolitan flavour and growing reputation for magnificence. Anne died in 1394 and Richard subsequently married Isabella of France. There was no heir from either marriage and so the question of succession became a thorny problem. In the final years of his reign Richard suppressed all opposition to his increasingly autocratic mode of kingship. He continued his vindictive pursuit of the Appellants and secured their death or banishment. Having also exiled Gaunt's son, Henry of Bolingbroke, Richard found himself politically isolated. His opponents took advantage of his absence on a military expedition in Ireland to promote Bolingbroke's claim to the throne, capture Richard, and secure his demise. Bolingbroke became king as Henry IV in 1399.

Chaucer experienced at first hand, and profited from, Richard's rule. His appointment in 1374 by the then king, Edward III, as customs controller in the port of London, continued under Richard's reign until 1386. Richard then appointed him clerk of the works at Westminster, the Tower of London, and other royal castles and lodges for the years 1389 to 1391. The king's warrant under the privy seal, using conventional language, is from 'Richard par la grace de Dieu roy Dengleterre e de France e signur Dirlande' (Richard by the grace of God king of England and France and lord of Ireland) to 'nostre bien ame [our good friend] Geffrey Chaucer'. The citation in a subsequent document is more direct and personal. In 1394, and for five years thereafter, Richard renewed under his private seal a life annuity of £20 to his 'dilectus armiger noster Galfridus Chaucer' (our beloved squire Geoffrey Chaucer) for good service.[67]

In spite of this evidence of royal favour, Chaucer is not to be thought of as a courtier coming and going at Westminster on a daily basis. The offices of the court were in the process of gaining some independence, that is, of becoming a civil service, and minor officials (such as Chaucer was) increasingly performed their routine work away from the court and at the behest of more senior employees of the Crown (such as Richard Lyons, assassinated by the rebels of 1381). And while Chaucer might depend upon the court for a living he was also careful not to become a victim of in-fighting. In the period surrounding the Merciless Parliament he severed many of his formal connections with Richard, even surrendering his annuities. He knew that the court could be an unforgiving place if he were to be too closely associated with the wrong faction.[68] In the Knight's Tale, Palamon and Arcite are two cousins of noble birth, mutual confidants who have sworn to advance each other's causes. Captured at Thebes and imprisoned by Theseus, they see his sister-in-law, Emelye, in the garden below and both fall in love with her. They quarrel bitterly, but the woman is out of reach, at least for the time being. Arcite compares their plight to that of two dogs fighting over a bone, but so engrossed are the dogs in their anger that a kite flies down and snatches the prize from between them. He concludes cynically, the word 'brother' having lost all sense of comradeship: 'And therefore, at the kynges court, my brother, | Ech man for hymself, ther is noon oother' (KnT 1181–2).

CHAPTER 3

THE LITERARY SCENE

THERE is a well-known image that is often reproduced in colour on the cover of books by or about Chaucer. Commonly referred to as the '*Troilus* frontispiece', it is taken from a book now at Corpus Christi College, Cambridge (MS 61). The manuscript contains a copy of Chaucer's *Troilus and Criseyde* and makes provision for an elaborate series of illustrations, although only the first was completed. The poem was produced between *c.*1415 and 1420 for an unknown person but he or she must have been of some standing since the opening illumination is in a lavish style. It shows a central figure, usually taken to be Chaucer, at a podium or pulpit from which he is reciting. His listeners, both men and women, are gathered round in a semicircle and in a variety of postures that register different degrees of attentiveness and response. Among them is a central figure, his face erased, who would appear to be a king. Some of the audience have their gazes fixed on Chaucer, others seem to be engaged in conversation. All are dressed in the colourful and fashionable clothes appropriate to a royal court. Behind Chaucer there is a rocky *coulisse*, set diagonally in the picture frame, and beyond that a scene at a city gate involving two groups of figures who face each other. They are dressed in clothes similar to those of the audience below. It is possible that the upper scene represents an episode from the narrative of *Troilus* as it issues from the mouth of the performer and unfolds in the imaginations of his listeners.[1]

The *Troilus* frontispiece seems to provide a privileged window on to the setting and circumstances of Chaucer's great poem. It is sometimes captioned as 'Chaucer reading *Troilus* to the court of Richard II'. That may be the effect the picture is trying to create but it does not necessarily convey an authentic account of Chaucer's relationship with that court, or of the circumstances in which he published his poem. Many elements of the composition derive from conventional ways of representing a medieval author before his audience; the image was made fifteen years or so after Chaucer's death and is to that extent a reconstruction; and it may be little more than a response to the illusion Chaucer himself creates within *Troilus*, of performing his poem to a group of sophisticated courtiers who see themselves and their preoccupations reflected in a romance about Trojan lovers.

Beguiling as it may be, the *Troilus* frontispiece does raise genuine questions about the literary scene that Chaucer knew. It alludes in general terms to matters already broached in the first chapter, namely the interaction of Chaucer's literary persona with his historical identity and the impact of patronage on his writing, but focuses more specifically on the court as a context for the production of literature. The image provokes curiosity, too, about the nature of his audience within and beyond the court—its constituent parts, their levels of literacy and expectation, their modes of response and engagement. That in turn leads to questions about the function of literature when Chaucer wrote. The *Troilus* picture gestures to a world where poetry was performed as well as read, and therefore experienced as a social event with all its opportunities for performance, entertainment, theatricality, and discussion. Publication through performance was something of a necessity in a culture without print technology, but oral performance has aesthetic implications too. Did the conditions of publication in part determine Chaucer's choice of material? What was the significance of Troy in the imaginative lives of his audience? Were his horizons generally as international as they seem to be from *Troilus*—based largely on a translation of Boccaccio's *Il Filostrato*?

Patronage

Chaucer was a survivor in the volatile court culture of the final quarter of the fourteenth century, but what are the implications of that for his literary output? In the first place, the court gave him access to French literature, introducing him to the dominance of French in courtly culture as the literary language *par excellence*. Chaucer's earliest lyrics may have been in French, and his translations show that he was fluent in the language. Otherwise, he could hardly have operated as a representative of the court, since French was also the language of international diplomacy, a *lingua franca* across Europe. However much Chaucer championed the use of English as a medium for literary composition, he remained indebted to French authors throughout his career. Other writers were more traditional. His contemporary,

Jean Froissart, a visitor to the English court, wrote entirely in French, and a significant part of Gower's output was in French.[2]

Second, the court gave Chaucer access to patronage, thereby providing him with income (however unreliable or intermittent), and so giving him the means to spend time writing poetry. There is a good demonstration of his survival instinct, and of his harnessing literary talent for practical ends, in a short poem, 'The Complaint of Chaucer to His Purse', addressed to Henry IV soon after the deposition of Richard and a year before Chaucer's own death.[3] The lyric is framed as a complaint, in which Chaucer addresses his purse as if it were his lady, complaining that 'she' is *light* in the sense both of wanton and empty. In the manner of a love-lyric, but with an allusion to his own advanced age, Chaucer announces that he would rather be laid on his bier if 'she' does not make him 'hevy chere'—that is take him seriously by becoming heavy with money again. Further witty and ambiguous plays on the idea of money as mistress now follow: he longs to hear her blissful sound, to see her colour 'lyk the sonne bryght', to be comforted by her. Then, in the five concluding lines, he addresses Henry directly as 'conquerour of Brutes Albyon' (i.e. the England founded by the legendary Brutus), endorsing his position as the rightful and true or 'verray' king, one who occupies his throne legitimately by 'lyne' (lineage) and 'free eleccion' (common assent). Chaucer is leaving Henry in no doubt that he enjoys his support and he, in turn, is expected to proffer his: 'ye, that mowen alle oure harmes amende [heal all our woes], | Have mynde upon my supplicacion'. The man who ended Richard's tyranny, bringing peace to the realm, must surely be able to extend his largesse to a loyal poet.

The patronage at issue here, though expressed in literary form, is political. In other words, Chaucer is suing for the continuation of the exchequer payments he received under Richard's regime. And it seems he was successful. The life records document Chaucer's exchequer annuities from Henry IV for the years 1399–1400.[4] Chaucer was also the continuing beneficiary of Gaunt's munificence, being the recipient of a life annuity of £10 in 1374. By then his wife was already being paid an annuity from Gaunt for having served as an attendant, or *demoiselle*, to his second wife, Constance of Castile. Politically speaking, the patronage of Gaunt would not have done Chaucer any harm—rather the reverse. The third son of Edward III, uncle of Richard II, and father of Henry IV, he was, to say the least, well connected, a kingmaker who was an international prince in his own right. He had aspirations of his own to be king of Castile, and although they were frustrated he did become duke of Aquitaine. In and out of favour with Richard, his absence from court could produce a power vacuum and a need for rapprochement. Gaunt's power, prestige and influence were such that Chaucer could be reasonably secure about the level of protection the duke's patronage provided against the stormy waters of court politics.

As we have seen in Chapter 1, Gaunt was also Chaucer's literary patron, since the *Book of the Duchess* commemorates the death of the duke's first wife, Blanche. Yet there is no payment from Gaunt's accounts that can be linked to the production of that poem, any more than there are records of payments from Richard's household to Chaucer for any of the 'courtly' poems (such as *Troilus and Criseyde*) that he wrote during his reign. True, there is the whiff of royal patronage about the *Legend of Good Women*, where Chaucer as dreamer is instructed to present his poem to 'the quene' at the royal palace at Eltham or Sheen, and there is further reference to Anne of Bohemia in *Troilus* where she is flatteringly described as a paragon of beauty, 'Right as oure firste lettre is now an A' (*TC* I. 171). But there is no documentary evidence that Chaucer received benefits in money or kind for any of the poems that seem to emanate from a court culture. In fact, there are no records to show that Richard commissioned any poet to produce literature for the court, although Gower records in his *Confessio Amantis* that he was asked to write that poem by Richard while travelling with him on the Thames in the royal barge.[5] The practice of the English court contrasts with that of the French court, where royal patronage was more visible and energetically pursued as a means of enhancing the repute of Charles V. It may be that in England patronage for literary endeavour was subsumed under the much larger patronage machine on which the political system depended; or it may be that Richard's interests were more focused on the production of works of direct concern to his ideas of governance. Richard was indeed a bookish person, but his personal library attests to a somewhat traditional notion of literature that was out of step with the more innovatory practices of Chaucer.[6]

What patronage of the political sort did bring Chaucer was direct involvement in some key events—for a writer, grist to the mill. As one of two knights of the shire for Kent in 1386, he attended the Wonderful

Parliament that lasted for fifty-nine days and which secured the dismissal, impeachment, and imprisonment of the lord chancellor, William de la Pole, earl of Suffolk, for embezzlement. De la Pole, with Richard's support, had wanted to secure parliament's approval for new taxation in order to propagate the war with France, but instead parliament channelled the money towards defensive measures. Further humiliation for Richard followed when he was obliged henceforth to govern with the assistance of a 'Great and Continual Council'. What Chaucer thought of his experience is impossible to know, but the Trojan parliament that meets in *Troilus* receives short shrift. Not unlike its English counterpart, it is full of factions, undercurrents, and a sense of crisis at a time of war, and in Chaucer's account is too easily swayed. It considers a proposal to exchange Criseyde for Antenor, a Trojan knight captured by the Greeks. Criseyde is the daughter of the soothsayer and traitor Calkas who has defected to the Greek side because he has foreseen the fall of Troy. Hector, a royal prince and ally of Troilus, protests that the proposed exchange is improper since Criseyde is not a prisoner, and that it is against precedent to exchange a woman as if she could be traded or sold. Rational discussion gives way to a 'noyse of peple' who object to Hector's case—their views, fanned by the urgency of the moment, raging 'As breme [fiercely] as blase of straw iset on-fire' (*TC* IV. 184). All they can see is the need to secure the return of a knight of Troy and they get their way, little knowing that it is Antenor who will later betray their city to the Greeks. The narrator, having invoked Juvenal on the tendency of people to take decisions against their better interests, uses the episode as an example of the ways in which a 'cloude of errour' has prevented an understanding of what is for the best (200). The impact of the decision on Troilus is, of course, devastating. As a result, he loses Criseyde. The political and the personal are closely entwined, and that may have been Chaucer's experience, too. A petition presented to the Good Parliament in 1376 had requested that all controllers of ports with life appointments should have their posts annulled 'because they were oppressing the people with extortions'. Chaucer retired from his posts as controller of the wool custom, and of the petty custom, in the port of London in December of that year.[7] And yet fate was to have the last laugh, as it did in *Troilus*. In 1430 his granddaughter, Alice, married an earl of Suffolk (William), who wielded considerable political power and influence as chamberlain to Henry VI.

Mirrors for Princes

The narrative that most fully reflects the circumstances, tendencies, and policies of Richard's rule is the Knight's Tale. It has recently been argued by Rigby that Chaucer's story takes account of the theories of kingship set out by Giles of Rome in his influential *De regimine principum* (On the rule of princes), written *c*.1280. If so, his work would have struck a chord with Richard. Giles's book was owned by his tutor, Simon Burley, who may have used it as a model for instructing his sometime pupil in the arts of governance.[8] In other ways, too, the reign of Theseus, duke of Athens, speaks to that of Richard II. The Knight's Tale ends with a political marriage between Palamon and Emelye orchestrated by Theseus and designed to heal the divisions between sworn enemies 'With al th'avys [advice] heere of my parlement' (KnT 3076), the Thebans and the Greeks. Richard, as we have seen, was eventually party to one such peacemaking marriage with Isabella of France. Like Richard, Theseus is a great patron of the arts, especially architecture, painting, and sculpture.[9] He galvanizes the artists and craftsmen of his dukedom with commissions for the amphitheatre in which Palamon and his rival, Arcite, are going to fight for the hand of the royal princess, Emelye:

> For in the lond ther was no crafty man   *craftsman*
> That geometrie or ars-metrike kan,   *arithmetic; knew*
> Ne portreyour, ne kervere of ymages,   *painter; sculptor*
> That Theseus ne yaf him mete and wages   *gave*
> The theatre for to maken and devyse.
>
> (1897–1901)

The amphitheatre here described is built to house a tournament, an activity that Richard was particularly keen to promote for the opportunity it provided to display his royal presence. The tournaments he staged at Smithfield in 1390 were elaborate affairs, partly modelled on French precedents, heralded by ceremonious processions and attended by numerous lords and ladies, including a significant number from abroad.[10] Chaucer captures something of the excitement attendant upon such an occasion when he describes the dazzling scene (spread over two days, as the Smithfield tournament was) as 'lordes upon steedes and palfreys' (KnT 2495–503) gather for the confrontation between Palamon and Arcite. There is preparation of armour 'uncouth [exotic] and so riche, and wroght so weel | Of goldsmythrye, of browdynge [embroidery], and of steel', gilded helms, mail coats, lords in rich robes and 'Knyghtes of retenue [in their service], and eek squieres | Nailynge the speres, and helmes bokelyng'. As clerk of the works, Chaucer had responsibility for erecting the scaffolds where the Smithfield jousting was to take place.[11]

The tournament Chaucer describes in the Knight's Tale, like that in London, features elaborate ceremony and formality. The noble Theseus rides 'Ful like a lord [magnate]' with Palamon and Arcite on either side, followed by the queen and her sister, Emelye, and after that others in due degree (KnT 2569–73). The opposing forces of Palamon and Arcite enter from facing sides of the arena, Palamon from the east with a white banner under a gateway that houses a shrine to his goddess, Venus; Arcite from the west with a red banner under a gateway containing an altar to his god, Mars. Other occasions, too, enable Theseus to display his magnificence through ritualized display. His return from Femenye with his newly wedded queen, Ypolita, is done with 'muchel glorie and solemnitee' (870), and the obsequies for Arcite are sumptuous and fitting to the death of a royal prince: leading the funeral procession are three large white steeds clad in glittering steel, adorned with the arms of Arcite. Their riders carry in turn the shield, spear, and bow of the dead knight. The noblest of the Greek lords follow, carrying the bier, winding their way through city streets hung with black.[12] Theseus and Egeus, his father, carry gold vessels full of honey, milk, blood, and wine.

This kind of theatricality would have appealed to Richard. After falling out with the London oligarchy over the matter of a loan they had refused he effected a reconciliation and staged an elaborate re-entry to the city in 1392, in which London figured as the second Jerusalem and he as Christ at the second coming, bestowing forgiveness on the penitent.[13] With increasing emphasis on royal splendour and rank or 'degree' (a recurrent word in the Knight's Tale) came a greater formalism and distance between king and subjects—an attribute Richard shares with Theseus, who appears to his subjects 'at a wyndow set, | Arrayed right as he were a god in trone' (KnT 2528–9). For all that, the remoteness of Theseus and the austerity of his decisions is ameliorated by the intercessory power of women. Widows of Greek knights killed at Thebes persuade Theseus to wage war on Creon; Ypolita and Emelye intervene to prevent his execution of

Palamon and Arcite. Similarly, Anne of Bohemia interceded at key points in Richard's rule, securing some clemency for the rebels of 1381, pleading with the Appellants for the lives of Burley and others in 1388, and asking Richard not to deal harshly with the Londoners who had refused his request for a loan.[14]

If the similarities between the rules of Theseus and Richard are too numerous and close to be coincidental, they should not be pushed to the point where Chaucer might seem to be doing little more than reflecting the glory of Richard's reign. The 'mirror for princes' tradition did not require poets merely to adopt a passive, adulatory role; it also enabled them to draw attention to problems and difficulties—to offer advice.[15] A key issue of Theseus's reign is the extent to which his own practice is called into question. Effective though he is at maintaining order through distance and ceremony, the consequence of the tournament is a blatant injustice: the victor, Arcite, does not win the prize—Emelye—but is instead unhorsed through the agency of Saturn and dies a revolting death. Thus the principles on which Theseus rules are called into question and the whole of Athenian society is plunged into despair. It is as much as Theseus can do, after an interval of some years, to explain to his populace that all is for the best in the best of all possible worlds. When he does so he sets out a hierarchical vision of the universe in which all created things, as well as the members of human society, have their allotted space and time under the rule of the deity, Jupiter. Anyone questioning or complaining about this state of affairs is designated a rebel to the godhead: 'rebel is to hym that al may gye [guide]' (KnT 3046). Acceptance is a necessity, resistance sheer 'wilfulnesse' (3057). His words are prescient of Richard's increasingly elevated sense of his own position. In 1398 he wrote in a letter of those who baulked at royal authority as rebels 'contriving wickedness against King Christ the Lord'—a notion of obedience among subjects that may have derived from Giles of Rome.[16]

Even more subversive of the status quo than Arcite's death is the Miller's Tale, which follows hard on the heels of the Knight's version of human affairs. As we have seen, the Miller (in the aftermath of 1381) provides an alternative account of what makes the world go round: not fancy ideas about governance, but desire, sex, trickery, and the need for freedom. So if Chaucer was a court poet who wrote mirrors for princes, he tended to identify difficult problems or contentious problems rather than merely providing a reflective surface for glory and pomp.[17] In any case, it would be difficult to put the label 'court poet' on Chaucer without serious qualification. True, *Troilus and Criseyde*, the Knight's Tale, Merchant's Tale, *Book of the Duchess*, *Legend of Good Women*, *Parliament of Fowls*, Franklin's Tale, Squire's Tale, and Wife of Bath's Tale all evoke courtly, or at least aristocratic, settings and to that extent imply an audience comfortable with the suppositions on which the narratives are based. But Chaucer does not opt for giving such an audience a comfortable time. Dorigen, the heroine of the Franklin's Tale, is a noblewoman of high status who becomes neurotic at the departure of her lord on service overseas; the hero of the Wife of Bath's Tale is a knight, but a rapist; the court of the Merchant's Tale is the setting for a plot of which the Miller would be proud. And so on. Even the courtly tales are to some extent anti-courtly, and the majority of the Canterbury Tales are not courtly at all. That being the case, what are the implications for the kind of audience Chaucer was addressing?

Audience

It is possible to identify by name some twenty individuals who qualify as members of Chaucer's first audience.[18] Either they are likely to have been patrons, like John of Gaunt or Queen Anne, or Chaucer names them within a poem, or they witness on their own account to their familiarity with Chaucer's work. What characterizes the group is its diversity and range. At one extreme is a family member, Chaucer's son Lewis, to whom in 1391, at the 'tendir age of ten yeer', he dedicated his *Treatise on the Astrolabe*. At the other extreme is the king, the object of an 'envoy' that concludes the short lyric, 'Lak of Stedfastnesse'. It exhorts Richard to respect God, the law, truth, and worthiness at a time of severe social instability. Of course an addressee is not necessarily a receptive member of an audience, or even a member at all. There is no way of knowing what Richard thought of Chaucer's attempts to offer advice, or whether he even knew of them at all.[19]

The other identifiable individuals are surer candidates. Mention has already been made in Chapter 1 of Deschamps, a French court poet present at Rheims (though on the opposing side) when Chaucer was captured there in 1360.[20] Chaucer used Deschamps's *Miroir de mariage* in his prologue to the Wife of Bath's Tale and Deschamps returned the compliment. His 'Ballade' of *c*.1385 is the first recorded tribute to Chaucer's literary powers. Deschamps writes that he longs to consume a *buvraige autentique* (authentic drink) from the stream of Helicon that Chaucer controls; his own work is by comparison *euvres d'escolier* (schoolboy work).[21] Another French poet, and also a knight, Oton de Grandson, was Chaucer's close acquaintance. Between 1368 and 1387 he worked in turn in the households of Edward III, John of Gaunt, and Richard II. Chaucer names Grandson in his *Complaint of Venus*, while Grandson's own work reveals the influence of the *Book of the Duchess* and the *Parliament of Fowls*.[22] As we have seen, the English poet Hoccleve, who was rather more on the fringes of court life, was also a disciple.

As might be expected, a shared experience of court culture is a recurrent theme among the members of Chaucer's audience, although their direct experience of court life varies considerably. With one or two exceptions, the court and its various functions provided them either with long-term employment, or occasional patronage, and certainly food for thought. Five members of Chaucer's audience (Clanvowe, Clifford, Montagu, Stury, and Vache) were Richard's chamber knights and therefore had close and regular access to the king and his preoccupations.[23] A number enjoyed the support of Gaunt. As a servant of the court, Chaucer's professional career was interlinked with theirs, although (fortunately for him) he was not a poet of Richard's innermost circle. Nor, with the occasional exception of Gaunt, and perhaps Queen Anne, did his audience comprise great lords and ladies of the sort suggested by the *Troilus* frontispiece. Rather, his audience was of people not unlike himself, some of whom were close to the centres of power and patronage while others (Gower, Hoccleve, Scogan) were decidedly more distant. It was a loose and shifting group, rather than a stable and coherent one, and quite diverse in its range of professional aptitudes. It included lawyers, and an Oxford theologian and philosopher, as well as chamber knights. It was not an audience so much as a series of audiences—some of its members having quite narrow horizons of expectation, others being quite catholic in their tastes. Predominantly, it was made up of people who, while they might be of gentry or mercantile background, nevertheless progressed and survived by dint of their own capabilities. Much as they knew each other as co-participants in a range of financial, diplomatic, and legal activities, a key interest, which they all shared, was in the production and reception of literature.

In the penultimate stanza of *Troilus and Criseyd*e 'philosophical Strode' is one of the two people to whom Chaucer directs that poem. They are asked to oversee all necessary corrections to the text through their 'benignites and zeles goode' (great kindness and concern). Radulphus Strode was a fellow at Merton College, Oxford, in 1359–60 and known for his work in logic.[24] Two of his compositions, *Consequentiae* and *Obligationes*, have survived, as has evidence of his debates with another, rather more famous, Oxford scholar, John Wyclif. Wyclif himself wrote two extant treatises detailing his responses to Strode's questions and arguments. There is also a late fifteenth-century record of a poem Strode may have written, called *Phantasma Radulphi* (Ralph's Vision). If the attribution is authentic it would have made him an especially fitting recipient of *Troilus*. It seems that Strode also trained as a lawyer and moved from Oxford to London. At his death in 1386 he was standing counsel for the City of London, and had previously been its Common Serjeant or pleader. In 1382 he and Chaucer are named in a legal document as the providers of surety for the good behaviour of a prominent London citizen, the draper John Hend, who was to become mayor in 1391–2.[25]

Strode's Oxford background opens up the possibility of an audience for *Troilus* that was scholastic in nature and quite different from the audience of lords and ladies suggested by the Corpus Christi frontispiece. The poem's philosophical content, derived from Boethius, and its theological debates on predestination and free will, would have had a strong appeal to the likes of Strode. He and others of a similar background would also have relished certain features of the *Canterbury Tales*. The portrait of an ascetic-looking and thread-bare 'clerk . . . of Oxenford' (GP 285–308) on a bony horse, spending more on books than he can rightly afford, is of a scholar who, like Strode himself, 'unto logyk hadde longe ygo' (studied logic for a long time). Strode himself switched to a more lucrative career, so from his point of view Chaucer's portrait of the Clerk is a 'there but for the grace of God' description. Then there is the sombre Clerk's Tale itself, borrowed from another great clerk, Francis Petrarch, about the virtue of patience pushed to its limits in a marriage between an over-bearing lord and his peasant wife, Griselde. At the other extreme are the salacious tales of the Miller and Reeve, with their vivid evocations of daily life in and around Oxford and Cambridge—places where, in various senses, scholars tend to come out on top.

Also quite at odds with the expectations set up by the *Troilus* frontispiece is the idea of an audience with legal training, yet that is the background Strode shares with the poem's second dedicatee, John Gower or 'moral Gower', as Chaucer calls him. Gower (*c.*1330–1408) was one of two people given power of attorney by Chaucer (for protection against lawsuits issued in his absence) when he travelled to Lombardy in 1378.[26] Gower is primarily known as Chaucer's fellow-poet who, as we have seen in previous chapters, wrote in a satirical and admonitory vein about contemporary abuses and social convulsions such as the revolt of 1381. Nor was he averse to espousing the cause of peace or advising King Richard in forthright terms about the perils of his policies, including those that resulted in heavy taxation. In various ways his writings register a growing disenchantment with Richard's rule.[27] Gower had independent means, is referred to as a squire, and was probably a member of the landed gentry. His training in the law may suggest a legal audience for Chaucer's writing. He was less reliant upon political patronage than Chaucer, but could be just as opportune: careful to describe the commissioning of his *Confessio Amantis* by Richard, the finished product is actually dedicated in 1391 to the king's eventual usurper, Henry of Bolingbroke. A writer of less range and narrower sympathies than Chaucer, Gower admired his friend's work, and at the end of the *Confessio* (*c.*1390) put into the mouth of Venus some generous words of praise. She says that Chaucer, pre-eminently, is 'mi disciple and mi poete', who in his youth 'Of Ditees and songes glade . . . | The lond fulfild'.[28]

Henry Scogan (*c.*1360–1407), tutor to Henry IV's four sons, straddles the scholastic and courtly spheres of Chaucer's audience. 'Lenvoy de Chaucer a Scogan', probably written around 1390, is correspondingly witty and sophisticated, and written not just for Scogan but for others in the know who would appreciate the personalities, allusions, jokes, posturing, range of voices, and rapid changes of tone.[29] It begins with inflated rhetoric and ends with a mixture of *double entendre* and abject begging. Chaucer describes cataclysmic discord in heaven ('Tobroken been the statutz hye') before turning more direct and blaming Scogan for a season of plague, this 'diluge of pestilence'. It is the gods' revenge for Scogan's mistreatment and neglect of his mistress. Henceforth, Cupid will have little interest in Scogan or Chaucer, who are in any case unlikely lovers since they are old and portly, 'hoor and rounde of shap'. Scogan, who could have been twenty years

Chaucer's junior, may not have appreciated the epithets. But Chaucer has now taken centre-stage: virile as he was in his youth, his 'muse' now rusts in its sheath. The poem ends with a playful plea to Scogan to 'Mynne [remember] thy frend' by sharing some of the generosity he receives at Richard's court and from which Chaucer, 'Forgete [forgotten] in solytarie wildernesse', claims to be excluded. The largesse which they did in fact share is somewhat more banal: in the 1390s both borrowed money from the wealthy London alderman and sometime sheriff, Gilbert Mawfield—as did John Gower and assorted dukes, earls, and bishops.[30]

That Scogan was a careful and attentive reader of Chaucer's writings is clear from his 'Morale Balade' of about 1407, addressed to the princes who had been his tutees. It advises them about the nature of virtuous behaviour, stressing that it is an innate rather than an inherited quality. In doing so, Scogan alludes to both the Monk's Tale and Wife of Bath's Tale, quotes from the latter, and proceeds to embed and attribute to 'my mayster' all of the stanzas of Chaucer's own lyric, 'Gentilesse'.[31] The Wife of Bath already enjoyed some notoriety among Chaucer's first readers. The addressee of 'Lenvoy de Chaucer a Bukton' is probably Sir Peter Bukton, who, like Chaucer, served John of Gaunt and also gave evidence in the Scrope–Grosvenor trial in 1386. Bukton became an esquire in the household of Queen Anne and was on the point of marrying or remarrying when Chaucer penned his lyric in the 1390s. It refers to the 'sorwe and wo' (misery and suffering) found in marriage, which is characterized as the 'cheyne | Of Sathanas' (Satan's chain) on which the devil gnaws, longing to be free. For all that, Chaucer advises his friend to take a wife, even though it will cause 'sorwe on thy flessh, thy lyf', in case he do something worse (although, given Chaucer's apocalyptic imagery, that would be difficult to imagine). This is gallows humour of the kind found among bachelor friends when one decides to surrender his freedom for the 'trappe' of matrimony. Chaucer ends by referring to his poem as 'This lytel writ, proverbe, or figure', designed to help Bukton steel himself for the rigours that lie ahead, and suggesting further reading: a work featuring a woman who well knew how to make a man his 'wives thral [slave]': 'The Wyf of Bath I pray yow that ye rede'.

Among the chamber knights who knew Chaucer's work, two, Vache and Clanvowe, stand out. Chaucer composed one of his short lyrics for Sir Philip de la Vache (*c.*1346–1408). It does not categorically mention the court, but to anyone caught up in its machinations Chaucer's words might well have given pause for thought.[32] The first three stanzas of the 'Balade de Bon Conseyl' (Good Advice), otherwise known as 'Truth', are full of exhortations to rely upon 'sothfast-nesse' (truthfulness) in preference to envy, ambition, and attempting to put the world to rights. More beneficial are the arts of content-ment, self-control, rest, and patience. These, if practised, will enable liberation: 'And trouthe the shal delivere, it is no drede [no doubt about it]'. Chaucer's culminating image is the familiar one of life as a wilderness, recognition of which should prompt a pilgrimage of the soul in search of truth. The tone of address becomes more impera-tive: 'Forth, pilgrim, forth! Forth, beste [beast], out of thy stal [stall]!' Then the last verse springs a surprise. It is addressed by name to Vache (in French, cow), and that creates a retroactive pun on the idea of a beast in a stall. So the tone turns playful, even as it cajoles. The implication is that author and recipient are on good enough terms to tolerate and enjoy the complex mixture of teasing and counselling. The records suggest that they were. Vache was a member of the landed gentry whose father had served Edward III as a garter knight.[33] Like Chaucer, he enjoyed financial support from John of Gaunt, receiving a grant from the Lancaster exchequer in 1374; in 1385 Vache and Chaucer, among others, were both given mourning livery (three-and-a-half ells of black cloth in Chaucer's case) for the death of the king's mother, Joan of Kent; and ten years later Chaucer, with others, was a witness for a transfer of some land to Vache as part of a larger transfer of properties in Kent (in the Greenwich and Deptford areas) from the archbishop of York to the archbishop of Canterbury and others.[34]

Sir John Clanvowe (1341–91) was a Herefordshire landowner who served in the French wars with the Black Prince. In 1373 he received a life annuity from Edward III and a gift from John of Gaunt. By 1381 he was a chamber knight in Richard's court, surviving—like Vache—the Appellant crisis of 1386–8. Thereafter he was a regular member of the king's council and active in a series of peace negotiations in France.[35] As well as being a witness in the Cecilia Chaumpaigne case, in 1385 he received mourning livery, like Chaucer and Vache, for the funeral of Joan of Kent; and the following year was a witness, like Chaucer and Bukton, at the Scrope–Grosvenor trial.[36] Clanvowe was an author in his own right, reading and absorbing Chaucer's Knight's

Tale and *Parliament of Fowls* and perhaps also the early version of the Prologue to the *Legend of Good Women*, as is evident from his dream vision, the *Boke of Cupid*.[37] It announces its debt with a quotation from the Knight's Tale—'The god of love, a! benedicite [lord have mercy] | How mighty and how grete a lord is he!'—before going on to describe the season of May when love stirs the narrator's heart 'al thogh I be olde and unlusty [not vigorous]'. On St Valentine's day he wanders into a wood full of flowers and singing birds and falls asleep by a melodious river. He dreams of a debate between a cuckoo and a nightingale on the trials and tribulations of love. It ends without resolution, but they decide to continue it the next day 'Before the chamber window of the Quene | At Wodestok [Woodstock]'—a reference to the palace of Queen Anne, for whom Clanvowe intends his poem. In 1385 Clanvowe had been named as an executor of her will.

Other chamber knights probably familiar with Chaucer's work were Clifford, Montagu, and Stury. Sir Lewis Clifford is the courier named by Deschamps for his 'balade' of 1385 addressed to Chaucer. Sir John Montagu mixed in similar circles and was praised for his poetry by no less a person than Christine de Pizan (though none has survived). Sir Richard Stury was a friend of Froissart who owned a high-quality copy of the *Roman de la Rose* (still extant) and knew the poetry of Deschamps. Clanvowe, Clifford, Stury, and Vache were survivors. Like Chaucer, they adopted a low profile during the Appellant crisis and lived to tell the tale. Montagu was less fortunate. After Richard's deposition he conspired to restore his master to the throne but was lynched for his loyalty by the citizens of Cirencester in January 1400.[38] He might have learnt a cautionary lesson from another keen reader of Chaucer's writings, the under-sheriff of Middlesex, Thomas Usk. Secretary also to John of Northampton, mayor of London (1381–3), Usk embroiled himself in city politics. When Northampton's rival, Sir Nicholas Brembre, became mayor (1383–6), Usk switched loyalties to him. Brembre, knighted by Richard in the aftermath of 1381, was a supporter of the king against those who were critical of his rule. In the midst of this factional turmoil, Usk penned his prose *Testament of Love*. It owes debts to Chaucer's *House of Fame* and *Troilus and Criseyde*, as well as to his translation of Boethius's *Consolation of Philosophy* (*Boece*).[39] In Usk's poem, Lady Love praises Chaucer as 'Myne owne trewe servaunt, the noble philosophical poete in Englissh' and recommends *Troilus* as a source of wisdom on the topics of foreknowledge and free will. Usk probably needed all the philosophical detachment he could get. Closely identified with Richard's cause, he became a target of the Appellants' purge of the king's supporters among London citizens and was executed in 1388, as was Brembre.

The individuals mentioned thus far are indicative of the kind of people for whom Chaucer wrote and who found his work entertaining and instructive. No doubt the size of his actual audience was considerably larger and it is possible to posit the existence of at least one further, if unnamed, group: women. Conspicuous by their absence (with the exception of Queen Anne) as named addressees, they do feature recurrently, and especially in *Troilus* and the *Legend of Good Women*, as a constituent part of Chaucer's imagined, or intended, audience.[40] The *Legend*, so its prologue would have us believe, is commissioned by the god of Love at the prompting of Queen Alceste, herself 'kalender [model] . . . | To any woman that wol lover bee' (*LGW* F 542–3). Love commissions the *Legend* to allow Chaucer an opportunity to remedy in women's eyes his apparent denigration of them in works such as *Troilus*. The narrator of that work includes women in his audience under the category of 'lovers', whom he addresses generally on several occasions and at the end as 'yonge, fresshe folkes, he or *she*' (*TC* V. 1835). The existence of a female audience receptive to and engaged with Chaucer's writings would square with what we know of court culture under Richard's rule. It incorporated women to an unprecedented, and sometimes scandalous, degree.

Performance Poetry

Chaucer's sense of an audience was acute. So much is clear from the extent to which he engages with his named recipients in a kind of dialogue, one based on subtle fluctuations in tone, and a shared frame of reference, all designed to be 'overheard' or witnessed by others as a kind of dramatic performance. He is also unusually adept at tempering his diction and style in response to the kind of audience he is addressing. His voice is tender and conversational with his son, 'little Lowys', impish and knowing with the courtier Vache. Indeed, much of his creativity springs from a strong connection with audience and the shared space that implies (architectural, emotional, cultural). Without an audience there would be little impulse to write, but audience reception is not the end-point of the process. As shown in the prologue to the *Legend of Good Women*, discussed in Chapter 1, reception entails interpretation, and the production of meaning is as diverse and unpredictable as the differences between one person and another.

In the *Canterbury Tales*, Chaucer makes capital of the audience's role by incorporating an imagined audience of pilgrims into the narrative framework. As one pilgrim tells a tale, others listen (or don't), interrupt, take umbrage, express approval, get bored, get involved, object, quarrel, offer alternative stories.[41] The case of the Miller's Tale, as a subversive response to the Knight's Tale, has already been mentioned. One of the listeners to the Miller's account of a cuckolded carpenter is the Reeve, also a carpenter by training. He believes that his fellow-pilgrim has launched a personal attack and so by way of riposte tells a story in which a miller is vilified. The Cook misses the point entirely, and takes a rather different moral from the Reeve's Tale. It is, he says, an 'argument of herbergage', a tale about the perils of offering accommodation to strangers. So he is in turn prompted to tell his own scurrilous (and unfinished) story about 'Perkyn Revelour', an apprentice lodger in London who outstays his welcome. There are many other examples of the ways in which the pilgrims interact, responding *as* audience before performing *to* an audience. The *Canterbury Tales* enacts the very process by which Chaucer himself reacted to his reading, and then incorporated his interpretations in new compositions for new audiences.

One reason that there is a strong performative element in Chaucer's poetry is because much of it was created to be heard as well as read.[42] While short lyrics, or individual tales, might circulate in manuscript among his friends and admirers, other works were designed for public events. The *Book of the Duchess*, probably written for a memorial service at St Paul's or Gaunt's Savoy palace, is a case in point. So is the Knight's Tale, with its four distinct parts, each corresponding to an hour or so of performance, perhaps on separate days. But the major example is *Troilus and Criseyde*, structured in five books so that each might be heard whole at a single sitting, the first four prefaced with stanzas that foreground the narrator as he invokes appropriate deities, rehearses the plot, and sets the appropriate mood.

Chaucer lived on the cusp between a literary culture in which hearing poetry read was the norm, and one in which private reading was more commonly practised. His poetry is full of double appeals, to hearer and reader, as the narrator asks his audience both to 'Listen, lordynges' and 'turn over the leef and chese another tale'. If Chaucer wrote for an audience still in the habit of listening to poetry, and composed works whose primary mode of delivery was performance, then certain consequences follow—consequences that tend to be undervalued, misunderstood, or missed entirely through the modern habit of quick private reading.[43] The context of performance affects the detail as well as the larger dimensions of his compositions. Perhaps the most obvious detail is to do with sound. A performance poet can, if she or he wishes, use pure sound to reinforce meaning. There is a well-known example in the Knight's Tale when Chaucer describes the onset of the tournament between Palamon and Arcite in a bravura passage, full of the noise of steel on steel, lance on shield, that needs to be said aloud for full effect:

In goon the speres ful sadly in arrest;	*firmly; lance rest*
In gooth the sharpe spore into the syde.	*spur*
Ther seen men who kan juste and who kan ryde;	*joust*
Ther shyveren shaftes upon sheeldes thikke . . .	*shiver, break*

(KnT 2602–5)

And so on. A listening audience is not necessarily going to hear every word, but they will get the gist in a passage like this. The same is true of repetition. Not unusually, Chaucer will repeat a key word at intervals to ensure that his audience has 'got the point'. An example from the Knight's Tale might be the word 'black', which occurs no fewer than thirteen times and in a variety of contexts: it is the colour of the clothes worn by the mourning widows, of the smoke caused by Saturn, of Arcite's pallor as he lies dying. So by the end of the poem it has accumulated a range of meanings to do with mourning, melancholy, and the forces arrayed against Palamon and Arcite, that take us to the heart of the poem.

Then there are the larger issues. Typically, Chaucer's poetry is sociable, not private—that is, it is predicated upon a social event such as a memorial service, a pilgrimage, or a public gathering of some other kind. Second, as we have seen, it tends to take account of a live audience (pilgrims, courtiers, lovers), envisaged as a key element in the process of creating new (if divergent) meanings. Third, given the variety of interpretation, the narratives tend to be open-ended rather than definitive. Chaucer prefers to leave his audience to debate and

decide individually what the meaning of one of his stories might be.[44]
At the end of the first part of the Knight's Tale, having described the
distinct but closely comparable fortunes of the heroes, Palamon and
Arcite, the narrator says:

> Yow lovers axe I now this questioun:
> Who hath the worse, Arcite or Palamoun?
> That oon may seen his lady, day by day,
> But in prison he moot dwelle alway;   *must*
> That oother wher hym list may ride or go,   *wishes*
> But seen his lady shal he never mo.
>
> (KnT 1347–52)

Thus the first episode of the narrative ends as a cliff-hanger to set
tongues wagging in anticipation of the next instalment. Finally,
Chaucer allows generous space for the role of a narrator, an alter ego
who—as we saw in Chapter 1—is both like and unlike his real-life
counterpart: a comic buffoon, a pilgrim who interacts with his fellow
travellers, or, as in *Troilus*, a failed lover. Chaucer as narrator fulfils a
vital part of his rhetorical strategy. The narrator does much to persuade a listening (and reading) audience that the work they are hearing is both entertaining and instructive. The inadequacies of the
figure they see before them are all part of the play: his deficiencies
invite remedies through their own experience or understanding.
Thereby, they become involved in the story and its interpretation.
Chaucer has their attention.

Chaucer's narrator is not merely a sophisticated, effective, and
highly imaginative rhetorical device. It is a role assumed by him, and
enacted by him before a live audience in the process of performing his
work. The potential for lifting the text from the page and rendering it
in dramatic form is huge. The pace of delivery, clarity of enunciation,
pauses for effect, body language, hand gestures, facial expressions,
the voicing of different characters, and perhaps the partial enactment
of some actions, all become possible and desirable adjuncts if audience attention is to be kept. The situation, of course, has its limitations as well as its advantages. The performer cannot afford to be too
original, too avant-garde, or the audience will have no frame of reference and quickly lose interest. On the other hand, mere repetition of
familiar plots and themes will induce boredom.

Troilus and Criseyde is a pyrotechnic demonstration of Chaucer's skill as a performance poet, and for all its shortcomings the *Troilus* frontispiece does capture something of his performative achievement. The poem engages in a balancing act between a well-known tale and a welter of new and unexpected meanings, defamiliarizing the received Trojan setting by relocating it in a London his audience knows only too well. And it is clear from what we know of Chaucer's audience, as well as from the aesthetic and intellectual demands of the poem itself, that their response, even as listeners, was likely to have been extremely sophisticated. He plays with their sense of themselves, their knowledge of him, their desires and aspirations, their myths, their familiarity with court life, of living in aristocratic households, of warfare and siege, of city politics, of love and religious belief, of history. The complexity of the poem's appeal as a performance piece is evident from the outset. The narrator announces, in a direct address to his audience, that before he leaves them, 'er that I parte fro ye', he is going to tell a familiar story, the 'double sorwe' of Troilus, a sad tale of love won and lost (*TC* I. 1–14). He then calls on the classical Fury, Thesiphone, to help him compose his 'woful' pagan tale—one, it seems, that is going to articulate non-Christian values, and one so affecting that the narrator weeps as he writes. Here the narrator is performing his writing of the poem, wanting his audience to imagine him writing it, and having done so Chaucer suddenly and characteristically hooks them in. Just as he is Thesiphone's instrument so now the narrator becomes theirs, 'the sorweful instrument, | That helpeth lovers, as I kan [best know] to pleyne [voice their complaints]'. And he frames his facial expression accordingly: 'to a sorwful tale, a sory chere'.

Having characterized (and thereby complimented) his audience as lovers, the narrator fastidiously puts himself in an inferior role. They serve Love, but not he, who serves them: 'I, that God of Loves servantz serve' (*TC* I. 15–35). He dare not even pray to Love because he is unsuitable and far from Love's reach. Nevertheless, if his poem should succeed in cheering the heart of any lover, or advancing their cause, he is thankful to them that his work will not have been in vain. Having been generous to them he now gives them the opportunity to be generous in return. He calls on their individual experiences of 'gladnesse', or former 'hevynesse', or knowledge of the difficulties other lovers have faced, and urges them to adopt a sympathetic and receptive attitude to the story they are about to hear. The task of praying to Love (and therefore of realizing the poem) now devolves to them, as also the task of praying to God himself that the narrator might show successfully the pain and woe endured by lovers in 'Troilus unsely [unhappy] aventure'. By such gambits narrator and audience appear to collude in creating the poem. The audience is made to feel implicated in its outcome.

Chaucer at Work

How did Chaucer go about the business of composing a major narrative such as *Troilus and Criseyde*?[45] His choice of story was determined by what his audience already knew. In a situation where his compositions were liable to be heard as much as read he could not afford to be too innovatory or confusion would ensue. The opening line of *Troilus*—'The double sorwe of Troilus to tellen'—reminds his audience that it is about to encounter a story whose plot is known. It is a tale with which they were already familiar through its previous incarnation in the French *Roman de Troie* of Benoît de Saint-Maure and in other versions reaching back to classical antiquity.[46] Furthermore, Chaucer's choice of subject-matter is tailored to the interests and preoccupations of those for whom he writes. In composing a story about love he can be assured of his audience's attention; and in setting it in Troy at a time of war he can also count on their interest. At this time London was known as Troynovaunt or 'new Troy', a name promoted by the court and a faction in the city. By describing the city walls, gates, streets, palaces, gardens, feasts, and parliament of the ancient city Chaucer is in effect describing his own London and its topography and institutions, with the activities and psychological state of its inhabitants conditioned by long-standing hostilities.[47]

Such considerations might make Chaucer seem derivative, little more than the passive recipient of literary and cultural influence (an impression he deliberately fosters). In practice, the common ground he establishes with his audience is the basis of his originality. His audience might have known the story of Troilus and Criseyde, but Chaucer introduces inflections and emphases that make the narrative seem new, contemporary, full of topical application. His art is therefore, in both a narrow and large sense, an art of rhetoric. It is at its most blatant when his narrator intrudes, as he does at the very moment when Troilus falls in love, to lecture his audience on the significance of the moment. It is at its most subtle when he transforms a key element of the received plot—Criseyde's betrayal of Troilus—to create a heroine whose motivations, fears, and insecurities are all too understandable. One of Chaucer's most successful rhetorical devices, used across his oeuvre, is the persona of the inadequate, passive, comical narrator. In *Troilus* the narrator represents himself deferentially as no more than the servant of the servants of love. He thereby credits his audience with direct experience of the emotions he describes and in so doing encourages them, through their own superior knowledge, to empathize with his protagonists.

Chaucer's narrator would have his audience believe that he is doing little more than translate the story from 'myn auctor', the elusive Lollius.[48] The stratagem allows the narrator to disavow responsibility for the work in hand, thereby giving Chaucer as poet a large room for manoeuvre. For while it is certainly the case that, as with so many other of his works, *Troilus* derives from a narrative by someone else, it is not a translation in the sense that Chaucer's *Boece* is a faithful rendition of the *Consolatio Philosophiae* by Boethius. In this case his narrative source was *Il Filostrato* by Giovanni Boccaccio (itself based on earlier accounts of Troilus and Criseyde), a fact that Chaucer nowhere acknowledges. He freely adapts it: although certain sections carefully follow Boccaccio's original, others are entirely made up. Not that any member of his audience would have been able to check: Boccaccio's writings were unknown in England, except perhaps among the Italian financiers and merchants who worked in London. Chaucer may have encountered *Il Filostrato* through them or, more likely, in the course of his diplomatic mission to Genoa and Florence in 1372–3. In addition to using Boccaccio, Chaucer goes to other sources such as Dante and, notably, Boethius, to create a combination or bricolage of material that achieves effects far removed from those of Boccaccio's 'original'.[49]

Another kind of change Chaucer effects concerns genre. *Il Filostrato* is conceived as a romance but Chaucer reintroduces some of the epic features of the Troy story. Within this framework, defined by a mixture of erotic intimacy and heroic deeds that will decide the fate of Troy, he incorporates or alludes to other genres.[50] They include both the philosophical treatise and the bawdy fabliau, but especially prominent is the lyric. *Troilus* can read like an anthology of medieval lyrics, and as an exploration of lyric moments—that is, of the experiences and occasions that give rise to short poems expressing heartfelt emotion. Thus, in a poem taken from Petrarch—the first English translation of one of Petrarch's sonnets—Chaucer provides his hero with the *Canticus Troili*, expressing the contradictory feelings of being in love (*TC* I. 400–20). Or, at the centre of the poem, first Criseyde and then Troilus recites an aubade that bemoans the onset of day and their consequent parting. Again, in the closing phase of the story the lovers exchange verse epistles. A new form of versification is, in *Troilus*, one of Chaucer's major achievements. The poem is the first extended elaboration of a stanza form Chaucer is credited with inventing, the rhyme royal. Adapted from French models, it provides an interlaced rhyme scheme of seven decasyllabic lines ending in a couplet (*ababbcc*). It is an instrument well suited to managing narrative pace, or giving pause for thought, or encapsulating a complex idea, or giving vent to lyric musing.

An example will help to illustrate some of Chaucer's working practices.[51] When Boccaccio describes the lovers' first night together, he describes Troilo and Cressida as equals, each charged with desire for the other, intent on undressing and getting into bed. Cressida creates a frisson with a flirtatious remark about the one garment she has not removed. Boccaccio then leaves the rest of the scene to his audience's imagination, having acknowledged the inadequacy of mere words:

It would be a long task to describe their happiness, and an impossible one to tell of the delight they shared when they were there. They undressed and entered the bed, where the woman, who still had one last garment on, asked him charmingly: 'Shall I take off everything? Newly-wed brides are shy on the first night.'

Troilo answered: 'Light of my life, I beg you to—so that I may hold you naked in my arms as my heart desires.' And she replied: 'See how I rid myself of it.' And throwing off her shift she at once enfolded herself in his arms; then clasping each other in a passionate embrace they felt love's power to the full.

What a sweet and much-desired night it was for these two happy lovers! Even if I possessed all the skill that any poet ever had, I should still be unable to describe it. Let those who have at any time advanced so far in Love's favour as these two had now think about it and they will have some notion of the lovers' joy.[52]

The equivalent scene in Chaucer's version is heralded by comic action that would not be out of place in a fabliau. Pandarus has encouraged Troilus to present Criseyde with a trumped-up story about the jealousy she has caused him to feel for a supposed rival, 'Horaste'. That is Troilus's pretext for entering her bedchamber. He kneels at her bed's head, on a cushion adroitly supplied by Pandarus, who is present for much of the scene. Criseyde graciously kisses Troilus and invites him to sit on her bed. She protests her innocence in the matter of Horaste with some eloquence and emotion, and breaks into tears. Dumbfounded, Troilus slumps once more to his knees, and this time faints. Pandarus comes again to the rescue, hoists Troilus into the bed, and tears off his clothes 'al to his bare sherte' (*TC* III. 1099). Gone is the sense that Troilus and Criseyde are somewhat hard-nosed consensual lovers on equal terms about to embark on the serious matter of sexual ecstasy. They are instead vulnerable, by turns bold and timid, subject to rapidly changing emotions, and caught up in an intricate network of desire and manipulation that places one, then the other, in a dominant position. The autonomy of Boccaccio's protagonists has gone: Troilus and Criseyde would not be lovers, Troilus could not even undress, but for the energetic and laughable interventions of Pandarus.

Such circumstances promote a sense of joy, and also a sense of inevitability, about what will soon follow. Contrived as the basic situation is, it is forever getting out of hand and flowing with its own energies. Criseyde is concerned for Troilus and helps Pandarus to chafe his wrists, palms, and temples in an attempt to revive him. As he regains consciousness she puts an arm around him, and kisses him again, to dispel his sorrows. At this point, Pandarus withdraws from the scene, taking the lighted candle with him, and a sense of intimacy rapidly develops. Criseyde forgives Troilus his jealousy; he, revived and encouraged, takes her in his arms. Pandarus, in his last comic moment of the scene, lies down to sleep as he comments, 'If ye be wise, | Swouneth nought [Don't faint] now' (*TC* III. 1189–90). Troilus, for once the assertive male, now declares that Criseyde is 'kaught' and alone so must of necessity yield (1205–11). In a quiet reply that speaks volumes for Criseyde's self-determination, she replies, 'Ne hadde I er now [Had I not before now], my swete herte deere, | Ben yolde [yielded], ywis [in truth], I were nought heere!' The decision to be where she is is hers.

However complicated and absurd human agency might make the amatory experience of Troilus and Criseyde, it is part of a larger natural process and not merely the result of acts of cognition and will as

Boccaccio seems to suggest. Criseyde, held by Troilus, is like a lark taken by a hawk. Sensing his ardour, she trembles like an aspen leaf. But once it is clear that their desire is reciprocal, their love mutual, the images cease to be predatory. Criseyde's fear and anxiety are replaced by joy and trust in Troilus's truth and honesty. The image is now of a honeysuckle's enraptured embrace of a tree. Who is the honeysuckle and who the tree is a moot point: 'as about a tree, with many a twiste, | Bytrent and writh [Encircles and winds] the swote wodebynde, | Gan ech of hem in armes other wynde' (*TC* III. 1230–2). Only now does Chaucer introduce the specifics of a sexual encounter. Deferral adds erotic intensity to the scene, but an eroticism that is intensely natural and joyful:[53]

> Hir armes smale, hire streghte bak and softe,
> Hir sydes longe, flesshly, smothe, and white
> He gan to stroke, and good thrift bad ful ofte
> Hire snowissh throte, hire brestes rounde and lite.
> Thus in this hevene he gan hym to delite,
> And therwithal a thousand tyme hire kiste,
> That what to don, for joie unnethe he wiste.   *he hardly knew*
>
> (1247–53)

As the reference to 'hevene' suggests, it is also an experience that is, for Troilus if not for Criseyde, intensely spiritual. Pausing in the middle of his love-making, he utters a three-stanza prayer to Love before adding an equally long commentary for Criseyde's benefit on the significance of his perceptions in the context of their relationship. Even this, seemingly solemn, moment has comic potential. Criseyde is not in the mood for philosophical speculation—'lat us falle awey fro this matere'—since she feels that they have in hand the more pressing needs of 'delit' and 'joies' (*TC* III. 1306–10). Both comedy and Boethian interpolations are beyond Boccaccio's range but, no less than Boccaccio's narrator, Chaucer declares that such a scene is beyond words, the lovers' bliss 'so heigh that al ne kan I telle!' (1323). The remark is disingenuous, to say the least, since he has just accomplished, highly successfully, the description of an extraordinary episode. Nevertheless, he insists on his inadequacy in relation to 'myn auctor, of his excellence' and that he has followed him faithfully, 'al holly [wholly] his sentence [meaning]', while slyly admitting that, under the inspiration of Love, he may have made one or two improvements with words 'in eched [etched in] for the best' (1325–35). The final judgement on such matters he leaves to his audience: 'Doth therwithal right as youreselven leste [wish]'. He further asserts that all of his words are subject to correction by those who, unlike him, have experience and aptitude in such matters ('felyng han in loves art'). He places his text at their disposal, to revise it ('encresse, or maken dymynucioun') as necessary. Such avowals flatly contradict the proprietorial sentiments directed at Gower and Strode at the end of *Troilus*, but then the way in which Chaucer, through his narrator, plays fast and loose with the role of authorship, is one of the fascinations of a work that, in practice, effect, and meaning, is far removed from *Il Filostrato*.

Manuscript Culture

Once composed, *Troilus* was performed to a live audience and was thereby published, in one fell swoop, to a significant number of people. Publication was not predicated on the rapid and mechanical reproduction of relatively large numbers of identical copies, intended for private reading. Chaucer wrote the best part of a century before William Caxton introduced printing to England (in 1476). The composition, production, and dissemination of literary works were accomplished through manuscript: handwritten copies which might then be read aloud.[54] There is a characteristic scene at the beginning of the second book of *Troilus and Criseyde*. Troilus, incapacitated by lovesickness, has agreed that his friend Pandarus should undertake the wooing of Criseyde on his behalf. Pandarus finds her at home, in a social setting, listening to a book being read. Interestingly, it is a work that answers to the military situation of Troy itself, so the reading is both a social distraction and a means of gaining a perspective on current preoccupations and anxieties. The same might be said of *Troilus* itself in relation to Chaucer's own society. Pandarus

> . . . fond two othere ladys sete and she,   *found; seated*
> Withinne a paved parlour, and they thre
> Herden a mayden redden hem the geeste   *read; story*
> Of the siege of Thebes . . .
>
> (*TC* II. 81–4)

The process of producing a manuscript copy of a lengthy poem like the *Siege of Thebes*, with its twelve books, or of *Troilus*, with its five, was expensive, time-consuming, and labour-intensive.[55] Quill pens were fashioned from goose or swan feathers and needed frequent trimming with a pen-knife. Crushed galls, from oak trees, mixed with copperas and gum, provided the black ink; other natural pigments (some very costly) the colours used for emphasis, decoration, and illustration; gold leaf the more sumptuous details. (Criseyde later refers to 'thise letters rede', the headings written in red ink or 'rubricated' to indicate chapter or book divisions.) The writing surface itself was parchment, a specially prepared animal skin, usually sheepskin, treated with lime, scraped smooth, and ruled. Paper was not commonly used until the fifteenth century. Multiple copies in limited numbers could be produced if there was sufficient demand, but in the first instance the author's concern would be to create an accurate single version of the work in question. It could then be used for reading aloud, or as an exemplar for subsequent copies.

Publication was a collaborative effort and a key figure was the scribe responsible for creating a fair copy of the author's original.[56] Authors register varying degrees of anxiety about the process. Gower supervised the production of copies of his works, to make sure that the spelling was correct and the presentation attractive. Hoccleve, a professional scribe, took the trouble to write out in his own hand a definitive copy of his collected works. Nothing in Chaucer's hand has survived; typically, he used a scribe to write out a fair copy of his work before making it public. His draft would have been on scraps of vellum, or possibly inscribed with a stylus on a wax tablet that could be easily erased and reused. Once the scribe had produced a fair copy it would be necessary to check it for errors and erase words as necessary by scraping the ink away with a pen-knife.

If the tone of a short lyric by Chaucer to 'Adam, His Owne Scriveyn [scribe]' is anything to go by, the production of a fair copy could be an exasperating business.[57] Adam's inaccuracies prompt a curse on the scribe's long hair, which will be afflicted with 'the scale', a scaly skin condition of the scalp, unless he mends his ways:

Adam scriveyn, if ever it thee bifalle
Boece or Troylus for to wryten newe,
Under thy long lokkes thou most have the scale,
But after my makyng thow wryte more trewe; *Unless; poetry*
So ofte adaye I mot thy work renewe, *must*

It to correcte and eke to rubbe and scrape,
And al is thorugh thy negligence and rape.   *haste*

The poem suggests a long-term working relationship, and not only on account of the ribbing Chaucer gives Adam. The title, though it may not be Chaucer's, refers to Adam as 'his owne' scribe, as if the connection is well-established; and the poem looks forward to a new writing out of Chaucer's translation of Boethius, or of *Troilus*, suggesting that Adam may have written them out before. These impressions are confirmed by recent scholarship, which seems to confirm the identity of Chaucer's scribe.[58] One Adam Pynkhurst became a member of the Scriveners' Company in about 1392, and his hand has been identified in the two earliest copies of the *Canterbury Tales*, known as the Hengwrt and Ellesmere manuscripts; in an early copy of *Boece*; and in a surviving fragment of *Troilus*. Pynkhurst is connected with the Mercers' Company from 1385, recording property transactions, writing a petition to the king, and, from 1391, keeping their accounts. He also produced a copy of Langland's *Piers Plowman* and part of a text of Gower's *Confessio Amantis*. It is possible, though not proven, that he worked under Chaucer's direction to produce the first version of the *Canterbury Tales* (the Hengwrt manuscript).

Pynkhurst's employment history is not unusual. The growing volume of vernacular poetry produced in London in the late fourteenth century was not the product of specialized workshops but of ad hoc arrangements with and among professional clerks and scribes. The focus of their activities was the St Paul's area of the city, where Paternoster Row and its adjacent streets became a centre for the production of books, attracting limners (decorators) and parchemeners (parchment makers) as well as 'textwriters'.[59] Such industry in turn gave rise to speculative trading by stationers, so-called because they were not itinerant but stationed in particular properties, many on London Bridge.[60] Stationers, who might also ply their own trades, say as limners or scribes, would commission for sale or hire works that were in demand, in booklet form. A booklet might contain a complete work, several short ones, or an excerpt from a larger work.[61] By this means an individual might obtain, say, a set of Chaucer's lyrics, or a tale or two from the *Canterbury Tales*. Either they would buy the booklet outright from the stationer, or commission a scribe to produce a clean copy of a booklet that had been rented from the stationer. Subsequently, several booklet-sourced items might be bound into a book by their owner. There, they might constitute a single long work built up incrementally; or parts of several works by different authors, linked by some theme; or have a fairly random and utilitarian feel and include prayers and medical recipes. Such processes of literary production and acquisition help to explain the variations in appearance, spelling, and content that characterize vernacular literary manuscripts of the period.[62] They also shed a light on the composite, anthology-like impression of many surviving books from the period, including the *Canterbury Tales* themselves.

London as a Literary Centre

There are other, complementary, explanations for the miscellaneous feel of the *Canterbury Tales*. The work was unfinished at the time of Chaucer's death; it was assembled by scribes like Pynkhurst from surviving fragments; and the pilgrimage framework produces clashes between tellers that send the sequence of tales off at a tangent and into unusual juxtapositions of register and genre (as the Knight's Tale–Miller's Tale pairing shows). But little prepares us for Chaucer's greatest *volte face*, the Parson's Tale. That he intended it as the last tale is clear from the Host's words in the Parson's Prologue, when he says the pilgrims need just one more tale: 'Now lakketh us no tales mo than oon' (ParsP 16). By this stage of the proceedings pilgrims and modern readers have become used to the freewheeling development of the sequence, the debates it provokes, the demonstration that the moral perspective of the teller is conditioned by the social estate of the teller and his or her experiences, and to the exhilarating display of literary technique, style, and genre. The Parson's Tale puts a stop to all that.[63]

The Parson's Tale adopts an absolutist position on morality and rejects literary artifice beyond the most basic variety. A treatise on the Seven Deadly Sins and penitence, it has few adherents among a twenty-first-century audience. But those who have troubled to read it through as the end-point of the *Canterbury Tales* attest to its extraordinary power to cause a rethink of all that has gone before. Ambiguity is replaced by certainty, hesitancy by conviction, doubt by faith, entertainment by instruction. Its impact extends to Chaucer the pilgrim and author, for in its aftermath he revokes those Canterbury tales that tend to encourage vice—'thilke that sownen into synne' (Ret 1085). The retraction of things literary has in fact begun much earlier. Called upon in a jocular manner by the Host to 'Tel us a fable anon, for cokkes [cock's] bones' (ParsP 29–47), such as they have just heard from the Manciple, the Parson dismisses fables and other 'swich wrecchednesse' as chaff by comparison with the 'Moralitee and virtuous mateere' that he plans. It will be entertaining up to a point, for he allows his audience 'plesaunce leefful' (legitimate pleasure), but states categorically that literary artistry is not a priority: his 'myrie tale in prose' will not be in the alliterative mode, nor in rhyme, and indeed its narrative joys are exceedingly meagre. Thus the Parson refuses the project of the *Canterbury Tales*, which, other than his tale and Chaucer's tale of Melibee, is all in rhyme; refuses a second major literary project then under way (alliterative poetry); and instead allies himself with a third, involving the production of religious prose. Some further consideration of his positioning will help us to understand more about the literary environment in Chaucer's London (Fig. 3).[64]

The Parson distances himself from alliterative poetry by identifying it as a phenomenon alien to the south of England, and by mocking its repetitive initial consonants.[65] He says: 'trusteth well, I am a Southren man; | I kan nat geeste [tell stories] "rum, ram, ruf", by lettre' (ParsP 42–3). In so doing he correctly identifies alliterative poetry as predominantly regional in its language and appeal, using idioms that to southern ears might be all but unintelligible. An outstanding example is *Sir Gawain and the Green Knight*, written in a north-western dialect and probably intended for an aristocratic household on the Lancashire–Cheshire border.[66] It is a Christmas and New Year tale of King Arthur, a romance divided into four books or fitts, each of which could have been heard at a single sitting during winter festivities. The narrative weaves together exciting incidents, such as the beheading of the green knight or the hunting of a boar, with lapidary close-up descriptions of indoor and outdoor scenes that are cinematic in their intensity. It pits the forces of nature (extreme weather, sexuality, hunger, survival) against the values of chivalric society (decorum, Christian faith, set codes of social behaviour); entangles Gawain in two sets of games in which he is the unwitting victim of magical stratagems; and ensnares him in a series of conflicting promises. Gawain's great ideal of 'trawthe'—truth, or personal integrity (the same quality Chaucer espoused in his lyric to Vache)—is revealed as too good to be true, and he returns to Arthur's court a changed, more introspective, person.

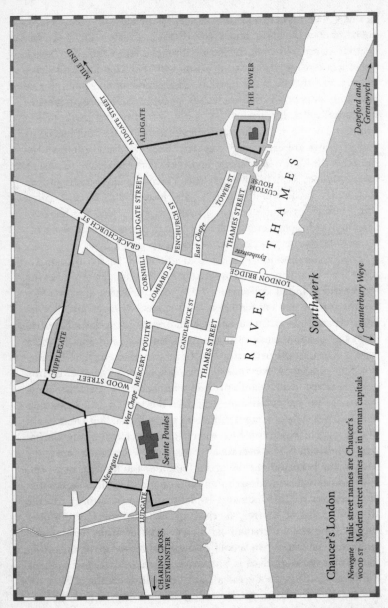

Fig. 3. Map of Chaucer's London.

Chaucer's London

Newgate Italic street names are Chaucer's
WOOD ST Modern street names are in roman capitals

Gawain continues to fire the imaginations of modern poets and readers, and is far better known now than it ever was in the fourteenth century.[67] Its dialect and provenance saw to that. Only one manuscript is known to exist, and it was not rediscovered until the early nineteenth century. Yet the horizons of the poem are by no means narrow or 'provincial'. It begins with a reference to that same masternarrative that haunts *Troilus*:

> Sithen the sege and assaut was sesed at Troye,
> The borgh brittened and brent to brondez and askes
> The tulk that the trammes of tresoun ther wroght
> Watz tried for his treccherie, the trewest on erthe.
> (Since the siege and assault ceased at Troy,
> The city destroyed and burnt to embers and ashes,
> The knight that wrought there the devices of treason
> Was tried for his treachery, the best example on earth.)

Here the Troy story is used explicitly as a myth accounting for the origins of chivalry and of cities. Aeneas the treacherous Trojan leaves his city in ruins and founds Rome; subsequently his grandson Brutus founds Britain, which is named after him. According to the *Gawain*-poet, Britain bears the imprint of its prototype: it is a place of marvel (*wonder*), but also of 'were and wrake', war and disaster, where peaceful happiness (*blysse*) alternates with 'blunder' or turmoil and strife. Brutus's direct descendant is Arthur and it is the values of his court and its chief representative, Gawain, that the poem opens to scrutiny. When it was written, Edward III was using the Arthurian myth as propaganda to legitimize his own political objectives. At one level, *Sir Gawain and the Green Knight* is a critique of the king's court.

Gawain also includes rhyme, so is anathema to the Parson on two counts. He might have found *Piers Plowman* more palatable, in spite of its alliterative lines. Its author, William Langland, was, like the Parson, a poor priest who used the Seven Deadly Sins as one way of representing and understanding personal and social aberrations. His outlook, too, is cosmic if more imaginative: human existence is described as a 'field full of folk', midway between heaven and hell—a 'toft' or hill surmounted by the Tower of Truth and a 'deep dark vale' where the devil dwells. The people in between lack direction: inclined to sin, they have intimations of a need to reform, and seek guides who can show them the way to Truth. Langland suggests a series of interconnected routes: the conscientious pursuit of work; the practice of contrition and confession; a pilgrimage of the soul rather than of the body.

Langland's concern is with society as a whole, and the forces that drive it, as well as with the individual. The use and abuse of money, the centrality of agrarian labour to the health of the economy, and the nature of charity, are among the topics he imbricates with the work of personal salvation. If he writes with conviction, the nature of that conviction, and of authority more generally, are opened to question. Langland recognizes, and satirizes, the corrupt practices and officers of the Church, the very people who ought to be guiding their folk to truth. In the absence of a dependable moral authority, the onus on individuals to determine their own path to Truth becomes more pressing. And while the poem begins as the report of a dream that seems to promise prophetic revelation, it is also full of doubt. The narrator himself, dressed as an itinerant hermit (a contradiction in terms), is aimless and searching for direction too, and unable fully to understand the purport of his vision.

Although he was from the Malvern area of Worcestershire (the setting of the opening scene of the poem) and wrote in a south-west Midlands dialect, Langland (like Gower) lived and worked in London.[68] It is his experience of London that fuels his imagination, moral indignation, and self-examination. After a panoramic sweep of the moral and spiritual landscape, Langland's focus narrows to the court, where a predatory cat (a figure for John of Gaunt) is causing mayhem, and then moves outside to the hustle and bustle of daily life, full of street cries (C. Prol. 230–4):

Cokes and here knaves cryede, 'Hote pyes, hote!	*their servants*
Goode gees and grys! Ga we dyne, ga we!'	*piglets; let's go*
Taverners til hem tolde the same:	*cried their wares*
'Whit wyn of Oseye and wyn of Gascoyne,	*Alsace; Gascony*
Of the Reule and of the Rochele the	*La Reole;*
roost to defye!'	*savour the roast*

London was fertile ground for Langland's art. First begun in the 1360s, he tripled the length of the poem in the 1370s, and then revised it again in the 1380s. At each stage, there is clear evidence of his response to contemporary developments such as the malign influence of Edward III's mistress, Alice Perrers, or the impact of the Peasants' Revolt.

The poem is an astonishing and exhilarating attempt to see the 'whole picture'—political, personal, spiritual, economic, moral, intellectual—and provide a coherent account of it in the face of forces bent on division and disintegration. In its ambition and scale and subtle use of the allegorical mode *Piers Plowman* stands comparison with Dante's *Divina commedia*. Nor did Langland want for readers. Some copies of *Piers* survive from the fourteenth century (which cannot be said with certainty about any of Chaucer's works); in total there are fifty-two manuscripts, only five fewer than the number surviving of the *Canterbury Tales*.

It is hard to believe that Chaucer did not know Langland's great work in one of its versions, using it perhaps to help him define what he was not (an allegorist, a theologian, confrontational) as much as what he was (a realist, of secular background, favouring indirection). Yet the two poets do share significant common interests, such as the court, London, social satire, the nature of authority. Even so, the differences in literary temper are more instructive than the similarities. Early in his poem (C. Prol. 66–84), Langland describes a Pardoner preaching with all the authority of a priest, but he is a seemer, an imposter bolstered by papal mandate and bishop's approval. What he offers (and what his real-life counterparts did offer) is an easy route out of the rigours of penance. In return for payment ('rynges and broches') he absolves them of further penitential acts and they are only too happy to comply, mistakenly believing that the indulgence granted by the pardoner is in fact a pardon, forgiveness itself. Thus the pardoner blinds the ignorant and adds insult to injury by using his ill-gotten gains to indulge his own sins of gluttony and lechery. Worse still, the racket is condoned by the parish priest, with whom the pardoner shares the loot.

Langland's vignette captures a number of his preoccupations: the degeneration of spiritual transactions into material ones; the abuse of money that should alleviate the suffering of the poor; the complicity of the Church in corrupt practices; the exploitation of ignorant people; and, worst of all, the proliferation of sin. Chaucer's portrait of his own pilgrim Pardoner (GP 669–714) touches on a number of the same issues, but he quickly ceases to be a representative pardoner and becomes an unforgettable individual one, fully conscious of his manipulative power and energized by his success in indulging his own sin of avarice while preaching against it. For the reader he has the fascination of an addict, unable to break out of the very vice that destroys him. And when he provides examples of his silver-tongued sermoning it is easy to understand how a congregation of believers might be hood-winked. Even Chaucer the pilgrim seems to admire his professionalism. So while Chaucer and Langland agree that the practices of pardoners are iniquitous their modes of representation and analysis are poles apart: Langland moves urgently to a categoric account of how and why pardoners as a species are deplorable; Chaucer shows what makes a particular one tick. Yet Langland's pardoner never gets his come-uppance; Chaucer's does. Carried away with his own rhetoric, he offers an indulgence to the no-nonsense Harry Bailly, inviting him to kiss his fake relics. The Host pierces the Pardoner's bogus importunity and hypocrisy with an obscene insult. He wishes that he might grab the Pardoner's testicles, cut them off, and enshrine them in a hog's turd. The loquacious Pardoner is rendered speechless.

Whether or not Chaucer knew Langland's work, it was being read in the London Chaucer knew.[69] A city of some 50,000 people, it was a lin-guistic melting-pot of regional accents, Italian, Flemish, Latin, Anglo-French, but above all the increasingly meaty and expressive language of choice: an east Midlands dialect of English. Its rapid rise in spoken and written forms in turn stimulated literacy in English, whether for sophis-ticated literary uses, keeping records, preaching sermons, or business transactions.[70] But the impression that the Parson creates, of there being an alliterative poetry alien to the south, is not quite right. Instead, there was a dynamic process of cultural exchange between London and other parts of the country, with texts passing back and forth.[71] Langland, though from Malvern, lived and wrote in Cornhill; *Gawain* and *Piers* might employ regional language, but they were in dialogue with issues generated by court, government, and Church—that is, institutions cen-tred in London but with powerful regional impact. One of the poems of the so-called alliterative revival, *Wynnere and Wastoure* (after 1352), has the same hallmarks. Linked to the north-west, it deals with the econom-ics of gaining and spending, mentioning Edward III and his chief jus-tice, William Shareshull, by name. It also refers to Edward's founding of the Order of the Garter (1348) and begins with an evocation of the Troy story similar to that found in *Gawain*.[72]

What alliterative poetry also points to is the existence of regional centres of literary activity and diverse regional audiences—some comprising aristocratic households, many others of gentry status, others yet made up of clerics. In the first half of the fourteenth century the vigour of regional literature in places such as Worcester, York, and King's Lynn outshone London itself, which came into its own as a literary centre only later in the century.[73] Chaucer ridicules the earlier regional poetry much as he ridicules its later manifestation, alliterative verse, as if he felt it necessary to establish his literary identity in contradistinction to others then prevailing. That earlier poetry is represented by the Auchinleck manuscript, a book Chaucer may have known and a miscellany of the sort previously discussed, containing saints' lives, prayers, and popular romances. The latter Chaucer lampoons mercilessly in his own pilgrim tale of Sir Thopas. He mocks their outworn descriptive conventions, proneness to long lists, emphasis on action for action's sake, predictable rhymes, repetitive rhythms, and general debasement of chivalric romance to a level more suited to popular consumption. His hero, Thopas—effeminate, vain, ineffectual, cowardly—is from Flanders. Chaucer describes him as a ludicrous, long-haired popinjay in terms normally reserved for describing female beauty that he mixes with incongruous details, domestic comparisons, and line-fillers. He then uses terms that might appeal to merchants used to dealing in cloth and other stuffs and in assigning monetary values to their commodities. The poem is on the point of getting out of control, as if its narrator does not properly understand the genre and can only imitate, not possess for himself, its key features:

Sir Thopas wax a doghty swayn;	*valorous young gentleman*
Whit was his face as payndemayn,	*fine white bread*
His lippes rede as rose;	
His rode is like scarlet in grayn,	*complexion; deep-dyed scarlet cloth*
And I yow telle in good certayn	
He hadde a semely nose.	
His heer, his berd was lyk saffroun,	*saffron (deep yellow)*
That to his girdel raughte adound;	*reached*
His shoon of cordewane.	*shoes; Cordovan leather*
Of Brugges were his hosen broun,	*Bruges; stockings*
His robe was of skylatoun,	*silken material*
That coste many a jane.	*Genoese coin*

(Th 724–35)

By the beginning of the third fitt the story told by Chaucer the pilgrim has got nowhere. Such is its numbing effect that the Host makes another of his timely interventions, and with the same criterion of value used for the Pardoner. He complains to Chaucer that his 'eres aken of thy drasty [worthless] speech' (Th 923–36). Chaucer protests that it is 'the best rym I kan [know]' but the Host has had enough, dismissing the tale as definitive doggerel rhyme, 'nat worth a toord [turd]'. As an antidote Chaucer offers 'a litel thyng in prose' about the virtues of prudence, the tale of Melibee.

Prose and seriousness go together in this literary world, contrary to modern expectations where prose, especially in the form of the novel, is the norm for literary endeavour serious or trivial, while poetry is its somewhat recherché cousin and a minority pursuit. When Chaucer wrote the reverse was the case: verse was the norm and could cater to matters light or heavy, while prose was reserved for serious matters catering to special interests in the shape, say, of philosophical discourse (*Boece*), scientific tract (*Astrolabe*), religious exposition (Parson's Tale), or admonitory advice (Melibee). But prose was making great headway, and composition in prose—much of it the outcome of translation from biblical, theological, and scientific sources—was a burgeoning activity in Chaucer's London, attracting a significant readership.[74] The Parson's Tale was not necessarily as rebarbative to Chaucer's contemporaries as it is to some modern readers.

CHAPTER 4

SOCIETY AND POLITICS

THE main emphasis of the present chapter is on some of the beset-ting and controversial issues catalysed by the traumatic experiences outlined in Chapter 2: plague, revolt, and war. Yet in concentrating on the destructive, the divisive, and the alienating it is easy to forget how resilient and adaptable Chaucer's society was. The ties that bound individual to kin, household, affinity, patron, or parish church could help to counteract and absorb some of the consequences of large-scale social crisis. The guild (a loose term that includes parish frater-nities, craft associations, and guilds of mayors and burgesses) is a particularly instructive example. A form of voluntary association with its own structure of authority that could cut across the conventions of hierarchy and gender, it offered an alternative route to individual and communal status and identity.[1] At the same time the guild was not merely a haven from social malaise: it manifested its own internal ten-sions and contradictions and provides a microcosm of social issues writ large elsewhere. Its *modus operandi*, as well as its dynamic, is reflected in the *felaweshipe* of Chaucer's Canterbury pilgrimage.

Evidence for the organization of guilds goes back to the twelfth century, but there is an especially rich cache of information dating from 1389. The parliament of the previous year, meeting at Cambridge, required all guilds to make a return detailing their constitution, mem-bership, and purpose. Parliament's decision may have been motivated by a sense that, post-1381, guilds might harbour sedition. In the event, no attempt was made to suppress them, but over 500 of the returns from the Cambridge census have survived. They reveal that guilds were of many different kinds. In Coventry, the Trinity guild, founded in 1364, attracted members from far and wide with an interest in the cloth-making industries central to the city's economy. Local farmers, as well as powerful magnates such as John of Gaunt, belonged to an organization that promoted the interests of a powerful élite. Those who aspired to the Trinity guild might first join the city's Corpus Christi guild and by that route seek civic office.[2] The merchant guilds of London, for their part, engaged in pseudo-courtly activities including feasts, liveries, processions, ceremonies, and entertainments that could involve literary activities.[3] At the other extreme, a fraternity associated with an altar in a parish church might have relatively few adherents and hardly any resources.

Differences apart, guilds had a number of features in common.[4] Members were bound by ordinances that reflected their common interests; and guilds tended to be much more inclusive of women than were other social groupings. All of them had a pronounced religious dimension, either through their dedication to the Virgin or a local saint, or—a recurring feature—their annual celebration of the feast of Corpus Christi. They thus provided an alternative to family and other social networks, much as they offered an alternative to the rigours of social hierarchy. The guilds also crossed the boundary between the living and the dead by commemorating deceased members in prayer and ritual. The sense of fellowship and continuity, of the guild's existing *sui generis* and in its own time-frame, was further enhanced by the particular history of its origins which a guild might possess and celebrate.

Many guilds were pilgrim-friendly—that is, they sponsored pilgrims from within their own ranks and offered succour to pilgrims from other places. The affinity between guilds and the emblematic figure of the pilgrim is instructive. It corresponds with the notion of guilds as associations that existed across and between other social structures and groups. The pilgrim is yet more liminal: a figure who leaves behind community and parish to join an ad hoc and temporary social group of other pilgrims in order to pass across and through other communities and parishes to a destination that promises a life-changing experience. Guild membership, like the role of pilgrim, offers some short-term immunity from the stresses and strains encountered in other social groupings, but it generates its own tensions. Guilds (like pilgrims) were particularly prone to reproduce in their own terms the issues that predominated in the wider social sphere. The records show that they were vulnerable to internal struggles based on power and status, to the competing claims of other social networks, to the divided loyalties of individual members as they negotiated their way through a variety of social identities, and to the impact of Wycliffite attacks on the eucharist (the sacrament celebrated at the feast of Corpus Christi).[5]

Wallace has argued persuasively that the guild, in all its complexity, is a valuable context for understanding Chaucer's account of pilgrimage in the *Canterbury Tales*.[6] Harry Bailly, the landlord of the Tabard Inn at Southwark, sets himself up as the governor of a *compaignye* bound by certain rules that have all the hallmarks of guild organization; the pilgrims have a common purpose; swear oaths of agreement; offer each other equal standing, as tale-tellers; engage in rituals of eating and drinking; are accommodating of women; have an ostensibly religious objective (worship at the shrine of St Thomas in Canterbury); and supersede existing social subgroups such as that of the Knight, Squire, and Yeoman, or Parson and Plowman. It is a transient and temporary community, existing outside of yet mimicking the more stable organization of a guild. Just as the social structures of guilds are under considerable pressure, so the Canterbury pilgrimage manifests similar stresses and strains and to some extent focuses and magnifies them. Whether in the fraught interactions of the pilgrims themselves, or in the tales they tell, the issues to which they revert are those that predominate in the history of the guilds: identity, authority, status, and gender.

Personal Identity

As members of Chaucer's society moved between different social groups either vertically into higher or lower estates, or horizontally into a guild, they assumed different roles and identities. Social crisis, with its loosening of traditional boundaries, tended to accelerate the frequency with which such changes became desirable or necessary, and also to raise consciousness about personal identity itself. Too frenetic and unsubtle an involvement in the social advantages of renegotiating one's personal identity could result in humiliation and disaster, as the case of Thomas Usk shows. A skilful manipulator of personal identity, such as Chaucer must have been, could hope to adjust to prevailing circumstances, survive, and prosper. Chaucer's own writing shows how fluid and subject to redefinition personal identity can be.[7] It is often difficult to distinguish between Chaucer the man and Chaucer the poet; he includes elements of his historical identity in his literary persona; and in the *Canterbury Tales* ventriloquizes a series of other narrators (the pilgrims) who in turn deploy a range of fictive characters with their own voices and idiosyncrasies.

The portraits of the General Prologue, so often seen as a gallery of colourful characters representative of Chaucer's society, might be read instead as a series of essays in the formation of identity.[8] Chaucer as pilgrim announces before and after his bravura descriptions that his focus will be on 'estaat' (social status), 'array' (clothing), and 'condicioun' or circumstances (GP 35–41 and 715–19). In practice, the portraits are made from a much richer palette of identity markers, including those related to estates satire, the science of humours, work practices, and place. By combining them Chaucer belies expectations set up by any one way of stereotyping individuals. Instead, he makes unusual juxtapositions that create the illusion of vitality precisely because each individual is an unstable amalgam of a number of possible identities. The sense that personal identity is not fixed but protean, its component parts in a perpetual process of recombination and renegotiation, is heightened by the pilgrimage. It opens individuals to scrutiny and interaction as, in one way or another, they give accounts of themselves. The critical eye of Chaucer the pilgrim, as *reporteur*, makes its own assessment. So the good-living Monk out of his cloister may be reprehensible by the standards of one stereotype, but Chaucer as pilgrim warms to him. Others are quick to note occasions when a fellow pilgrim's identity overflows into unexpected categories. The Reeve adopts a homiletic stance in the prologue to his tale. 'The devel made a reve for to preche' (RP 3903) is Harry Bailly's wry observation.

The Merchant provides an interesting illustration of the process, for constructing and maintaining a particular kind of identity is unusually important to this pilgrim, a relative newcomer to traditional accounts of medieval estates (GP 270–84).[9] His array, full of rich materials and details, suggests affluence: he wears expensive, particoloured cloth; a hat in the Flemish style made of beaver fur; and boots with elegant clasps. To match his power-dressing the Merchant contrives an imposing physical presence, with his forked beard and his elevated riding position on a high saddle. His speech and reported actions are also designed to impress. The Merchant voices his opinions 'solempnely', loses no opportunity to reiterate his success in making a profit ('th'encrees of his wynnyng'), expresses professional anxiety about the security of sea-trading between England and the Low Countries, and is skilful at trafficking in foreign currency.

In short, he lives on his wits, but he also lives on the edge: his estate, array, self-importance, and vaunted financial dealings are a mask: 'Ther wiste no wight [person] that he was in dette, | So estatly [digni-fied] was he of his governaunce [demeanour], | With his bargaynes and his chevyssaunce [financial dealings]'. The Merchant's credibility in the markets depends upon confidence in his financial acumen and the figure he cuts is crucial to that perception. His portrait, where he is twice described as 'worthy', is an exercise in the relative evaluation of worth—financial, social, and personal. What the Merchant's pro-fessional acquaintances see is what he wants them to see, but the care-fully constructed image disintegrates before the scrutiny of Chaucer the pilgrim.[10] And the Merchant's window-dressing comes at a cost. The commerce of 'eschaunge' (exchange) and 'bargaynes' has replaced social commerce of a more personal kind, while the necessary conceal-ment of debt entails withholding a key element of his identity. He thus remains to some extent inaccessible. It is not by chance that a key marker of personal identity escapes the pilgrim narrator: 'sooth to seyn [if the truth be told], I noot [don't know] how men hym calle'.

There is another shift in the tectonic plates of the Merchant's identity in the prologue to his tale. It is not so much what he reveals as the fact that he reveals it at all. His unhappy marriage is consistent with the desolation of the Merchant's personal life, but gone is his emphasis on maintaining appearances and instead personal confes-sion is the order of the day. The historical figure behind Chaucer the pilgrim had plenty of opportunity to observe the dynamics of mer-cantile identity, and this is not the only occasion on which he linked marital hollowness to the showiness and obsession with profit that are the hallmarks of the merchant's world. He does so again in the Shipman's Tale, where, while the husband is away on business, a mer-chant's wife exchanges sex with a family friend (who happens to be a monk) for the price of a new gown. The money the monk uses has been given to him for safe-keeping by the husband. The wife 'repays' her husband with more sex. Their marriage seems like a model of harmony and good practice by the side of the pilgrim Merchant's. Married for just two months, he has known nothing but 'Wepyng and waylyng, care and oother sorwe' (MerchP 1213–28). His wife is a match for the devil himself, a 'shrewe' full of 'hye malice'. The Merchant describes himself as a text-book victim, a representative speaking for a particular social category of 'wedded men' who live 'in sorwe and care'. He has become a comic figure quite different from the solemn man of the General Prologue. His carefully considered 'resons' or opinions are now a barely controlled emotional outburst.

His tale also is a saga of identities in flux, focusing particularly on young May, the focus of old January's desire. The very names of the chief protagonists signal one key stratum in the formation of their identities. According to the iconographic schemata visible in count-less manuscript illustrations and stone carvings of the labours of the months, May was associated with outdoor activities such as hawking, hunting, and wooing. January, on the other hand, was pictured in domestic interiors, sometimes as a two-faced lord who eats and drinks as attendants come and go. The idea that January and May might enjoy enduring, harmonious union is ludicrous. The relationship between these months, as some medieval poems describe it, is one of contention: old winter attempts to suppress young spring but is even-tually defeated. At the end of Chaucer's tale the quarrel that erupts between Proserpine, goddess of spring, and Pluto, who holds her in thrall under the earth, underscores the same theme. At this seasonal level of meaning it is as inevitable that May will gain the upper hand over the sixty-year-old, white-haired duke of Pavia as it is that spring will follow winter. She is, after all, like May personified: 'lyk the brighte morwe [morning] of May, | Fulfild of [Full of] alle beautee and plesaunce' (MerchT 1748–9). It is also inevitable that May will fall for January's young squire, Damyan. Young squires are familiar components of May calendar images. The pilgrim Squire is 'as fressh as is the month of May' (GP 92).

But the Merchant's May also has a number of other identities. There is of course her sexual identity, detailed as the object of January's fantasy—'Hir fresshe beautee and hir age tendre, | Hir myddel smal, hire armes longe and sklendre' (MerchT 1601–2)—on which he plans to feast. Desire blinds him, as does the arrogance that prevents him from listening to the sage advice of his counsellor, Justinus. For January overlooks another aspect of May's identity that might have given pause for thought to a person of his high position. Although renowned for her beauty, May is no more than a 'mayden in the toun' and so of low status, 'of small degree' (1623–5). So old January will have to contend with her different social background as well as with her sexual vitality and her spring-like youthfulness.

May has no say in the matter of her marriage and is initially an inert participant in the transaction, but a psychological identity does emerge. After she has been brought to the bridal bed 'as stille as stoon [stone]', January with his stubbly beard ('thikke brustles of his berd unsofte') labours all night until, at daybreak, and apparently pleased with his efforts, he sits up and sings loud and clear while 'The slakke skin about his nekke shaketh' (MerchT 1818–50). May is no more enchanted by the horseplay than she has been by the foreplay and its aftermath:

> But God woot what that May thoughte in hir herte,   *knows*
> Whan she hym saugh up sittynge in his sherte,
> In his nyght-cappe, and with his nekke lene;
> She preyseth nat his pleyyng worth a bene.
>
>   (1851–4)

However reprehensible May's subsequent actions, they are at least understandable in the circumstances.

What those circumstances rapidly become is a fabliau plot, even though the opening phases of the tale, with its aristocratic setting, high-flown language, and lovestruck squire, are in the romance idiom. Increasingly, May behaves to all intents and purposes like a fabliau heroine. She is no Guinevere but a waif and stray from a story such as the Miller's Tale, where the energetic and ingenious Alisoun, no less than *hende* Nicholas, acts according to her sexual urges and has little time for 'romance'. It is an identity appropriate to May's social origins as 'mayden in the toun', exactly the kind of person and setting featured in fabliaux. Gradually, too, like the month after which she is named, May becomes more vital and assertive. Thus she takes a practical and unromantic approach to the urgency of responding to Damyan's lovestruck overtures. Having received from him a secret letter, couched in flowery language, she makes an excuse to leave January's company, reads the letter, tears it into small pieces, and unromantically discards it: 'And in the pryvee softely it caste' (MerchT 1954). Once she has replied in kind Damyan makes a remarkable recovery from his bedridden state, but they are suddenly restricted by the onset of January's blindness, which makes him pathologically jealous and possessive. May is up to the challenge. Having counterfeited the key to January's private garden, Damyan enters and awaits her in a bush. Signalling with a cough and hand gesture that he should climb a laden pear tree, she feigns an appetite for the fruit and persuades

January to help her into the branches. Her lover wastes no time: 'And sodeynly anon this Damyan | Gan pullen up the smok, and in he throng' (2352–3). Witnessing the act, Pluto is enraged and gives January back his sight in time to see May and Damyan *in flagrante*. Such is the state of January's inner blindness that May, with Proserpine's help, is able to persuade him that what he has seen was no more than a hallucination.

January leaves the garden a happy man, thinking that his wife has not, after all, deceived him, and believing her to be pregnant with the heir he longs to have: 'on hir wombe he stroketh hire ful softe' (MerchT 2414). Whether the child will be his or not is a moot point. January, once so dominant, is now utterly under May's control. How has she effected the transformation from passive sexual property to the driving force of the marriage? At a seasonal level, of course, the garden is her natural habitat, one where the energies of May are fully displayed—just as the ducal hall, with its feasting, drinking, and attendants, was the place where January held sway. But there is much more going on in the garden than a struggle between seasonal figures. It is a place where new identities for May flourish and proliferate. For instance, January's image of May as his 'paradys terrestre' (earthly paradise), for whom he builds an Edenic garden in which to enjoy her, enables the garden to be read as a black comedy version of the fall of man with its tree, fruit, and trio of protagonists in which Damyan the demon plays the Satanic tempter, January plays Adam, and May, Eve (1332). Even more outlandish is the idea of May as the Virgin Mary, yet this is where January's warped piety leads. In the garden, he addresses his wife with a pastiche taken from the biblical Song of Songs: 'Rys up, my wyf, my love, my lady free! | The turtles [turtle dove's] voys is herd, my dowve sweete' (2138–9). However literally January construes what he says, the words were traditionally taken as figuring the relationship between Christ and Mary.

Such identities are offered as it were for audience consumption, as possible templates for interpreting May's behaviour, or as a way of understanding the extent of January's dotage. May herself does not lay claim to them, but the way in which she attracts a range of possible interpretations indicates something about her magnetic power. Certainly she exerts that power by behaving like a heroine in a fabliau where quick wits and youthfulness triumph over folly and old age. But her power derives more specifically from her abilities in manipulating her manifold identities. In the garden she may act like a maiden of the town but she affects the dignity and manners of a lady of the court, asserting that she is 'a gentil womman and no wenche' (MerchT 2202). She speaks 'Benyngnely' (with kindliness) and with feeling, weeping as she affirms her undying fidelity to January in eloquent terms: for the sake of her soul, her honour, her wifehood and body given to him in matrimony and blessed by the priest, and for fear of shaming her family or damaging her reputation, she will never be untrue (2186). No matter that she protests too much, this is just what January wants to hear and from the kind of woman he wants her to be. But it is all a sham. May's words are spoken with Damyan already in the garden and at the ready, just before she signals to him to climb the infamous pear tree. It is small wonder that to a woman of such exceptional skill in the management of her personal identities her old, blind, rich husband should want to give all he has. January promises that the next day charters will be drawn up assigning to her all his wealth and property, 'al myn heritage, toun and tour' (2172).

Authority

The Merchant has been prompted to reveal the state of his own marriage, and to tell the story of January and May, out of sheer incredulity at the preceding tale, told by the Clerk about the marriage of Walter and Griselde. He declares that there is a 'long and large difference' between the great patience of Griselde and the 'passyng crueltee' of his own wife (MerchP 1223–5). In the Clerk's Tale, the cruelty belongs to the husband, for Walter subjects his wife to a series of outrageous tests in order to measure the depth of her loyalty and affection. He feigns the murder first of their daughter and then of their son; secures documents from the pope that permit a divorce in favour of a younger woman of higher birth; shames Griselde in public view by sending her home in nothing but a smock; invites her back to his palace, similarly dressed, to organize his wedding festivities; and, only once the guests are seated, reveals that his new bride is in fact their daughter, and her brother, their son. It is small wonder that Griselde, reunited with the children she believed dead, collapses, her mettle proved beyond all reasonable doubt. She resumes her former position as Walter's wife and thenceforth enjoys his unalloyed devotion. Throughout her ordeals she has remained patient, loving, and steadfast.

The Clerk's Tale sets up a number of the issues that the Merchant then paints in an alternative, more cynical, light. If January squanders his inheritance, Walter safeguards his by ensuring that the woman who bears his heir possesses true—that is, innate—nobility. Although his people expect him to marry a wife born 'of the gentilleste and of the meeste [most high]' (ClT 131) he insists, like January, on making his own decision. His people are anxious about his childless state and the threat it represents to his 'heritage' and their governance (134–40). The woman he chooses is, like May, of a much lower social position. She is the daughter of a peasant, Janicula, the poorest man of a poor village. But Griselde makes up for her lack of material possessions in the richness of her other qualities: she is sober, hardworking, and treats her father with respect, reverence, and tenderness. Walter concludes that social status is no indicator of personal worth, for 'under low degree | Was ofte vertu hid', although he later uses Griselde's origins as an excuse for mistreating her (425–6). Janicula himself has misgivings about the match, thinking that a lord such as Walter will discard his daughter once his desire (*corage*) is slaked, for he will then think Griselde socially demeaning: 'it were a disparage [degradation] | To his estaat so lowe for t'alighte' (908–9). However, Walter is not driven by the same lecherous urges as January. He has gazed at Griselde 'noght with wantown lookyng of folye | . . . but in sad [serious] wyse' (236–7), admiring her womanly virtues.

Once married, those virtues are put severely to the test but, unlike May, Griselde does not splinter into a variety of identities overt and covert. Griselde's *benygnytee* is not mere airs and graces, no 'semblant of roialtee', but the expression of a natural nobility associated with patience, discretion, humility, and loyalty (ClT 925–31). The intense personal pressures Griselde endures strengthen and deepen her qualities, rather than corrupt them. Unassuming in her innocence, she remains true to her promise to be obedient to Walter, acknowledging subservience and conformity as necessary components of her married state. Given the extremity of the tests Walter devises, she might well be expected to change her approach, to fragment her identity, but she remains steadfast in adversity. In a word, she preserves the integrity between her inner and outer selves and, try as he might, Walter finds no 'variance' in her: 'She was ay oon [always one] in herte and in visage' (710–11). He concludes at last that she is 'constant as a wal, | Continuynge evere hire innocence overal' (1047–8).

Her speech at the lowest ebb of her fortunes, when she is 'divorced', banished from Walter's household, and sent all but naked back to Janicula, is full of dignity and pathos. Contrast May, who, given everything by January, speaks with a forked and flattering tongue; and January, who loses what authority he had.

By the end of the tale it is clear that Griselde is made of finer stuff than Walter. He has caused her unnecessary suffering; she has endured it and emerged triumphant. The marital authority may have been his but he has abused it; the moral authority is hers. There is more at issue here than the power relations within a marriage. By means of the relationship between Walter and Griselde the tale makes a wider emphasis on the uses and abuses of authority in the social and political domains.[11] One strand concerns the value of respecting authority. Griselde emerges triumphant only by submitting entirely to the authority structure devised by Walter, baleful though it is: 'as ye wole [will] youreself, right so wol I' (ClT 361). Walter himself accepts the paternal authority of Janicula, asking his permission before inviting Griselde to be his wife. Janicula, as the marquis's 'lige man', has little option but to agree: he blushes, is abashed, and trembles before asserting that his lord should 'governeth this mateere' (322). Walter nevertheless insists that Janicula should be present when he asks Griselde for his hand and to submit to his 'reule' (326–7). So the authority that invests their marriage is involved with and reflects the hierarchical authority that obtains in the family and in society at large.

As Walter's terminology of government and rule indicates, marriage is but one aspect of governance and is enmeshed with others. For instance, the citizens of Saluces are quick to recognize the natural authority of Griselde in dispensing justice for, thanks to her own good self-governance under Walter's marital regime, she is able to appease their discord, rancour, and disputes to the benefit of social harmony: 'The commune profit koude she redresse' (ClT 431). Her good 'governaunce' is again in demand at the time of Walter's supposed second wedding. Walter, for his part, uses trumped-up public opinion as an instrument of marital policy. He persuades Griselde that his people are murmuring against their marriage because they resent the idea that 'the blood of Janicle' (632), the poorest of the poor, should succeed him. Consequently, he claims, it is expedient for their son to be slain. Public opinion is actually less hidebound. As the Clerk reminds his audience, Walter is being slandered 'ofte and wyde' for his cruel heart, for his exploitation of a woman from a poor background, and for the murder of his two children (722–8).

The authority that Walter uses to manipulate his wife, the authority to which she accedes, is underpinned by an ideology to which Walter's people also subscribe and which vindicates the exercise of such authority whether in its personal, marital, familial, judicial, or political form.[12] That authority system and its ideology are indistinguishable from those that informed Chaucer's own society, and their foundation is in biblical texts. At the root of biblical authority is an author—ultimately God—whose scriptures (as interpreted by clerks) may be used to justify the authority structures that govern society. There are periodic allusions to this divinely ordained textual substructure throughout the Clerk's Tale. Griselde's suffering is of a piece with that of biblical precedents. Men may speak of the humility of Job in the face of his trials, comments the Clerk, but no man can match the humility and constancy of a woman such as Griselde when faced with commensurate suffering. Griselde, in her poignant farewell to Walter, declares that, by being banished from Walter's presence, she is in effect returning to her former state and going home naked, just as 'Naked out of my fadres hous . . . I cam' (ClT 871–2), thus using words spoken by Job in his affliction (Job 1: 21). Since Job was held to be a prefiguration of Christ and his suffering, Griselde is in illustrious company. She is aware of Christ's model precisely at the moment when her own suffering reaches its peak, with the removal of her second child, marking the boy with the sign of the cross of He who 'for us deyde upon a croys of tree' (554–60). Her affinities with Christ are also indicated by her poor origins, to which God sends his grace as into a 'litel oxes stall' (207). To reinforce the analogy, the Clerk urges that his story be read as an exemplum of the patience that should rightfully be shown to the inscrutable ways of God.

Such patterns of meaning invite an interpretation of the Clerk's Tale as a vindication of male, hierarchical authority, with all its iniquitous consequences for women, as endorsed by biblical text and commentary. The Clerk's Tale does indeed make a forceful statement about the orthodox position. It is all the more surprising, therefore, to find that it also contains the basis for a critique. All of the tale's considerable emotional charge favours Griselde, the victim whose plight inspires 'routhe' (compassion) and 'pitee' (ClT 893). Nor does Walter escape censure. The Clerk goes on record as having serious misgivings about the marquis's course of action and does not mince his words about its terrorizing effect: 'as for me, I seye that yvele [evil] it sit | To assaye [test] a wyf whan that it is no need, | And putten hire in angwyssh and in drede' (460–2). He reiterates his views, leaving his audience—and especially the women in it—in no doubt that his sympathies lie with Griselde. At the end of his narrative he stresses that it is emphatically not to be taken as a model of the humility appropriate to wives, for such suffering would be 'inportable' (intolerable). Rather, it is to be construed as a general lesson to all, whatever their 'degree', to be constant in adversity, like Griselde, and submit to God's governance (1142–7).

There is then a sudden and extraordinary coming down to earth that seems to leave the world of west Lombardy not just far behind but turned upside-down. In six stanzas headed 'Lenvoy de Chaucer'— that is, a lyric attributed directly to him though still in the voice of the narrator—the Clerk switches to the here and now of the pilgrimage, and the experience he shares with his listeners. He declares that it would be hard to find 'now-a-dayes | In al a toun' (ClT 1164–5) anyone of Griselde's temper, since women have become more like brittle brass than malleable gold. He proceeds with a song that celebrates the death of Griselde and her patience, 'bothe atones [at once] buryed in Ytaille' (1178), and which advises men not to test their wives' patience, for they will most certainly fail. The carnivalesque inversion of the tale proceeds apace with a parade of caricatures—the chatterbox, the shrew, the flirt—and a mythical cow called Chichevache, of legendary leanness because its sole diet is patient wives. Wives, says the Clerk, should shirk humility and not remain silent or be tricked on account of their innocence but turn the tables and assume control: 'sharply taak on yow the governaille' (1192). Husbands are not to be feared or reverenced. Nothing they can do is a defence against the 'crabbed eloquence' of a wife, whose efforts to keep him jealous will ensure that he is in thrall: 'lat hym care, and wepe, and wrynge, and waille!' (1201–12). This is a world that the Merchant knows only too well.

The Clerk invokes the sanctioned ideals of hierarchical authority only to ridicule them. He describes a theory of authority, but flinches at the suffering it causes. The Clerk's ambivalence points to a disjunction between ideal and practice that the Merchant himself registers. The latter's experience of authority is that it does not work: the received hierarchy is inverted since marital dominance, supposedly the prerogative of the husband, is in practice unenforceable. This questioning of orthodox structures is part and parcel of a challenging of authority within Chaucer's own society. The revolt of 1381 was an attack on authority and targeted lawyers and royal officials. If the authority of the king remained intact for the time being, by 1399 Richard had been deposed after a series of struggles with his magnates.[13] In the religious sphere there were comparable developments. The schism within the Church and the existence of two popes—one in Rome and one in Avignon—did little to enhance the authority of the Church; nor did the perceived and manifest corruption of its representatives, as chronicled by Gower, Chaucer, and others. The wide-ranging evaluation of the institution, organization, doctrine, and practices of the Church undertaken by the Oxford don, John Wyclif, created a framework and terminology within which authority did not have to be taken on trust but was open to critical examination. A major feature of the Wycliffite movement was its relatively liberal and progressive attitudes towards the biblical text, literacy, and interpretation. One of its key projects was the translation of the Latin Bible into English. Those who could read it—and the Wycliffites actively encouraged literacy, among women as well as men—could then engage in acts of interpretation hitherto the preserve of a clerical élite. Chaucer's attitude to his own writing is similarly unorthodox. He is a notoriously unauthoritative writer, who prefers polyvalent endings to definitive closure, who refracts his ideas through multiple voices, and who transfers authorship to others. The Clerk is one such voice, but he in turn denies authorship: he claims to have learnt his story at Padua from a 'worthy clerk', Petrarch, 'Fraunceys Petrak, the lauriat poete', who is an authority in his own land, having 'Enlumyned al Ytaille of poetrie' (ClP 26–33). The attribution recurs at the end of the Clerk's Tale: 'Petrak writeth | This storie' (ClT 1147–8). Chaucer is nowhere to be seen.[14]

Status

May and Griselde may react to their respective situations differently, but they share one experience: the sudden transformation of their status from low to high. In each case it is an extreme and rapid change of social identity. May is a mere 'maiden in the town', Griselde a peasant's daughter, and each becomes *gentil* by means of marriage to a nobleman. However, each construes her new-found condition differently. May realizes that she is in a position of power which she can turn to her own advantage, and stands on her acquired dignity, reminding January that she is now 'a gentil woman and no wenche' before behaving as wenches do. Griselde, unaffected by the trappings of power, behaves as she has always done, with constancy, love, submission, and patience—virtues that mark her out as a truly *gentil* person in spite of her 'low degree'. Taken together, the two tales indicate that a *gentil* status is hereditary but may also be acquired; that it is associated with power, influence, wealth, possessions, and standing; and that it is cognate with moral virtue.

Just as the ambivalence about authority in the Clerk's Tale may be related to uncertainties in the expression and acceptance of authority in society at large, so Chaucer's treatment of status has parallels in the non-literary sphere.[15] As we have seen, one effect of the Black Death was to ease and accelerate transitions from one estate to another. The result was a heightening of anxiety about the nature of social differences and the means of controlling those differences.[16] The Statute of Labourers and sumptuary laws might seek to maintain the traditional markers of social division, whether through wage legislation or by regulating clothing, but the poll tax legislation shows the extent to which such markers were being effaced in favour of taxable values. Yet there was one key indicator of social difference that remained resistant to such pressures, in part because there was no clear-cut way of marking it by clothing or monetary means: the intangible but highly desirable state of being *gentil*.

The term *gentil* is an identity marker based on social status. It signifies a high level of perceived worth. A *gentil* person wields influence and enjoys esteem and is expected to act with generosity, consideration, and disinterest. It is automatically part of the condition of being noble—the birthright of a magnate such as John of Gaunt. But it can also be acquired through education and action, as in the case of Chaucer or mayor Walworth, or through marriage, as in the cases of May and Griselde.[17] Since *gentilesse* is a moral quality as well as a social condition—as Chaucer's separate lyric, 'Gentilesse', makes clear—cases arise where those of *gentil* status act in ways that are anything but virtuous (e.g. May), and where those not of *gentil* status display a natural affinity for *gentil* behaviour (e.g. Griselde). Anxiety about the elusive requirements of gentility—material, social, ethical—is likely to be especially acute among those who have recently acquired it, and among those who see it as a desirable acquisition but who remain excluded. Such is the case with Chaucer's Franklin.

The Franklin is on the cusp between *gentil* and non-*gentil* status.[18] The General Prologue portrait describes a man who is a wealthy householder, hospitable, generous, and good-living. He plays a prominent role in the county hierarchy, presiding over court sessions and being, 'ful ofte', a knight of the shire, like Chaucer, and so a member of parliament (GP 331–60). He is also a sheriff and a lawyer and is, in short, a 'worthy vavasour'. *Vavasour* denotes landowner and it is possible that such a person, especially someone as well networked as the Franklin, would have acquired *gentil* status. He would certainly aspire to it. So he is either an aspirant or a parvenu.

The status anxiety that accompanies the Franklin's middling, in-between position as a wealthy stalwart of county systems of justice and administration emerges in the prologue to his tale. The Squire, *gentil* from birth, has been regaling the pilgrims with an exotic romance set in 'Tartarye' and featuring a magic mirror, a flying horse, and a miraculous sword. The Franklin—whether through envy or exasperation—has had enough, and interrupts him. The dramatic intervention expresses a larger social impatience, much like the Miller's riposte to the Knight's Tale. Here, the Franklin has been made uncomfortable by being reminded of the huge gap that separates the Squire, scion of the Knight, from his own son. He recognizes that, however dissociated from the 'real world' the Squire's story might be, he has acquitted himself 'gentilly' (SqT 673–87), that is by telling a tale in a genre appropriate to his estate, and by telling it well. Considering the relative youthfulness of the Squire, he has, says the Franklin, spoken 'feelyngly' and with a promising eloquence that has been a pleasure to hear. His own son lacks such fine qualities, such judgement, such 'discrecioun'. Wealth, what the Franklin calls 'possessioun'—which he and his son have in abundance—is nothing 'But if a man be virtuous withal!' The virtue or quality that the Franklin has in mind is of the *gentil* variety so amply displayed by the Squire. In spite of continual reprimands, the Franklin's son shows no interest in social improvement and would rather play at dice and spend and lose all his money. He mixes with the wrong people, such as young, untutored servants and their ilk: 'And he hath levere [rather] talken with a page | Than to comune with any gentil wight [person] | Where he myghte lerne gentillesse aright [properly]' (692–4).

Harry Bailly, ever on the look-out for incursions from one estate to another, has little time for such aspirations: ' "Straw for youre gentillesse!" quod oure Hoost' (SqT 695). But the Franklin's preoccupation with what it means to be *gentil* is not so easily dislodged. His tale is an examination of *gentilesse* in practice and one that ranges across different estates. Once again the focus of attention is a woman, Dorigen, although in this case she is not of low birth but from the opposite end of the social spectrum. She is 'of so heigh kynrede', comes from such a high-born family, that Arveragus, the knight who loves her and who is of lower status, hardly dares express his love (FrankT 729–43). But he does, and she is persuaded of his merits, which include 'worthynesse' (admirable qualities) and 'meke obey-saunce' (humble compliance), so they marry. Their relationship thus far has followed the familiar pattern of courtly behaviour, whereby the woman assumes the dominant role and the man is the supplicant. After marriage, it would be customary for Arveragus to turn the tables, assume 'maistrye', and treat Dorigen as his inferior. Such is the type of arrangement that Walter perpetuates and that the Merchant expects in his own marriage, only to be disappointed. Indeed, for the sake of appearances, and in order to prevent shame to his 'degree' and preserve his reputation, 'soveraynetee' is what Arveragus does assume (744–60). But within the marriage, as a private *modus operandi* between husband and wife, he proposes a radically different arrangement. Arveragus, of his own free will, promises Dorigen as much latitude or freedom in their marriage as she has enjoyed during their courtship, namely that he will 'take no maistrie' against her will, obey her, and do her bidding. She, in turn, recognizing that his offer springs from innate 'gentillesse', freely promises to be a 'humble, trewe wyf'.

Freedom, the condition of being free, thus becomes a keyword for the tale, its exercise a litmus test of whether or not an individual has what it takes to be *gentil*. As in the marital agreement between Dorigen and Arveragus, freedom has an ethical dimension in that it entails a surrender of self-interest, but it is also a word associated with social status. The 'free' person, socially speaking, is one of independent means who owes no service to an overlord and who is not in trade. The tale proceeds to show that ethical freedom is not necessarily the preserve of a social élite, that the free-born do not have a monopoly on freedom of thought and action. More immediately, the Franklin celebrates the freedom granted by Arveragus because it is the best way to preserve love. Love is, by definition, free as any spirit, and will not tolerate constraint: 'Love wol nat be constreyned by maistrye' (FrankT 764). Freedom, he says, is also the state to which all men and women aspire by their very natures—a truth known only too well to the rebels of 1381, who had their own views on the artificiality of social inequality, and for whom 'freedom' was a battle-cry.

After a year or two of wedded happiness, Arveragus leaves his home of Armorik in Brittany for Britain, in order 'To seke in armes worshipe and honour' (FrankT 811). This is not an inexplicable and reprehensible abandonment of his wife, as it has sometimes been represented, but a necessary and expected course of action for a knight, and especially one in Arveragus's position. More than is usually the case, given his social inferiority, he needs to demonstrate his continuing worthiness, and if possible enhance it, by engaging in meritorious conduct according to the precepts of chivalry. Dorigen, meanwhile, faces dangers of her own. The aristocratic culture that is her natural milieu, and which is designed to embody and enable the practice of 'freedom', is, paradoxically, a threat to the love, freely given and freely taken, that she enjoys with Arveragus. The Franklin introduces us to a world—alien to him, and one of which he is suspicious—which is claustrophobic, artificial, and inclined to hysteria. It is one just as prone to magic and deception as that described by the Squire and is in its way no less immature.

In the absence of Arveragus, Dorigen becomes distraught—'She moorneth [mourns], waketh, wayleth, fasteth, pleyneth [laments]' (FrankT 818–19)—but the Franklin is unimpressed because this is what such women do in such circumstances: 'As doon thise noble wyves whan hem liketh [when it pleases them]'. Arveragus sends letters, her friends comfort her, and gradually Dorigen's 'derke fantasye' (844) abates. But it soon finds another outlet, an external embodiment. Dorigen's castle is by the sea and to pass the time (there being little else for her to do) she sits on the high cliffs, staring downwards 'fro the brynke' at the 'grisly rokkes blake' below (857–94). They make her heart quake with fear, and she questions the wisdom of a God that would allow such 'feendly' things a place in his otherwise fair creation; for they bode destruction to those who, like her husband, travel by sea, and she wishes them 'sonken into helle'.

Dorigen's friends realize that it is not such a good idea to leave her brooding alone on the edge of a high cliff, and so distract her with idle pastimes, including walks, chess, and backgammon, in the course of which she in turn becomes the object of another's obsession. Significantly, the key encounter is in a paradisal garden similar to the one found in the Merchant's Tale (except that this garden is open, rather than enclosed), full of 'beautee with plesaunce [delight]' (FrankT 917–22). It is the kind of place a woman of her estate might frequent and one associated in romance with erotic fantasy. After eating, her friends dance and sing—activities the preoccupied Dorigen cannot share, 'For she ne saugh [saw] him on the daunce go | That was hir housbonde and hir love also'. But someone at the party is keen to fill the gap: Aurelius, a 'lusty squier, servant to Venus', and the very epitome of his estate. His courting of Dorigen is straight out of the best romance. He has been in love with her for over two years but has said nothing, sublimating his desire with lyric verse—'Songes, compleintes, roundels, virelayes' (925–98)—that expresses the extremity of his suffering. Seeing his chance, Aurelius plucks up courage and in well-turned but somewhat wooden courtly language declares his love: 'My gerdon [reward] is but brestyng of myn herte'. Dorigen will have none of it—'shal I never be untrewe wyf'—but then 'in pley' (and the excessive amount of play in which she has been able to indulge may be part of the explanation for what she now does) she promises to be the mistress of Aurelius if he will clear the coast of rocks. If he fulfils her fantasy, she will fulfil his.

Arveragus returns safely and Dorigen's life gets back to its version of normality. The wretched Aurelius endures 'In languor and in torment furyus' (FrankT 1101) for another two years until rescued by his brother, who puts him in touch with a magician, a clerk of Orleans. For a thousand pounds (a vast sum) the clerk undertakes to make the rocks disappear and does so through 'illusioun' and 'apparence' (1264–5). Aurelius, now revitalized, reminds Dorigen of her promise. The blood drains from her face as, true to form, she resorts to her self-dramatizing mode: she weeps, wails, and faints to excess, uttering a complaint on the vindictiveness of a Fortune that has trapped her between the devil and the deep blue sea. Her outpouring is as high-flown and inconclusive as her previous musings on God's wisdom, but much longer. For over a hundred lines she lists role-models who chose death over shame: the daughters of Phidon, who drowned themselves in a well; the maiden Stimphalides, slain while clinging to an image of Diana; the wife of Hasdrubal, who committed suicide at Carthage; and some twenty other precedents. The deadpan Franklin concludes: 'Thus pleyned [complained] Dorigen a day or tweye [two], | Purposynge evere that she wolde deye [die]' (1457–8). Instead, she opts for compromise, and tells Arveragus everything. By contrast, he is calm, plain-speaking, and brief, responding in a *gentil* manner 'with glad chiere, in freendly wyse' (1467–9). He comforts her in a down-to-earth way, asking 'Is ther oght elles, Dorigen, but this?', adding that what's done is done and that things may yet work out for the best. He does, however, insist on one important detail: that she keep her promise to Aurelius. A promise is a promise and must be kept in order to maintain 'trouthe'. That lost, all claim to *gentilesse* goes begging. At which point Arveragus himself breaks down and cries, for he runs the risk of losing both the fidelity of his wife and thereby the honour on which the perception of *gentilesse* depends.

Disconsolate, and now a truly pitiful figure, Dorigen heads for the tryst with Aurelius. Inevitably, it has been arranged for the private space of the garden, but she encounters her lover instead in a public place, the busiest street of the town. Hearing of Arveragus's insistence that his wife should maintain the integrity of a promise, though it cost her husband dear, and recognizing Dorigen's misery, Aurelius experiences an involuntary emotion: 'And in his herte hadde greet compassioun | Of hire and of hire lamentacioun' (FrankT 1515–44). He now sees his own role as socially degrading, 'cherlyssh wrecchednesse'. Acknowledging that Arveragus, by comparison, has displayed 'grete gentillesse', he frees Dorigen from her promise in order to show that he, Aurelius, can also do the decent thing: 'Thus kan a squier doon a gentil dede | As wel as kan a knyght'. A burden lifts from Dorigen, but Aurelius must face up to the huge debt he owes the magician, and fears he will have to sell his heritage and become a beggar. Once he hears the story of Arveragus the clerk too is caught up in the contagion of free and generous actions. He recognizes that Arveragus and Aurelius have acted 'gentilly til oother', but so much is only to be expected by virtue of their estates: 'Thow art a squier, and he is a knyght' (1607–11). However, *gentilesse* is not their prerogative alone: 'God forbede . . . | But if a clerk koude doon [knew how to do] a gentil dede'. So he in turn releases Aurelius from his debt. By this point in the narrative there is a sense that, by acting freely and generously, Aurelius and the clerk have escaped the make-believe world of romance and grown up, just as Dorigen too has faced up to her responsibilities. The Franklin ends by asking his audience to evaluate the protagonists. His question plays simultaneously on ethical, social, and existential registers: 'Which was the mooste fre, as thynketh yow?' (1622).

Women and Gender

The Franklin's sardonic remarks on Dorigen's emotional excesses should not obscure the fact that she is an educated woman. She has access to exempla from Greek and Roman legend and history; uses them to reflect on her own situation; and engages in philosophical discourse. Her education is a by-product of her aristocratic status and was accessible only to the privileged few. It was denied to the likes of May and Griselde. Griselde, however, does display some biblical knowledge, and for women of her low-born status the Church provided a route to instruction in the stories of the Bible and the tenets of the Christian faith. Others with a religious inclination might seek learning and literacy by taking holy orders, although that option too is associated with higher-ranking women. Chaucer's Prioress, for example, affects the manners of a courtly lady. For the vast majority of women, education and literacy, and therefore access to professional careers, were simply not options.[19] With some notable exceptions—the notorious Alice Perrers, the multilingual Anne of Bohemia—women did not attain positions where they could exercise political power, although there is evidence that their presence at the court of Richard II was enjoyed and encouraged by the king.[20]

Women are similarly disregarded within accounts of the three orders, although, again, the poll tax categories tell a rather different story. They could not fight, were a small and not very influential part of those who prayed, and were therefore subsumed in the general category of workers. Women's work took a number of different forms but for many it was menial, domestic, and associated with child-rearing. The trades with which they are most frequently associated are those of spinning, weaving, and brewing. Estates literature sometimes represents women as a distinct category, existing in a kind of parallel universe, with its own subdivisions that describe stages in a woman's life history: maiden, wife, widow.[21] The inferior status of women in society was underpinned, and to some considerable extent caused, by Church dogma, which demonized woman, in the form of Eve, as the cause of Adam's fall from grace in the garden of Eden. Women were the high road to sin, and legendary in their ability to subvert maleness, undermining its alleged rationality and spirituality with their own proclivities for emotion and sensuality.[22] There is something of this prejudice in the Franklin's attitude to Dorigen, while the Clerk's Tale represents women as either victims or caricatures: as a woman safe within the bounds of fiction Griselde stirs the empathy of the Clerk, but in his version of the real world women are out to eviscerate men.

Given the prevailing social conditions, it is all the more remarkable that Chaucer creates narratives that empower women.[23] The experiences of Griselde and May suggest that, even with the disadvantages of low birth and little learning, women are quite capable of thriving in a man's world, and of dominating it. Dorigen, for her part, is doubly empowered by her high social status and by the freedom she enjoys from male control of her married life (a freedom which, as she learns, has its limits). In these cases, women are the focus for Chaucer's exploration of status, authority, and identity, especially as these issues emerge within the context of marriage—marriage being, as we have seen, a model for wider social relations. That exploration is undertaken through a series of thematically connected narratives, sometimes referred to as 'the marriage group', although marriage itself is not so much the topic as the means of representing other issues. Thus the plot of the Franklin's Tale, with its garden and amorous squire, echoes that of the Merchant's Tale while offering a contrast to the jealous constraints of January's world. The Merchant's Tale is a riposte to the Clerk's and he in turn has in mind another narrator, the Wife of Bath, to whom he ruefully dedicates his palinode: it is 'for the Wyves love of Bathe— | Whos lyf and al hir secte [sex] God mayntene | In heigh maistrye' (ClT 1170–2).

It is the Wife of Bath's intervention in the sequence of pilgrim tales that galvanizes a debate centring on women. Her name even features in the middle of a scene at January's court when Justinus refers to her as an authority on marriage, as well she might be, having had 'Housbondes at the chirche door' five times between the ages of twelve and forty (GP 445–76). By that means she has become an exponent of women's power, 'expert in al myn age' on the tribulations of marriage (WBP 173–4). She is a particularly effective expert within the Canterbury tale-telling game because she is a 'here and now' woman, contemporary with Chaucer and his audience, present and boisterously interactive with the other pilgrims, unlike May, or Dorigen, or Griselde. She is exceptional also in her awareness and rejection of the categories by means of which men, especially clerks, construct female identity; the extent to which she challenges that authority which regards women as inherently inferior; and the force of her claim that women's status is the equal of men's.[24] She goes yet further by demonstrating the mainsprings of women's power in gossip and female community; sexuality; and alternative forms of belief.

Dame Alys's account of the identity categories that bedevil women is succinct: 'Deceite, wepyng, spynnyng God hath yive [given] | To wommen kyndely [in their natures]' (WBP 401–2). In other words, it is their God-given lot to be deceitful, to endure life in a state of sorrow, and to work at spinning thread. The stereotypes hark back to the Genesis story of Eve's role in the garden of Eden, where, at the serpent's behest, she encouraged Adam to do what God had expressly forbidden: eat fruit from the tree of knowledge. For their disobedience God ejected Adam and Eve from paradise and as further punishments condemned Adam to hard manual work, and Eve to pain in childbirth. Their post-Edenic state is traditionally represented in medieval imagery with Adam digging the ground while Eve spins, often with a baby nearby (Fig. 4). Wretched destiny as it was, it represented a kind of equality: 'When Adam delved [dug] and Eve span | Who was then the gentilman?' went the jingle used by the rebels in 1381. Thanks to the Genesis story, woman can be made to bear a heavy responsibility for a deplorable chain of events that goes far beyond the initial narrative: the origin of sin itself, the misery of human existence, the death of Christ, the perdition of the human race. As Alys later observes:

> Of Eva first, that for hir wikkednesse
> Was al mankynde broght to wrecchednesse,
> For which that Jhesu Crist hymself was slayn,
> That boghte us with his herte blood agayn.
> Lo, heere expres of womman may ye fynde,   *categorically*
> That womman was the los of al mankynde.
>
> (715–20)

Fig. 4. After the Fall: Adam digs while Eve spins and cares for their children (c.1430).

Alys does not contradict the core of the biblical narrative, but she does quarrel with its interpretation, with the authorities that have used it as a pretext for the subjugation of women. The story of Eve that she cites occurs in a compilation possessed by a former 'clerk of Oxenford', her fifth husband, Jankyn. As well as containing the myth of Adam and Eve, his 'book of wikked wyves' (WBP 685) includes the biblical story of Delilah's deception of Samson; an account of the shrewish behaviour of Xantippe, wife to Socrates; writings against women by St Jerome; excerpts from Ovid; and numerous other examples of the misery visited upon men by women. As a collection of antifeminist lore it represents in miniature a misogynist tradition stretching back to antiquity, endorsed by the Church Fathers, and still actively propagated in Christian culture of the fourteenth century. Jankyn has the endearing habit of reading juicy passages from his book aloud to his wife. On one occasion she is so incensed that she rips three leaves from the volume and lands a blow on Jankyn's cheek with her fist. The brawl that ensues is a dramatic realization of the conflict between male dominance, enshrined in books and institutionalized in marriage, and female power—what Alys earlier refers to as the altogether sufficient power of 'experience'. Her prologue begins: 'Experience, though noon [no] auctoritee | Were in this world, is right ynogh for me' (1–2). She thus posits a counterforce, comprising common sense, practical action, and life knowledge, to the bookish theorizing of clerks. To make her point she observes that the very reason there are so many stories hostile to women—except those that concern female saints—is precisely because they were written by men. Had women been able to write they would for their part have revealed 'moore wikkednesse | Than al the mark of Adam may redresse' (695–6).

Alys applies her commonsensical approach also to the interpretation of biblical texts, and the results add up to a comic but challenging reworking of traditional exegesis. Christ, she says, spoke to the Samaritan woman who, like her, had been married five times, and reproved her for not being married to the man who was then her partner. But Christ did not explicitly prohibit serial marriage: 'Yet herde I nevere tellen in myn age | Upon this nombre diffinicioun' (WBP 24–8). 'Wexe and multiplye' is a text she can readily understand (even though its original application is to the propagation of children rather than husbands). The case of Solomon, who had many wives, demonstrates that the practice of exuberant sexuality may be a blessing from God: 'As wolde God it leveful were unto me | To be refresshed half so ofte as he!' (37–8). Abraham and Jacob also married more than once, and even St Paul affirms that widows are free to marry. Marriage is no sin, and although Paul prizes virginity he does not command it but advises it, leaving the decision to the individual concerned. In any case, universal virginity would lead to the extinction of that very virtue he extols: 'if ther were no seed ysowe, | Virginitee, thanne wherof sholde it growe?' (71–2). Other biblical pronouncements less conducive to her life-style Alys dismisses out of hand, rejecting both the interpretation and the writing that conveys it: 'After thy text, ne after thy rubriche [rubric] | I wol nat wirche as muchel as a gnat' (346–7).

Embattled, militant, and truculent as Alys is, her fracas with Jankyn has a surprising outcome. He is enraged by her blow, and in turn strikes her on the head with his fist so hard that she falls to the ground, apparently senseless. Full of remorse, he cedes to her 'governance of hous and lond' (WBP 814), the same 'lond and fee [property]' (630) which she had given to him at their marriage as an expression of her love. She thus acquires total domination, 'By maistrie, al the soveraynтее' (818). Jankyn allows her freedom to control both her honour and his 'estaat' or social standing, thereby recognizing something fundamental in woman's nature: 'We love no man that taketh kep or charge | Wher that we goon; we wol ben at oure large' (321–2). Yet, far from being triumphal, Alys chooses to be kind and faithful, as Jankyn now is to her. Each having freely relinquished the exercise of 'maistrye', they have no more quarrels and live in harmony and equality: 'After that day we hadden nevere debaat' (822). There are intimations here of the key theme of the Franklin's Tale, the tale that concludes the 'marriage group'.

Such moments apart—and the moment soon passes, for Alys is widowed yet again—there is an argument for regarding the Wife of Bath as a pastiche confected by Chaucer from popular clichés and writings by Jerome and others. To that extent she is a misogynist's nightmare come true: rebellious, self-willed, out to browbeat men with outrageous behaviour, ruinous expense, and perpetual nagging. While this might be the textual core of Chaucer's creation, he goes beyond written authority to embed Alys in the world of experience and so provide a glimpse of a more authentic woman's world.

The rampant sexuality of women is a prominent aspect of antifeminist writing, but Alys discounts its negative implications. Instead, she celebrates and revels in her sexuality as a natural force to be used, enjoyed, and recognized for what it is rather than treated coyly as a source of shame. Ridiculing clerks who claim that the genitals were made solely for 'purgacioun | Of uryne' she insists that they were also made for 'ese | Of engendrure [procreation], ther [so that] we nat God displese' (WBP 119–29). She refers to her vagina as a *queinte* [cunt], and uses a range of alternative, colourful terms (*bele chose*, *chambre of Venus*) in explaining how she put it to good use as a bargaining tool with her earlier husbands (three of whom were rich and old), or as a source of sheer pleasure, as with Jankyn, who was young. Similarly, misogynist writers might denigrate the loquacity of women, but Alys revels in her success in browbeating her husbands with 'continueel murmur or grucchyng [grumbling]' (406): 'God it woot [knows], I chidde [chided] hem spitously [without mercy]' (223). But there is more to this claim than exuberance. When Alys says of her husbands that she 'quitte hem [answered them] word for word' (422) she is referring to their antifeminist sentiments, culled from St Jerome, as well as to domestic tit-for-tats. Hearing one such authoritative statement along the lines of 'women hide their vices and shortcomings until they are married', she retorts: 'Wel may that be the proverbe of a shrewe [fool]!' (284). So the spoken word, at which women excel, is pitted against the written word, which is men's domain. In this case, at least, the spoken word—pithy, colloquial, new-minted, quick-witted—emerges victorious over the hoary truisms of clerkly culture.

The success of female orality in counteracting male structures of authority, based on the written word, is further illustrated through Alys's social network. It likewise depends on word of mouth, and constitutes a highly effective means of controlling male behaviour, and of providing information about it. Alys mentions a number of its members: a maid, her niece, another 'worthy wyf', and the key figure, her boon companion or 'gossib', called Alisoun, who knows Alys's heart and secrets better than that local representative of male authority, the parish priest. There is little that her husband can say or do, no secret he might divulge, without its spreading through gossip to this group and so causing him 'shame': 'hadde myn housbounde pissed on a wal' it would have been round the network in no time

(WBP 534). In matters of confession the parish priest is outclassed by the belief system to which this group of female parishioners pays heed. Alys alludes to enchantment and a superstitious belief in what dreams portend in order to lure Jankyn—tricks learnt from her mother. And when it comes to explaining her drives and desires she resorts not to Christian morality but to astrology. Her incompatibilities with Jankyn are a consequence of their being 'children' of different planets, ones that are inherently opposed. She, as a child of Venus, loves 'ryot and dispence'; he, as a child of Mercury, 'wysdam and science [knowledge]' (699–700). But if 'Venus me yaf [gave] my lust, my likerousnesse [appetite for pleasure]', it is Mars who 'yaf me my sturdy hardynesse [rebellious boldness]' (611–16). Mars was ascendant in Taurus (a sign ruled by Venus) when Alys was born, so her inclinations are driven 'By vertu of my constellacioun'. She thus incorporates both male (Mars) and female (Venus) characteristics, an indication that maleness and femaleness are not to be thought of, as they tend to be in clerical discourse, as confined by gender. According to this account, being a woman is a much more complex mode of existence than traditional stereotypes, and their framework of belief, allow.

Chivalry

The Wife of Bath's prologue is more than twice the length of her tale. The Friar calls it 'a long preamble'—ill-advisedly, since he is then attacked in turn by the Summoner and Alys herself. Given her loquacity and desire to set the record straight, the prologue's relative length is perhaps not as surprising as the nature of tale she tells. It is an Arthurian story set 'many hundred years ago', far away in a Britain of magic and faery, before friars (so Alys says) became the new elves and incubi causing dishonour to women. At first encounter the tale does not seem to match the immediate, riotous, and slapstick qualities of Alys's peroration, which seem to anticipate more of the same rather than the decorum of courtly manners. Indeed, there is some manuscript evidence to suggest that Chaucer first intended for his Wife of Bath the narrative now known as the Shipman's Tale, summarized above: a fabliau with a contemporary urban setting, mercantile values, and full of sexual innuendo and trickery. Instead, he assigned her a Breton lai, a sub-genre of romance that anticipates the Franklin's Tale, which is of the same ilk. On closer inspection, however, the tale does portray—albeit in an aristocratic setting—some of Alys's pre-occupations: a woman's world, in which female subtlety overcomes the crudeness of masculine mentalities; sexuality; the marital struggle for 'maistrye'; and the possibility of gender equality. Where the tale parts company with the prologue is in its treatment of *gentilesse* (another foreshadowing of the Franklin's Tale), linking it in particular with the practice of chivalry.[25]

The male protagonist of the Wife of Bath's Tale is a knight of King Arthur. While out riding he finds a solitary maiden and, in spite of her protestations, rapes her. There is outrage at court and Arthur condemns him to death but the queen, Guinevere, intervenes. She grants the knight his life if he is able to say, to the satisfaction of her court of ladies, what it is that women most desire. Although the knight has a year and a day to discover the answer he despairs of doing so because he can find no agreement. Some say that women most desire wealth, others status, others sexual satisfaction, others regular remarriage. Returning despondently to court, he catches sight of some beautiful women dancing by the edge of a forest, but on approaching them they disappear, to be replaced by an old hag. She convinces him that she has the right answer to his question and whispers it in his ear, on condition that in return he will give her whatever she demands. They return to court together and the knight discloses to Guinevere and the assembled ladies that what women want is sovereignty. No one demurs, and the old hag now reminds the knight of his promise. She demands that, in return for saving his life, he marry her. Appalled at the prospect, he goes through with the ceremony, but proves somewhat unenthusiastic on the wedding night. His wife chides him, and offers him a choice: either she can remain old and ugly, but faithful; or she can become young and beautiful and fickle in her affections. He leaves the choice to her, thus ceding control, and she in return transforms into a beautiful, young, and faithful woman. They live happily ever after, in a state of mutual respect and love.

Told like this, Alys's tale might seem little more than a wish-fulfilment fairy story, a fantasy of how relations between men and women might be in an ideal world. Yet it is freighted with other meanings. In the first place, the transposition of Alys's preoccupations, urgent and immediate as they are, to aristocratic culture, suggests that they are issues not peculiar to her but ones that are endemic. Second, her narrative is tethered to ongoing debates about *gentilesse*, its connections with social status, and the implications for chivalry itself. The knight's revulsion at having to marry the old hag is based on his perception of her status as much as her appearance: 'Allas, that any of my nacioun [family] | Sholde evere so foule disparaged be [brought low by a mis-marriage]' (WBT 1069–70). When he is 'daungerous' (standoffish) on their wedding night, she affects surprise and reminds him that she is his beloved, his wife, and the person who saved his life. He believes that nothing can be done to remedy the situation because she is ugly, old, and low-born, 'so loothly [loathly], and so oold also, | And therto comen of so lough [low] a kynde' (1090–1101). She does not agree that the situation cannot be remedied, as she later demonstrates by magical means. But she begins the process of transformation by argu-ing for a change of attitude on his part. She does so in the first instance by subjecting the concept of *gentilesse* to a re-examination.

The idea that *gentilesse* is acquired at birth she dismisses out of hand: 'Swich arrogance is nat worth an hen' (WBT 1109–90). The truly *gentil* man is he who strives to do virtuous deeds, both in private and in public, 'Pryvee and apert'. Christ himself is the true originator of *gentilesse*, not our ancestors. They might provide wealth and inher-itance, and a claim to an impressive family tree ('heigh parage'), but they cannot bequeath 'vertuous lyvyng'. If *gentilesse* were to occur as a natural trait within a certain family, then none of its members would be able to prevent themselves from acting virtuously and shunning 'vileynye or vice'. But in fact virtuous deeds are not tied to wealth and inheritance: 'genterye | Is nat annexed to possessioun'. So much is clear from witnessing 'A lordes sone do shame and vileynye'—sins the knight himself has committed by raping a defenceless woman. No matter that a lord's son is born to a 'gentil hous' with forebears who were noble and virtuous: if he abhors virtue he is not *gentil*, whatever his received social status; rather, the opposite, for 'He nys nat gentil, be he duc or erl, | For vileyns [base] synful dedes make a cherl'. *Gentilesse* stems from God alone; it is given by his grace and not bequeathed. It follows that, even though the wife's ancestors may have been uncultivated she is nevertheless *gentil*, and therefore the equal of her husband, provided that she is resolved to 'lyven vertuously, and weyve [avoid] synne'. The knight's accusation of pov-erty his wife dismisses by reference once more to Christ, who chose to live in 'wilful poverte', and by pointing again to the disparity between social and moral estates: the rich, covetous person is poor for not possessing what he craves; the poor person who covets nothing is correspondingly rich, 'although ye holde him but a knave'. As for the knight's reproof of his wife's old age, she reminds him that it is customary among the so-called *gentils*, according to their code of conduct, to show respect to older people.

The force and effectiveness of the wife's reasoning prepares the ground for her husband's acceptance of her sovereignty and for the miraculous events that ensue. Her speech is also a comprehensive and successful challenge to the moral basis of the knight's claim to be her superior. It goes far beyond the analysis of *gentilesse* in the Franklin's Tale and constitutes a wide-ranging attack on the ethical standards according to which men such as the knight conduct their lives. Previous references to Gower and Brinton indicate that Chaucer was not the only writer exercised by the behaviour of the knightly estate, whether on account of their flamboyant tournaments or their failure to act in the revolt of 1381.[26] While it is possible to explain such concerns as manifestations of a satirical tradition reaching back through Dante, there is also evidence to suggest that the chivalric class had reached a point of intense self-scrutiny. Knights, the practitioners of chivalry, could justify their existence only if they could be seen to be acting in a *gentil* manner; otherwise chivalry was little more than licensed violence which could lead to the kind of excess described at the beginning of the Wife of Bath's Tale. The war with France, of course, amply demonstrated the need for knights and, provided they won victories, the benefits they brought. But with stalemate and defeat came a more introspective mood about war and its practitioners. Wyclif and his followers were especially strident in their attitude to warmongering, pointing out its contradictions with a gospel that espoused peace—a matter further complicated by the fact that both sides in the war were allegedly Christian.

In truth, the upholders of knighthood did not bother themselves over-much about the tangled affiliations between chivalry and its Christian credentials, which do not bear too close a scrutiny. Chivalry was in essence a secular ethic condoned by the Church and useful to it as a means of protection and of propagating crusade.[27] The Church's support gave chivalry part of its *raison d'être*, but its representatives could be nuisances if they interfered too much in political or practical matters. Froissart cites numerous instances of well-meaning bishops or papal legates, anxious to broker a truce, who were sent packing by princes equally anxious not to lose an opportunity for chivalric glory. Chivalric glory is indeed Froissart's main topic, and the sense of nostalgia that seeps from his pages is in itself indicative that, by the time he wrote his chronicles in the later fourteenth century, the glory days were over. Nevertheless, his is an invaluable testimony to chivalry as a practice that, whatever the cause of the conflict or the gruesomeness of the outcome, united enemies of a certain social status in a set of shared values. For instance, Sir John Chandos (whose herald was later the biographer of the Black Prince) and Sir Jean de Clermont, both 'young and in love', are reconnoitring the other's army when they meet by chance and recognize that each wears on his left arm the same emblem of 'a lady in blue embroidered in a sunbeam'. They bicker about who has the right to wear it, having inadvertently discovered that they are rivals for the favours of the same woman. Again, after his brilliant victory at Poitiers, the Black Prince provides a lavish feast for the king of France and other high-ranking captives, seating them at a high table. As a mark of deference and respect for the king as a renowned warrior he refuses to sit with them, but instead serves the food. King Jean is taken to London and imprisoned in the Tower. He is treated with such 'courtesy, good faith, and honour' that, some time after his release on parole, he returns voluntarily to make amends for his son Louis, also a hostage, who has broken his parole terms. Jean is greeted royally and entertained at Gaunt's palace, the Savoy, along with other distinguished French hostages, and dies in London the following year, 1364.[28]

Such episodes may strike a modern reader as absurd and quaint, but they are indicative of an unquestioning faith in the principles and 'game' of chivalry that, by the 1380s at the latest, was beginning to wane, at least among its more thoughtful practitioners. An instance of this disillusionment is provided by Chaucer's associate, Sir John Clanvowe, a soldier who had served in France and then became one of Richard's chamber knights. His Wycliffite leanings emerge in *The Two Ways*, a treatise written soon before his pilgrimage to Jerusalem, where he died in 1391. It concerns the moral choices that determine whether we travel the narrow and straight way to heaven or the broad and crooked way to hell. Clanvowe writes disparagingly of a world he knew inside-out as, unquestionably, a road to hell. To do so he isolates a key word, 'worship', or renown, that cornerstone of chivalry comprising the public acclamation on which the good name of a knight depends.

What men desire so much, 'the worsshipes of this wrecchid world', he writes, is not worthy of the name. Before God, only virtue deserves worship, but in this world the reverse is true for 'worship' is given to the sinful ways of knights hell-bent on conquest, the display of largesse and magnificence, and the upholding of their reputation (i.e. what knights customarily do):

ffor the world holt [holds] them worsshipful that been greete werreyeours [warriors] and fighters and that distroyen and wynnen manye loondis [lands], and waasten and geven [give] muche good [gifts] to hem that haan ynough, and that dispenden [spend] oultrageously in mete, in drynke, in cloothing, in buyldyng, and in lyvyng in eese, slouthe [sloth], and many oothere synnes. And also the world worsshipeth hem muchel that woln [would] bee venged proudly and dispitously [pitilessly] of every wrong that is seid or doon to hem. (lines 485–93)[29]

Men write books and songs about such people, so that their glory might be perpetuated, for long-lasting renown is something that they greatly prize. God, however, views matters differently, and regards such knights as 'right shameful'—shame being the very opposite of what knights seek to uphold at all costs: their honour.

Others too felt that the energies of chivalry needed to be harnessed to more constructive ends. Such exhortations were as old as chivalry itself, but fifty years into a protracted war between Christian neighbours they had a particular relevance and application.[30] Philippe de Mézières, tutor to Charles VI of France, chancellor of the king of Cyprus, and a knight of international celebrity, made a series of interventions in Anglo-French politics that analysed the ills of chivalric practice while seeking to redirect it. For Philippe, the crisis in chivalry was symptomatic of a wider malaise evident in comparable disorder within the other estates. One fundamental cause was the war itself, so the first remedy was peace, to be effected through a strategic marriage between Richard and a French princess. The second remedy was a healing of the papal schism, responsible for so much antagonism across Europe. The third was a joint crusade by a newly united Christendom against the infidel Turks, who were making significant advances in the eastern Mediterranean. Philippe set out his ideas in a widely circulated open letter to the English king, his *Epistre au Roi Richard II*, and subsequently proposed the creation of a new crusading order, the Order of the Passion—a proposal which Richard may have supported.[31]

Peace

To what extent was Chaucer aware of, and involved in, what might loosely be called the 'peace movement'? If he himself was not a close associate of the king, he worked with people who had their fingers on the pulse of political life. Sir Richard d'Angle, one of Richard's tutors, was Chaucer's companion in the mission of 1377 to Montreuil to discuss possibilities for a marriage between Richard and a French princess. A Frenchman who had been taken prisoner at Poitiers, d'Angle then joined the English side and served the Black Prince. At his coronation Richard made him earl of Huntington.[32] A more significant figure was another royal tutor, Sir Simon Burley, an influential *magister* (master) who became Richard's confidant. Richard rewarded Burley in 1377 by making him vice-chamberlain, a role that enabled him to control access to the king. Of gentry background, Burley was never ennobled but consolidated his power by acquiring the extensive Leybourne estate in Kent—to the consternation of established landowners. In 1384 Richard gave him yet more control of the county by appointing him constable of Dover and warden of the Cinque Ports.[33] Commissions of the peace for Kent, such as the one on which Chaucer sat in 1386, could not be held without Burley's presence. A target of the Appellants, he was executed in 1387.

Other associates of Chaucer close to the king were Sir John Clanvowe and Sir Richard Stury. They were also closer to Chaucer in aptitude, background, and outlook than the likes of Burley. Clanvowe and Stury were both of gentry background and favoured by Richard as chamber knights. In the 1390s they were also regular attendees at the king's council, meeting at Westminster, which determined war policy in consultation with the king. More prominent members of the council included Gaunt and the chancellor, Thomas Arundel.[34] When, in 1380, Chaucer was released from a charge of *raptus* (rape or abduction) by Cecilia Chaumpaigne, Clanvowe was one of the witnesses. The personal histories of Chaucer and Stury are even more intertwined. Both were members of Edward III's household, their names appearing in the accounts for the receipt of winter and summer robes. Both were ransomed by the king in 1360 after being captured in France—Stury (styled 'king's esquire') for £50 as against Chaucer (a *valettus*) for £16. In 1377 both participated with d'Angle in the marriage negotiations at Montreuil, and in March 1390, following severe floods, they

were both made commissioners for walls and ditches between
Woolwich and Greenwich.

The pursuit of peace was interlinked with another long-term question, the nature of the king's counsel: the quality of the advice he
received, the motives of his advisers, their tendency to fall foul of
parliament.[35] The examples of de la Pole and Burley have already
been cited. In the Tale of Melibee, Chaucer as narrator, in the guise
of a pilgrim to Canterbury, offers some perspectives on the nature of
counsel as it pertains to war and peace. There is no evidence that
Richard knew Chaucer's work or was influenced by it. Nevertheless,
it is designed to raise consciousness about the pursuit of peace at a
time when peacemaking was very much on the king's agenda. And it
would have struck a chord, given Richard's interest in promoting
himself as a ruler steeped in wisdom and prudence.[36] The tale also
prompts wider questions about the function of Chaucer's writing in
relation to the court, or to court circles. He is intervening in a current
debate and offering advice or counsel of his own in the manner of a
traditional 'mirror for princes'.[37]

The story begins with an outrage against the ruler Melibeus,
'myghty and riche'. While out of his house his enemies enter through
the windows to beat his wife, Prudence, and severely wound his
daughter, Sophia, leaving her for dead. At one level, the work is a
psychomachia, as a ruler listens to the promptings of prudence and so
regains wisdom (*sophia*). But it is construed as a series of dramatic
dialogues conducted under threat of armed conflict. The issues are
pressing, the decisions crucial to the well-being of the land. Inclined
to immediate vengeance and sudden war, Melibeus calls together a
'greet congregacioun' to seek its advice. Its chances of providing dis-
interested or unified counsel are not good. It comprises

surgiens, phisiciens, olde folk and yonge, and somme of his olde enemys
reconciled as by hir semblaunt [seemingly] to his love and into his grace; |
and therwithal ther coomen somme of his neighebores that diden hym rev-
erence moore for drede than for love, as it happeth ofte. | Ther coomen
also ful many subtille flatereres and wise advocatz [lawyers] lerned in the
lawe. (Mel 1004–6)

The surgeons favour the healing of divisions, but the physicians
the medicine of war. An advocate counsels delay until Melibeus is
well provisioned, but the young people want immediate action and

clamour for hostilities to begin. An old, wise man reminds them that war is easy to begin but difficult to finish, and unpredictable in the suffering it causes: 'ther is ful many a child unborn of his mooder that shal sterve yong by cause of thilke werre, or elles lyve in sorwe and dye in wrecchednesse' (1040). To make matters worse, Melibeus finds that many members of his council advise one thing in private and 'the contrarie in general audience' (1049), but the consensus is in favour of armed aggression.

Before he can take any action, Melibeus is asked by his wife, Prudence, to reflect more deeply. It is another occasion on which masculine tendencies are gradually realigned by feminine ones. Prudence urges caution, distrusting the opinion of the 'greet multitude' (Mel 1067) and suggesting a better counsellor, 'heighe God' himself (1115). Turning to God for guidance, she suggests, will negate the force of those emotions and motives hostile to good decision-making, namely anger, greed, and haste. Melibeus should also 'keep his counsel', that is proceed secretly and without broadcasting his intentions, for many of the counsellors who surround him are flatterers and, in practice, his enemies. Her own view is that the wickedness he has suffered should be countered by goodness, war with peace, and by praying to Christ for his guidance and protection. Vengeance is God's prerogative, not the ruler's. Melibeus counters that the law itself espouses redress, not longsuffering, for wrongs inflicted. He has the resources, so should seek justice through war. Prudence believes it is foolish to put trust in riches or in war when the outcome is so unpredictable. Better to make peace, for Christ said, 'Wel happy and blessed been they that loven and purchacen pees, for they been called children of God' (1679). Melibeus thinks that such a policy would be an affront to his honour and renown, but Prudence insists that his adversaries can be won over. She becomes an intermediary, a peace negotiator or conciliator, patiently explaining to her lord's enemies the advantages of peace and the perils of war. They are persuaded to come to court and confess their guilt. At first wanting to exile them, under Prudence's guidance Melibeus grants a full pardon and a merciful forgiveness, modelling his approach on that of Christ, 'so free and so merciable' (1885) to the repentant.

A network of connection with men such as Burley, Clanvowe, and Stury—not to mention Gaunt himself—meant that Chaucer had direct access to issues, such as the king's counsel and peace-making, that preoccupied court and parliament. In Richard's reign the war with France was pursued sporadically, with little enthusiasm, and less success. Certain factions—Gaunt's among them—advocated a more aggressive policy, but there was little appetite for the heavy taxation entailed. A truce was agreed in 1389 that enabled peace diplomacy to flourish.[38] Gaunt was appeased by being granted the duchy of Aquitaine. After protracted negotiations a new amity between England and France was sealed at Ardres in 1395 when, with a lavish display of magnificence on both sides, Richard took Isabella, the six-year-old daughter of Charles VI of France, as his new bride (Anne having died the previous year). If the tale of Melibee is any indication, Chaucer would not have been displeased at this happy outcome.[39]

CHAPTER 5

INTELLECTUAL IDEAS

JOHN WYCLIF dominated English intellectual life in the later four-teenth century. Other thinkers, especially William of Ockham but also Thomas Bradwardine, were more profound and subtle, and had considerable influence on philosophical thought, but Wyclif's ideas had more impact and reach.[1] That was primarily because his teach-ings were not confined to philosophical or theological speculation; they were also polemical, and had practical and radical applications. The objects of his attention were the institution, doctrines, and prac-tices of the Church, many of which he viewed as in need of urgent reform. Since the Church was guardian of the ideology on which the whole of society rested, Wyclif's ideas had an unsettling effect. Their impact and reach were further increased by his direct involvement in political activity, by the patronage of the rich and powerful, and by the enthusiasm with which some took up and pursued his cause. As far as Chaucer is concerned, the question is not so much the extent to which he was aware of and influenced by Wycliffite thought, as the way in which that body of thought operates as a context for under-standing and interpreting his narratives.

Among writers that appealed to Chaucer as providing a coherent body of thought distinct from conventional Christian doctrine, none is more influential than Boethius. Chaucer translated his *Consolation of Philosophy* and incorporated his ideas in a number of works, not-ably the Knight's Tale and *Troilus*. Chaucer's fascination was for a writer who, though living in the Christian era, chose not to apply the obvious Christian solutions to the problems he faced. Instead, by sto-icism and force of thought—what Boethius calls 'feathers of philoso-phy'—he rose above the harsh contingencies of his existence and reconciled himself to the forces arrayed against him, embodied in the pagan figure of Fortune. She is held responsible for the extreme con-ditions in which Boethius, a political prisoner under sentence of death, found himself (in both senses). To counteract the reductive effects of Fortune Boethius articulated a Platonic account of love as a universal principle that binds together all of God's creation. His exposition had a profound effect on Chaucer's understanding of the human experience of love.

Another intellectual space that appealed to Chaucer was that of the classical past, ostensibly free of Christian dogma. It was therefore an excellent vantage-point from which to survey the 'added value' represented by the story and meaning of Christ's life. *Troilus and Criseyde* is one such exploration of the Christian through pagan mythology. The ancient world provided a means of representing, and thinking about, 'pagan' forces embedded in Christian culture and which in various ways threatened its disruption: erotic love, violence, Fortune, or the gods themselves, felt through the influence of the planets named after them: Mars, Venus, Saturn. The ancient past also provided Chaucer with a rich source of narrative and imagery whether from ancient mythology, the Trojan story, or Ovid.

In moving through, and gaining knowledge of, different systems of belief and explanation, Chaucer encountered different versions of reality and different ways of giving value to moral and emotional phenomena. As often as not, those alternative versions were compatible with the Christian scheme of things, but sometimes they were not. Chaucer's writings register his understanding of how a sense of reality varies according to the historical moment and cultural setting, and how it varies according to gender and status. His work also reveals an aesthetics of reality because different literary genres order reality in different ways. For romance, reality is in the realm of ideas, for fabliau in things and bodies, for the saint's life in the spiritual domain, for the dream vision in mental images. Chaucer's acute awareness of the subjective, relative, and constructed nature of reality finds a context in philosophical speculations about the nature of the real associated with the work of Ockham, Bradwardine, and Wyclif, among others.

Heresy

John Wyclif (*c*.1330–84) was a 'clerk of Oxenford' who first attended the university as a student in about 1354. He became a fellow of Merton College and, in 1360, Master of Balliol. A prominent scholar, he lectured on theology from about 1370. In that role he developed his views on the nature of the Church and its beliefs, and produced a series of influential written works (some 132 in total) including a

complete biblical commentary. The Church, he argued, was not syn-
onymous with the body of priests who worked within it; rather it was
the elect, or chosen, known only to God, who comprised the Church.
It followed that some priests were not elect and that therefore the
traditional role of priest as mediator (of absolution, or penance) was
questionable. For Wyclif, the relationship of the soul to God was
direct, and did not need such intermediaries. And just as the grace of
God determined who was elect, so it determined true lordship,
whether in the secular estates or in the Church. The temporal power
of the pope, or the temporal possessions of the Church, were not
sacrosanct, but accidents of history. In arguing his case, Wyclif referred
again and again to the authority of the Bible. Scripture was for him
the touchstone of truth: it fed his thinking, provided the evidence for
his arguments, and was itself an object in need of reform. He believed
that it should be made as accessible as possible, by means of an English
translation, 'so faithful people, those meek and humble of heart, of
whatever station, cleric or lay, men or women, applying themselves to
the logic and eloquence of Scripture, will find there the strength to do
well'.[2] Then others could see that the Bible provides no precedents
for popes, or for the Church's temporal power, or for such doctrines
as that of transubstantiation—the belief that the bread and wine of
the eucharist is miraculously transformed, in the priest's hands, to
the actual body and blood of Christ. The latter issue, more than any
other, became a *cause célèbre*.[3]

Wyclif argued his case with passion and rigour. His oratorical and
polemical skills, as well as his arguments, attracted political interest.
His views on the power of the pope and the influence and wealth of
the Church could be put to good use by those keen to curb papal
authority and jurisdiction, or to extract more money from the Church
in support of the war. In 1374 he was one of seven English ambassa-
dors sent to Bruges to meet the pope's delegates over the vexed questions of provisions (the direct appointment of clergy by the pope) and
papal taxation. By 1376 Wyclif was enjoying the patronage of John of
Gaunt, who employed him to preach against William Wykeham,
bishop of Winchester and a former chancellor who had been prominent among Gaunt's accusers in the Good Parliament. Inevitably,
Wyclif's activities and ideas provoked fierce resistance and hostility.
By the autumn of 1377 pope Gregory IX had issued bulls detailing
nineteen of Wyclif's errors. Chief among them were his views on

the eucharist. Three years later his teaching on this topic was the subject of a commission set up by the university authorities at the instigation of his clerical detractors. In 1381 he was obliged to stop teaching and retire to his living at Lutterworth. The following year a council at Blackfriars, in which bishop Brinton played an active role, condemned fourteen of Wyclif's propositions as erroneous, and ten as heretical. He died two years later, in 1384.

Wyclif's ideas were not so easily suppressed. As in the case of Sir John Clanvowe, they fitted well with a kind of introspective piety, growing in popularity, that was not well served by more conventional means. Clanvowe was a long-serving chamber knight but his is not a unique case. Chroniclers record the names of others at court sympathetic to Wyclif. They include Sir Richard Stury, Sir Lewis Clifford, Sir John Montagu, and Sir William Neville, as well as others, known collectively as the 'Lollard knights'. ('Lollards', applied disparagingly to Wyclif's disciples from *c.*1387, is from the Dutch *lollen*, to mumble.) Three—Clanvowe, Clifford, and Stury—were the executors of Queen Anne's will. However, it would be misleading to suggest that the Lollard knights were subversives at the heart of a conservative Christian court.[4] Wyclif's ideas were not a monolithic structure to be adopted wholesale or rejected out of hand. Rather, they represented a series of positions on a set of related topics, positions which an individual might separately accept, or not: his views on the papacy, for example, but not on the eucharist. It was possible to be both orthodox and heterodox. Not until 1401, with the statute *De heretico comburendo* (On the burning of heretics) did pro- and anti-Wycliffite beliefs become consolidated and polarized.

Nevertheless, a significant number of clerics actively propagated Wyclif's thought before and after his death.[5] He had recognized the need for a body of priests who would convey the unadorned meaning of Scripture to the faithful. In practice they streamlined his ideas, emphasizing and developing some aspects, and carried through his great project, the first complete translation of the Latin Vulgate Bible into English. The first version was a literal translation; the second, completed by 1397, an eminently readable text. Together they amount to over 230 surviving manuscripts. Some Lollard priests are known from the records that detail their prosecution by the Church authorities. Nicholas Hereford and John Aston were Oxford men found preaching heretical doctrines in the Winchester diocese and in Leicester.

There, they were assured of a warm welcome by Philip Repingdon, canon of St Mary's. Archbishop Courtenay summoned all three to the Blackfriars Council of 1382 where they were forced to acknowledge the errors of their ways. Aston and Hereford soon relapsed: in 1387 they were prohibited from preaching in the Worcester diocese, along with William Swinderby of Leicester. Persecution of the Lollards had a political slant: appearing when it did, in the early 1380s, Lollardy could be readily associated with sedition. The politicizing of Lollardy meant that it became increasingly difficult for those in authority to remain openly sympathetic. For instance, in 1395 Richard II obliged Sir Richard Stury to abjure heresy on pain of execution.

It was not difficult to argue that the ideas of Wyclif's followers were seditious. In the same year there had appeared nailed to the doors of St Paul's and Westminster Hall a document entitled 'Twelve Conclusions of the Lollards'.[6] A petition addressed to 'the lordis and comunys [commons] of the parlement', it would have made any archbishop apoplectic. The Church is represented as the home of Antichrist, a 'blynde and leprouse' oppressor, maintaining a 'proude prelacye' to the great detriment of the people. The Church, contrary to what it should be, is a place of 'michil privy falsnesse' (much secret deceit), an institution out of joint and in need of urgent reform. In support of its polemic the document cites Wyclif's views, including those on the elect, the eucharist, the separation of spiritual and temporal power, and against war. It also develops arguments that provide further contexts for ideas found in Chaucer's writings. It argues against the offering of special prayers for the deceased in lavishly endowed chantry chapels. It attacks pilgrimage and sainthood (especially that of St Thomas of Canterbury) as a spiritually bankrupt activity beguiling the people by encouraging them to make idolatrous prayers and offerings to 'blynde rodys [crucifixions] and to deve [deaf] ymages of tre and of ston'. And it attacks priests' 'feynid' (pretend) power of absolution as a means of enhancing their pride and increasing their wealth by exerting their supposed powers for payment, 'for a busschel of qwete [bushel of wheat]'—an abuse and pride that stem from the pope himself.

That Chaucer was aware of the kind of controversy embroiling Church and reformers is clear from the epilogue to the Man of Law's Tale, when the Host first invites the Parson to contribute a story: 'Sir Parisshe Prest,' quod he, 'for Goddes bones, | Telle us a tale' (MLTE 1166–77). But the Parson objects to Harry Bailly's oath, to which the

Host, ever on the look-out for indicators of identity and affiliation, retorts: 'I smelle a Lollere in the wynd'—swearing and blasphemy being another of the Lollards' *bêtes noires*. The Host now anticipates a sermon, a 'predicacioun', such as Lollard preachers used to spread their views: 'This Lollere heer wil prechen us somwhat'. In practice he has to wait until the end of the journey to Canterbury to hear the Parson's views on sin and penance, but long before that, or the Host's observations, the Parson's Wycliffite credentials have been on view.[7]

The General Prologue portrait describes a 'good man . . . of religioun', not addicted to material wealth and, though poor, 'riche . . . of hooly thoght and werk' (GP 477–528). He is, as Wyclif and his followers were, 'a lerned man, a clerk' who makes the focus of his teaching and preaching the unadorned 'Cristes gospel'. Devoted to his community (community being a focus of Lollard concern), he adopts a benign, diligent, and patient attitude towards his parishioners, not browbeating them with his power over them (e.g. by cursing them for not paying tithes), but rather showing them charity: he shares with the poor his possessions, and the offerings made at church. Again, the charitable use of money was a Lollard preoccupation. The Parson is assiduous in visiting on foot, staff in hand, both the high and the low, whenever sickness or misfortune befall them and no matter where they live in his far-flung parish. By these and other means he teaches by example in the manner of Christ himself—'first he wroghte, and afterward he taughte'—and using the same biblical metaphor of a shepherd caring for his sheep. He does not leave them to a hireling, running 'to Londoun unto Seint Poules | To seken him a chaunterie for soules', but stays at home to protect his flock against 'the wolf' because 'He was a shepherde and noght a mercenarie'. Encountering sinners, he treats them not with scorn, disdain, or undue dignity, but is instead discreet, kind, and fair, persuading them to virtue by good example. But in the case of obstinate sinners he is no respecter of persons and treats high and low with the same sharp rebukes. Pomp, reverence, and an over-fastidious conscience are not for him, but rather the teaching of biblical truth, that of 'Cristes loore [lore] and his apostles twelve', first following it himself.

The Parson is the Lollards' imagined ideal, an antidote to the corruption they see as endemic to the Church. The portrait is built on a series of details of what the Parson is not (the corrupt priest of Lollard polemic) contrasting with what he is. The Parson's nemesis is the

Pardoner, a definitive mercenary devoted to avarice, not poverty or
charity. He preaches only 'To wynne silver' (GP 713) and make his lis-
teners 'free'—not free from sin, but free with their money: 'free | To
yeven hir pens, and namely unto me' (PardP 401–2). He cares nothing
for their souls—they can go to hell for all he cares—and despises wilful poverty of the sort espoused by the Parson when he can 'wynne
gold and silver' (440–7). The apostolic life of poverty, manual labour,
and begging for his sustenance is not for him. The model embraced
by the Parson the Pardoner categorically rejects: 'I wol noon of the
apostles countrefete'. The integrity of the Parson is replaced by a
readily acknowledged hypocrisy. An expert on his topic, the Pardoner
preaches against the very vice he embodies, using the biblical text
Radix malorum est cupiditas (Greed is the root of evil): 'Thus kan I
preche agayn that same vice | Which that I use, and that is avarice'
(427–8). The Pardoner's Latinity is of the superficial variety, used to
flavour his sermons and make them sound more impressive, to 'saf-
froun with my predicacioun | . . . to stire hem to devocioun' (345–6).
He is not the textual scholar that the Parson is. And just as the Parson
practises humility, so the Pardoner practises an oppressive arrogance,
using the pulpit to settle scores with anyone who has defamed him or
his 'bretheren'. He is all vindictive, snake-like rhetoric and bombast
where the Parson is measured and plain-speaking: 'Thus spitte I out
my venym under hewe | Of hoolynesse, to semen hooly and trewe'
(421–2). A wolf in sheep's clothing, the Pardoner preys on the likes of
the Parson and his flock:

. . . whan that he fond	*found*
A povre person dwellynge upon lond,	*parson; in the country*
Upon a day he gat hym moore moneye	
Than that the person gat in monthes tweye;	
And thus, with feyned flaterye and japes,	
He made the person and the peple his apes.	*fools*

(GP 701–6)

The power and authority that the Pardoner wields, however heinous, are entirely orthodox, legitimate, and sanctioned. He is a representative of that very 'proude prelacye' denounced by the Lollards.
The Pardoner comes straight from the papal court, his wallet crammed
full of pardons with the ink hardly dry, 'from Rome al hoot [hot]' (GP
687). His brand of religion is one that depends on the ostentatious

show of the external trappings of authority, the signs rather than the substance. In order to impress a congregation he displays his documentary credentials, including the bishop's seal on his 'patente' (ecclesiastical licence). These he uses to warn any priest or clerk not to disturb him in 'Cristes holy work'—taken to be synonymous with his extortions—and further buttresses his authenticity with 'Bulles of popes [papal edicts] and of cardynales | Of patriarkes [high-ranking prelates] and bishopes' (PardP 335–76). The entire Church hierarchy, it seems, is complicit in what the Pardoner does. What he does, other than preach to considerable effect, is display his supposedly authentic holy relics that are, in fact, worthless junk, 'longe cristal stones, | Ycrammed ful of cloutes [rags] and of bones'. They include a mitten which, if worn, increases crop yields, and the equally miraculous shoulder-bone of a holy Jew's sheep. If washed in a well, its water will thenceforth cure the ailments of animals, increase their fertility, and heal a man's jealousy even if his wife has 'taken prestes two or thre'. The efficacy of the relics is guaranteed only if his listeners 'offre pens, or ellis grotes'.

The Pardoner's chicanery depends for its success on the gullibility of a rural congregation, and on its preoccupations with harvest, cuckoldry, and livestock. The process of conferring power on talismanic objects comes close to the hocus-pocus or 'nigromancie' of exorcism and blessing condemned in the Lollard Conclusions. The psychology of belief he encourages borders on the idolatry they also decry: things worthless in themselves are invested with magical potency. Worse, offering money to the relics results, so he would have his listeners believe, in the forgiveness of sin: 'whoso . . . wol come up and offre . . . I assoile him, by the auctoritee | Which that by bulle ygraunted was to me' (PardP 387–8). The Pardoner leaves such communities spiritually and financially bankrupt, the authority of the parish priest in shreds, but with hardly a care in the world:

> I wol have moneie, wolle, chese, and whete,
> Al were it yeven of the povereste page,   *peasant*
> Or of the povereste wydwe in a village,   *widow*
> Al sholde hir children sterve for famyne.
> Nay, I wol drynke licour of the vyne,
> And have a joly wenche in every toun.
>
>   (448–53)

This world of superstition and hypocrisy, where money buys forgiveness, and the material has replaced the spiritual, greed has supplanted charity, and the poor suffer, is symptomatic of and enabled by the institutional corruption of the Church. It is precisely what the Lollards attacked.

Do the portraits of the Parson and Pardoner make Chaucer a Lollard?[8] Foxe and other Protestant authors liked to think so. The virulence and impact of Lollard and anti-Lollard polemic was such that Chaucer could hardly have been ignorant of it. But his investment in the terms of a current debate does not make him a partisan. In any case he is, as ever, refracting issues through the mouths of characters each with his own agenda and dramatic rationale. And there are a number of other ways in which the Lollard tag does not stick. In the first place, if the Parson were a card-carrying follower of Wyclif and his ideas, he would not be going on a pilgrimage. To do so conflicts with his dedication to staying put and ministering to his parish community, and runs counter to the Lollards' avowed hostility towards pilgrimage. They regarded it as fostering the idleness, drunkenness, lechery, idolatry, and extravagance that led to ruinous debt. At the very least, he would not be heading for the shrine of St Thomas of Canterbury. The Lollards abhorred the cult of saints, and reserved special opprobrium for archbishop Thomas Becket. As chancellor of England he had wielded that temporal power which, for the Lollards, was not the province of the Church; and he died defending his rights to temporal power (jurisdiction over the clergy). Nor is the Pardoner entirely a Lollard shibboleth. His bravura is breathtaking, the gulling of his congregation has a comic side, the relish with which he reveals his *gaudes* or tricks is infectious, his tale is spell-binding. It is difficult not to harbour, along with Chaucer the pilgrim, a sneaking regard for his single-minded professionalism and its success.

Then there is the small matter of the *Canterbury Tales* themselves, organized around the framework of a pilgrimage. Were Chaucer a Lollard, he would hardly have used this motif as a framework for his narratives. On the other hand the case of the Pardoner, who is a kind of travelling shrine, suggests that offering at relics is nothing more than a confidence trick perpetrated by the Church on the credulous. And making offerings at relics (the shrine of St Thomas, which contained his mortal remains) is exactly what Chaucer's pilgrims will do on arrival in Canterbury, as an early fifteenth-century continuation of

Chaucer's work, the *Tale of Beryn*, makes clear. The issue here, then, is not pilgrimage itself, or offering at relics as such, but the authenticity of those practices. The Pardoner's self-exposé reveals his practices as a sham—and by extension those of others within the Church—and his relics as so much rubbish. It does not follow that devotion to pilgrimage and the saints is necessarily worthless. Harry Bailly captures the distinction vividly at the end of the Pardoner's Tale when the Pardoner ill-advisedly turns to him as one 'envoluped in sinne', inviting him to 'kisse the relikes everychon, | Ye for a grote! [groat] Unbokele anon thy purs' (PardT 944–55). The Host's robust reply amounts to a recognition that the Pardoner's motivation (greed) and the nature of his relics (false) render such a transaction not only worthless but positively risky, spiritually speaking. It would incur 'Cristes curs', for the Pardoner would swear, if he could, that his shit-smeared breeches were a relic. Then, in wishing the Pardoner's testicles themselves 'shryned [enshrined] in a hogges toord [turd]', the Host swears by a true relic, that of the 'croys [cross] which that Saint Eleyne fond', indicating that he for one has not had his faith in relics, and therefore pilgrimage, undermined.[9]

The working hypothesis on which Chaucer proceeds is that the Lollard critique has tremendous force and validity in revealing the corruption of the Church and the need for a kind of reform that would take it back to its first principles. But he resists the atomizing or polarizing that might ensue and which, historically speaking, did ensue. Instead, the religious ideas that underpin the *Canterbury Tales* are catholic in the true sense of being inclusive. The Host and Pardoner are at daggers drawn, but all the other pilgrims are in fits of laughter as the Knight intervenes to effect a reconciliation. He persuades them to kiss, so that the 'pleye' of story-telling on the road to Canterbury might continue. Later, as the pilgrims approach the city, the Parson invites them to regard their journey as emblematic of life's pilgrimage towards salvation, envisaged as a heavenly city, 'Jerusalem celestial'. The squabbles of individuals, much as the dissensions within the Church, look insignificant by comparison with heartfelt piety.

Love

If Chaucer's position on Lollardy is ambiguous, he was an inveterate and acknowledged acolyte of another notorious sect—that of love.

Deschamps went so far as to call him 'd'Amours mondains Dieux en Albie' (the god of earthly love in Albion), but to Gower he is merely a 'disciple' of Venus, her 'owne clerk', enjoined by her to write his own 'testament of love'. For Usk, too, he has an intermediary role as Love's 'owne trewe servant'.[10] If the testimony of Chaucer's persona is anything to go by, his writings on love soon led him into error. In the Prologue to the *Legend of Good Women* the god of Love complains that Chaucer is an impediment to the true faith. He has hindered Love's servants from expressing their 'devocyoun' with his translation of the *Roman de la Rose* 'That is an heresye ageyns my lawe' (*LGW* G248–57). The harsh accusations of Love in this mock trial are mollified by the advocacy of his queen, Alceste, who presents a case for the defence. To show his penance for past misdeeds, Chaucer agrees to write a more orthodox work, modelled on the genre of saints' legends, describing the lives of women who loved virtuously.

The other composition for which Chaucer stands condemned is *Troilus and Criseyde* because it contains an account of 'How that Crisseyde Troylus forsok [betrayed], | In shewynge how that wemen had don mis [amiss]' (*LGW* G265–6). The poem is indeed the fullest exposition of Chaucer's doctrine of love.[11] The first half of it would cause no accusations of heterodoxy; it is a text-book exposition of the religion of love as invented by the troubadours in twelfth-century France, codified by Andreas Capellanus, developed by Chrétien de Troyes, and replayed with feeling in countless late medieval romances.[12] Troilus is a sudden convert to the cause and, like many such converts, an extreme case. He has made the mistake of ridiculing his fellow Trojan knights for the ardour of their foolish rituals or 'lewed observaunces' in the pursuit of love, while he prides himself in having 'no devocioun . . . to non [no one]' (*TC* I. 187–98). His attitude enrages the god of Love, who avenges himself with a characteristic action, found for example in the *Rose*: he shoots Troilus through the eye with an arrow and so pride has its fall. Troilus is now love's subject. What this means, translated into personal experience, is that Troilus sees Criseyde and falls in love at first sight. Significantly, the key event happens in a temple during a service in honour of Palladion. The idol which is the focus of the Trojans' celebrations is now replaced in Troilus's heart by Criseyde, who becomes the object of his private devotions. The narrator exclaims: 'Blissed be Love, that kan thus folk converte!' (I. 308).

Thus begins the double life of Troilus. Outwardly still the valiant knight, inwardly he is helpless, incapacitated by fantasy and desire. He does, however, affirm his new-found piety to the god of Love, thanking him for the turn of events that has brought him Criseyde— 'But whether goddesse or womman, iwis [in truth], | She be, I not [do not know]' (*TC* I. 425–6)—and dedicating himself to the deity's service. Once his friend, Pandarus, discovers Troilus's plight he becomes a kind of officiating priest at the rites of love. Finding Troilus bedridden and groaning with lovesickness he presumes (correctly, as it turns out) that it is the onset of a spiritual crisis, a 'remors of conscience' that makes him express sorrow 'for thi synne' (I. 554–6). Having discovered the cause of Troilus's anguish, Pandarus insists that he beat his breast and pray 'I me repente' to the god of Love—advice Troilus immediately follows, asking forgiveness for his mockery (I. 932–8). In representing Troilus's case to Criseyde, Pandarus emphasizes the Trojan's piety and recalls an occasion when he overheard Troilus praying to Love to have pity on his pain. Troilus, he says, acknowledged his former rebelliousness with a '*mea culpa*, lord, I me repente!' before making 'confessioun' in anticipation of 'penaunce' (II. 525–30). Troilus is now only too keen to perform all the correct rites, 'observaunces | That til [to] a lovere longeth [belong]' (II. 1345–6). His devotions, along with Pandarus's energetic ministrations, produce results. When Criseyde eventually agrees to be Troilus's lover, sealing the moment with an embrace and a kiss, Pandarus falls to his knees, looks up to heaven, holds his hands high, and thanks the 'Immortal god . . . that mayst nought deyen [may never die], | Cupide I mene' (III. 185–6).

The principle of using the ritual, gestures, language, and practice of Christian devotion to describe the experience of erotic love was well established when Chaucer wrote.[13] But it is only one aspect of his doctrine of love. Its comic side is never far from the surface. Brought by Pandarus's machinations to a secret room allowing access to Criseyde's bedchamber, Troilus becomes fearful. He plucks up his courage by praying to every god under the sun (and the sun itself) that his fortunes will prosper: Venus, Jove, Mars, Phoebus, Mercury, Diana, the Fates. But Pandarus is dismissive: 'Thow wrecched mouses herte, | Artow agast [afraid] so that she wol the bite?' (*TC* III. 736–7). Pandarus is not the only one who thinks that Troilus takes himself and his devotions a little too seriously. At last alone with Criseyde and

in bed with her he stops in the middle of their caresses to deliver a
lengthy prayer of thanks to Venus. For Criseyde there are more pressing matters to attend to: 'Gramercy [thank you], for on that is al my
trist [trust]! | But lat us falle awey [turn aside] fro this matere [sub-
ject-matter]' (III. 1305–6).

The energy of the scene favours Criseyde: it is sensual, carnal,
erotic. Troilus strokes 'Hire armes smale, hire streghte [straight] bak
and softe, | Hire sydes longe, flesshly, smothe, and white', and then
'Hire snowissh throte, hire brestes rounde and lite [small]', delight-
ing in this very earth-bound 'hevene' (*TC* III. 1247–51). But although
the scene favours a celebration of sexuality, the possibility of transcendence is never far away, however absurd it may sometimes seem.
Crucially, it is not a transcendence that seeks to replace flesh with
spirit, but rather one that insists on the co-existence, and mutual
dependence, of the two. Troilus fully discovers the spiritual side of
love only by virtue of making love to Criseyde. There is an indication
of this in the opening line of his inopportune prayer, in which he
addresses Love as 'thow holy bond of thynges' (III. 1261), that is as a
force within but also beyond their immediate, ecstatic, intimacy. The
force of love, it seems, extends also to the relations between other
things in nature.

The idea has been broached by the narrator at the beginning of this
third book of *Troilus*, when he invokes Venus as a formidable power in
the universe: 'In hevene and helle, in erthe and salte see | Is felt thi
myghte' (*TC* III. 8–13). Love is an animating principle affecting
'man, brid, best [beast], fissh, herbe, and grene tree'. It is the basis of
God's relationship with his creation: 'God loveth' and will not deny
love to any living thing. Without it, life is worthless and cannot
endure. In social terms it has many beneficial effects by ennobling
hearts, whether 'heighe or lowe' born, unifying kingdoms and families, and sealing friendships (III. 27). His words are counterbalanced
at the end of Book 3 by those of Troilus himself, who at the same time
echoes his 'bonds of love' prayer. In the second *Canticus Troili*, a
hymn sung by Troilus to Pandarus as they walk in a garden (holding
hands to signify their own bond of friendship), he describes the revelation that has resulted from his loving of Criseyde. Love for him is
Platonic or what we would now call a principle of ecology, governing
earth, sea, land, peoples, fellowships, and couples in an integrated
system. It regulates the elements, the sequencing of day and night,

the tides, keeping the world stable 'with feith' (III. 1744–71). It is exactly the same force that God uses in a divine embrace 'To cerclen hertes alle and faste bynde'.

The second *Canticus Troili* is modelled closely on a metrum or lyric in a work that Chaucer translated, the *Consolation of Philosophy* by Boethius (*c*.480–524).[14] The narrator's prayer to Venus derives from the same author: although taken from Chaucer's narrative source, *Il Filostrato*, Boccaccio was himself drawing on Boethius. The idea of there being a 'fair chain of love' that binds together all aspects of existence is Platonic in origin, but it combined well with the Christian notion of a God who created the universe and who expressed himself through love. That combination of ideas is one of the central consolatory motifs of Boethius's work. Written while he was in prison at Pavia prior to his execution for political crimes, the *Consolation* is cast in the form of a dialogue between Boethius and Lady Philosophy. Through the exercise of reason, she encourages him to regard the misfortunes of his life with some detachment, and to believe that the changeable world of experience is worthless and insubstantial by comparison with the higher truths such as the benevolence of God. The key words here, echoed by Troilus, are faith and love: Boethius must needs have faith that, in spite of his suffering, the universe is ordered according to 'stable feyth' and 'bounde with love' (*Bo* II, metrum 8) and that, therefore, these should be the guiding principles of human relations.

Troilus's commitment to faith and love is soon put severely to the test. Criseyde is exchanged for a Trojan knight held captive by the Greeks and, although she has vowed to return, Troilus is plunged into despair. He rides alone through the streets of Troy a woeful pilgrim and gazes at her desolate, empty, dark house. It is to him, in a fore-shadowing of the fate that awaits the city at large, a ruin, a shrine bereft of its relics. His object of devotion, the focus of his piety, has left behind nothing but empty space: 'farwel shryne, of which the seynt is oute!' (*TC* V. 553). Pandarus attempts to comfort and distract his friend, but gradually it becomes clear that Criseyde will not return. Pandarus advises that Troilus transfer his affections to another woman, but Troilus will have none of it, and Pandarus the giver of good advice is at last silenced. Criseyde has in fact found the succour and protection she needs with a Greek knight, Diomede. When Troilus confronts the evidence of her infidelity—a brooch given by

Troilus to Criseyde appears on a tunic captured from Diomede—he curses the day he was born, asking, 'Where is youre feith, and where is youre biheste [promise]? | Where is youre love? Where is youre trouthe?' (V. 1675–98). For all this, Troilus does not have it in himself to reply in kind: 'I ne kan nor may, | For al this world, withinne myn herte fynde | To unloven yow a quarter of a day!' Driven now by bitter anger to pursue his enemy, he dies on the battlefield, slain by Achilles.

The practice of faith and love would therefore seem to have resulted in a personal tragedy. But it is only Troilus's body that has died. His spirit, that part of him that has perceived the spiritual dimensions of love, rises free of his corpse and up through the very elements and planets that Boethius described. From his new vantage-point Troilus sees that the universe is indeed held in harmony by love. The word used is 'embraced': the sea encompasses the land, the air the sea, the spheres of the elements and planets the earth itself, and so on up to heaven itself, as the Sphere of John Pecham (Fig. 6) showed (*TC* V. 1814–17). Right at the centre of that universe, as Troilus has known it, and at the centre of Chaucer's narrative, is his embrace with Criseyde. The interactive connection of body and spirit is confirmed. From this perspective Troilus laughs—laughs at the woe of those who mourn his death, not out of mockery but because of the insignificance of human preoccupations when seen *sub specie aeternatis*. His 'trage-dye' is thus transformed to a 'comedye'—what it always had the potential to be—that is, a story with a happy ending (V. 1786–8). His discovery of faith and love through his affair with Criseyde, and his practice of those principles, have been vindicated.

The Pagan Past

Troilus is a virtuous pagan, which is to say he has an intuitive grasp of the central ideas that were subsequently embodied in Christianity. Unfortunately for him, he lived in ancient Troy, and so could not enjoy the full benefits of the later dispensation. He is near to it in intelligence, but far from it in historical terms. He receives his reward in a pagan heaven but is denied the full revelation of that Christian truth known to Chaucer and his audience. Chaucer captures the sense of simultaneous closeness and distance when, having asked his audience to envisage the ascent of Troilus's spirit to the 'holughnesse of the eighthe spere', he directs them to 'up casteth the visage [face]' in a different direction, and imagine not Troilus but another figure who sits 'in hevene above', one also associated with suffering, faithful love, and indeed its paradigm: Christ's love far exceeds anything known to Troilus, 'for he nyl falsen no wight [no one]' (*TC* V. 1807–46). As virtually an honorary Christian, Troilus was in good company. It was a status accorded by medieval theologians to Plato, for example, whose thought-patterns fitted so well with those of the early Church Fathers; and to Virgil, whose fourth eclogue was interpreted as a prophecy of the birth of Christ. Virgil also had the honour of being Dante's guide to hell and purgatory (a guise in which Chaucer knew him) but not to heaven: that was Beatrice's role.

Chaucer's sense of debt to the classical past, and the non-Christian literary tradition within which he works, is evident in the closing lines of *Troilus*. He personifies his great poem and asks that it follow humbly in the footsteps of 'Virgile, Ovide, Omer, Lucan, and Stace [Statius]' (*TC* V. 1792). There is some window-dressing here. The immediate debt is to his contemporary, Boccaccio (nowhere mentioned by name), who wrote the version of the Troilus story on which Chaucer's account is based. However, Chaucer's direct use of classical texts, though more common in his earlier writings than his later, is frequent and extensive.[15] A story from Ovid's *Metamorphoses*, that of Ceyx and Alcione, is retold in the *Book of the Duchess* and sets in motion the consolatory mechanism of the poem. Virgil's narrative of Dido and Aeneas dominates the early part of the *House of Fame*. The *Legend of Good Women* and the Monk's Tale are full of exempla taken from classical legend. Chaucer's practices reflect the value set on the pagan inheritance by Christian thinkers. Aristotle's writings on logic were the cornerstone of scholastic discourse. Ovid's *Metamorphoses*, suitably sanitized with Christian moralizations, was a widespread text. And in the fourteenth century certain friars such as Robert Holcot, whose work Chaucer knew, were enthusiastic students of classical authors.

Given the extent of Chaucer's real and rhetorical interest in ancient authors and the worlds they inhabited, and the receptiveness of his culture to classical texts, it is odd to find the narrator of *Troilus* biting the hand that fed him. He denounces pagan belief in round terms in the antepenultimate stanza of the poem:

> Lo here, of payens corsed olde rites!   *pagans'*
> Lo here, what alle hire goddess may availle!
> Lo here, thise wrecched worldes appetites!
> Lo here, the fyn and guerdoun for travaille   *end; reward*
> Of Jove, Appollo, of Mars, of swich rascaille!   *rabble*
>
>   (*TCV*. 1849–53)

It is difficult to take these words at face value when the same narrator
has spent the previous 8,000 lines describing in loving detail ancient
customs, the 'appetites' of Troilus and Criseyde, and the gods' part in
their fate. It is possible that Chaucer has now removed his narrator's
mask as the servant of love's servants, and is speaking more *in propria
persona*. Having just reaffirmed his Christian credentials, and before
he goes on to address his friends Gower and Strode, he may be wanting to leave his audience in no doubt about where he as Geoffrey
Chaucer stands on 'paganism', however seductive its claims on his
imagination as a poet. Then again this is only one of a number of
tables that have been turned in the exhilarating but perplexing final
stanzas of the poem. A body has become a spirit; a tragedy a comedy;
a pagan past the Christian present; and now we discover that the narrator, who has been so empathetically involved in his story, in fact has
a love–hate relationship with it. Or perhaps it is just the case that
Chaucer could not resist a good palinode such as also occurs in the
Retraction to the *Canterbury Tales*.

But if Chaucer's intention is impossible to ascertain with any certainty, it is at least possible to be clear about the effect of the narrator's
words. Coming immediately after a stanza which refers in pious and
reverent terms to Christ's crucifixion and its meaning for all mankind, his denunciation of Troy highlights a sharp sense of difference
between one world and another. Put in stark terms, as it is here, the
ancient world is false and the Christian one, true. The difference and
otherness of 'payens' is precisely their usefulness to Chaucer. The
pre–Christian past represents an imaginative space distinct from that
of his own culture. Within it, he is able to consider topics, such as the
nature and meaning of erotic love, to which medieval Christianity
allowed only limited access. The final effect may be to reinforce a
sense of the limitations of 'paganism' and, given Chaucer's Christian
context, such a conclusion is inevitable. Yet the conclusion does not
square with the argument of the poem, for, on closer inspection, this

apparently despicable world of Troy has a remarkable similarity to the London (also called 'New Troy') that Chaucer and his audience knew, complete with its opulent town-houses, protracted war, fortifications, parliament, and pursuit of love and chivalry. So to examine the pagan world of Troy as both distinct from and similar to the present experience of Chaucer and his audience is to shine a rather searching light on his own cultural moment. He can explore features of it not otherwise accessible and in so doing raise questions, implicitly or not, about the values that dominated in his day. One question might concern the Church's traditional hostility to sensuality and sexuality when—as Chaucer knew from Dante—they are intimately connected to the love of God for his creation. Another might concern the place of a practice such as chivalry, which traditionally originated in Troy, within a belief system supposedly dedicated to peace and amity— issues that would have interested Sir John Clanvowe.

The same observations hold true of the belief system of Troy: it holds a mirror up to that of Chaucer's world. Ostensibly, it is quite at odds with the Christian scheme. In Troy, humans are merely caught up in the consequences of old scores that the gods are intent on settling. There is an overbearing sense of inevitability, of the power of fate to determine the outcome of events, and of the impotence of individuals to do anything about it. Calkas, Criseyde's father, is a soothsayer who has defected to the Greek camp because he has foreseen the fall of Troy. It is for the same reason that he demands his daughter join him in exchange for Antenor (who is later to betray Troy to the Greeks). Thus fate determines the end of Troilus's affair. The experience of being its victim is compared, time and again, to the condition of being Fortune's victim. Lady Fortune is a blind goddess who never stops turning her wheel (Fig. 5).[16] She embodies the constancy of change. Those who love, who seek riches, or have political ambition, or engage in war, are especially vulnerable to her effects. Just as she can bring success and happiness so, just as inevitably, she brings failure and misery to those who cling to the rim and the spokes of her wheel. Its rise and fall maps Troilus's progress. The narrator announces he will tell of the 'double sorwe' of Troilus as he moves from 'wo to wele, and after out of joie' and there are recurrent further references to Fortune as her unending circular motion describes the inevitability of Troilus's fate (*TC* I. 1–4). No sooner has he won Criseyde than he begins to lose her and someone else replaces him.

pres ce que philosophie

Et dit de son vouloir partie

On ne pou se taist et puis parole

Car selon la vraie parole

De trop parlez et desire nuis

Fig. 5. Blind Lady Fortune turning her wheel (*c.*1400).

The narrator calls Fortune a seemer who appears true only to deceive. She laughs and pulls faces when someone is thrown from her wheel, as Troilus soon will be:

> From Troilus she gan hire brighte face
> Awey to writhe, and tok of hym non heede,　　　　*turn*
> But caste hym clene out of his lady grace,
> And on hire whiel she sette up Diomede . . .
>
> （IV. 8–11)

One way of dealing with a downturn in the favours of Fortune is to play her at her own game. While luck may be running out in one area, it may be increasing in another. Pandarus is an adroit and canny player of Fortune's wheel, and he speaks of love's fluctuations like a gambler: 'in the dees [dice] right as ther fallen chaunces, | Right so in love ther come and gon plesaunces [pleasures]' (*TC* IV. 1098–9). Love is a game of chance governed by fickle Fortune, so when Troilus loses Criseyde—so Pandarus advises—he should cut his losses and find another woman. Criseyde, too, is aware of the need to adapt to the changes wrought by Fortune. Although she finds herself involuntarily drawn to Troilus, she calculates the odds, the pros and cons, of loving him. To some extent she is a creature of Fortune and shares some of the same characteristics, being not rigid but adaptable, not steadfast but 'slydynge of corage' (V. 825): she knows how to let things go and how to take hold of the next opportunity, how to survive. Not so Troilus, who, in terms of what passes for faith in the city of Troy, is a fool. Fortune embodies change but he remains constant and suffers the consequences. One consequence is a bout of existential *Angst*. When he hears of the plan to exchange Criseyde for Antenor he falls into despair and goes alone to a temple to pray at length and question the meaning of his existence. The sudden turn in events makes him feel like a lost plaything of destiny: 'Thus to be lorn [lost], it is my destinee' (IV. 959). Divine foresight (*purveiaunce*) knew about Criseyde's departure; therefore it was destined to happen. Humans have no say in the matter: 'We han no fre chois' (IV. 980).

A sense of Fortune's power and pervasiveness, and of the issues raised, was not the preserve of ancient Troy. The wheel of Fortune is familiar from Christian contexts too. For example, there is a splendid image of it on the pilgrim route to Canterbury, in Rochester cathedral, bishop Brinton's church. Fortune is Boethius's nemesis in his

Consolation, the antagonist that Lady Philosophy confronts. Similarly, when Chaucer wrote he could draw on a debate about the place of free will within a universe ruled by an all-knowing God. Did not his very omniscience preclude the possibility of personal choice? And if there was no free will, did that not render moral decisions meaningless? The conclusion that Troilus reaches is the one rehearsed by Boethius— foreknowledge (God's preserve) does not entail necessity—but the terms of his self-questioning are entirely contemporary. Troilus alludes anachronistically to the opinions of tonsured Christian theologians— 'That han hire top [head] ful heighe and smothe yshore [shaven]' (*TC* IV. 996)—not Boethius, but clerics such as Thomas Bradwardine (*c*.1290–1349), who wrote a treatise, *De causa dei* (On the causality of God) that covered the relationship between free will and divine *purvei-aunce*. The relentless march of oppressive and destructive events, of the sort that provides a context both for Troilus's musings and Bradwardine's writing, was especially apparent in the fourteenth century. Bradwardine, a confessor to Edward III, was present at the battle of Crécy and the siege of Calais. When archbishop John de Ufford died of the plague in 1349, only a few months after his appointment, Bradwardine replaced him. Returning from Rome, he himself fell victim to the Black Death, and died at Rochester just forty days after his own consecration. Fortune had got her way.

Reality

Another way of thinking about the differences between Christianity and paganism in *Troilus and Criseyde* is as representations of altern-ative orders of reality. One is bound by Fortune and the gods, the other is liberated and enlarged through the self-sacrificing love of Christ. Troilus is the bridge between the two: he has intimations of another, transcendent reality in the course of his love for Criseyde and after death he gains access to it. From his new perspective he is no longer anxious but relaxed, no longer miserable but happy, no lon-ger time-bound but in an eternal realm. From the reader's point of view, the reality of the central scene of the story, in which Troilus and Criseyde make love, is transformed. Until Troilus's death it was the spindle of a perpetually turning wheel of events. After the ascent of his spirit it is the central embrace within a nest of concentric spheres contained and informed by the love of God. But it is not only different ideologies that produce different accounts of reality. Even within the confines of a single belief-system there are multiple, if overlapping, versions of what constitutes the real. Chaucer explores them also in relation to identity, gender, social status, genre, and consciousness.

The Wife of Bath is a case in point. We have already seen how she rejects the received clerkly reality of women as shrews who lead men to sin. Instead she constructs a world in which she, as an individual woman, might well fulfil certain misogynist expectations, but one where she is fully conscious of them, contemptuous of their reductive tendencies, aware of the economic needs that shape her behaviour, of her susceptibility to desire and love, and of her groundedness in a network of social relations and practices which she shares with other women. The end result is an outlook, a sense of reality, diametrically opposed to that of clerks such as those responsible for Jankyn's *Book of Wicked Wives*. That differences in social status produce different versions of reality is clear from the Knight's Tale and Miller's Tale. The high-falutin idealism and introspective, nostalgic tendencies of chivalric society are categorically rejected as inappropriate to the lives of 'those who work'. Instead, the Miller suggests, it is the here and now of bodies, sex, trickery, and everyday objects (ladders, tubs, beds, windows, coulters) that constitutes reality.

The genres allocated respectively to the Knight and the Miller, romance and fabliau, speak volumes abut their competing outlooks. Romance fosters a preoccupation with hierarchy, order, deference, decorum, ceremony, rules, and obligations; fabliau exults in transgressing all such boundaries and in releasing anarchic tendencies. Bring the two genres together within a single narrative, as happens in the Merchant's Tale, and the result is impending social and dynastic chaos as two orders of reality struggle for dominance. The same principle holds true in other cases: different genres generate their own accounts of what is real. The Second Nun's Tale is a saint's life that tells the story of St Cecilia. She eschews what might conventionally pass for reality (what we know through our senses) and instead apprehends another plane of existence. Cecilia insists on celibacy within her marriage in order to maintain her focus on this other, greater, reality, identifying its presence in the mysterious perfume of flowers (lilies) that she alone can detect. She defends her faith against her pagan persecutors precisely on the issue of reality: they, she says, worship stones thinking they are gods; she worships the invisible God who informs all creation. Subjected to torture and mutilation she remains serene and, until the end, sings the praises of her maker. Her tale is a graphic account of the disparity between pagan and Christian reality found in more muted form in *Troilus and Criseyde*. From the saint's perspective, human sensory experience is insubstantial, fleeting, and, as we might say, unreal. Reality lies in the spiritual world that lies behind the veil of sensory experience, and in the heavenly hereafter.

So reality is for the most part various and relative, affected by the contingencies of personal identity, social estate, gender, and belief. It becomes absolute only in the afterlife; until then, reality is provisional and fluid. In the meantime, there is much negotiation to be done. Different genres enabled Chaucer to represent different orders of reality, but even within the strict confines of a single genre, and in the case of two individuals of identical cultural background, opposite accounts of reality emerge. Palamon and Arcite, the main protagonists of the Knight's Tale, are Theban princes and blood relatives (cousins) captured by Duke Theseus at the siege of their city and imprisoned in Athens. One day, from their high prison window, they each see in turn the same woman, the duke's beautiful sister-in-law, Emelye, walking in the garden below. Both fall instantly in love, but at the same time their apprehensions of reality diverge. Arcite, who is governed by Mars, sees Emelye as a woman to be won by force and enjoyed physically. Palamon, ruled by Venus, regards her as a goddess to be adored. From these differences much anguish ensues. Arcite renounces his chivalric obligation to support his sworn brother-knight, Palamon, in all his endeavours; they shed much blood in armed single combat; and Arcite eventually dies a hideous death, hours after he has won Emelye at a tournament by defeating his rival. Theseus does his level best to manage their rivalry within the precepts of chivalric practice and belief, but he is trumped by a higher reality when Saturn takes charge of events.

Such narratives raise questions about the relationship between the objective world and the subjective perception of it. To what extent is reality independent of the observer? To what extent is it constituted by him or her? And if the individual understanding of a single sight (as in the case of Palamon and Arcite) can vary so much, to what extent can we talk of a shared reality? Is the common denominator here the two knights' subjection to the gods who rule them and, as it turns out, events in Athens generally? One genre in particular, the dream vision, allowed Chaucer to explore in some depth the interplay between objective and subjective reality. Insofar as dreams happen inside the head the dream vision explores the alternative reality of the mind operating as it were in a state of altered awareness. But characteristically dream visions incorporate episodes of intensified realism which seem to beg the very question about the relationship of mental image to waking consciousness, of what is 'in here' to what is 'out there'. At the same time dream images, however real, often seem to suffer from a superfluity of possible meanings, as if the genre is wanting to articulate the importance of interpretation in the creation of reality, rather than to urge the acceptance of one dominant and uniform account of it.

An episode from the *Book of the Duchess* will help to exemplify some of these points. It is one of those moments when the world seems to have been temporarily perfected and become hyper-real. The poem has opened gloomily, with an insomniac narrator in a despondent and melancholic state of mind. Now he is asleep and his dream has effected a miraculous transformation. His dark bedchamber is bathed in light; the night has become a May morning; formerly introverted and cerebral, the dreamer now focuses on his naked body and its susceptibility to sensory stimulus. On the roof tiles birds sing a glorious, heavenly melody such that the room echoes to their harmonies. The windows are fully glazed (a sign of opulence) and engraved with the 'story of Troye', while the walls are painted in fine colours with the 'text and glose' of all of the *Romance of the Rose* (*BD* 326–38). The windows are shut and through the glass the sun shines from a blue and cloudless sky on to the dreamer's bed 'With many glade gilde [golden] stremes'. The scene is one of intense joy and expectation: the dreamer seems cured, rejuvenated, alert to his surroundings. But if the vitality of the outer world affects the conditions of his inner awareness, the inner world has also affected the outer. It is by virtue of an imaginative process—responding to Ovid's tale of Ceyx and Alcione by praying to the god of sleep—that the narrator has entered his dream world. And the idea of imaginative process is sustained by the window engravings and wall decorations, which are both of narratives fundamental to Chaucer's creative development. The image of sun rays, shining through the story of Troy on to the recumbent poet, captures the process of literary transmission and transformation. The audience is included in the imaginative transactions. If, as seems likely, the poem was first performed as part of a commemorative service, then the dreamer's allusions to echoing choirs, and to light passing through historiated windows, would have had correlatives close at hand. But the poem soon spirits the audience away, calling on them to envisage a secular setting, a solitary not a sociable scene, and a persona other than the Geoffrey Chaucer who stands before them, who has in turn dreamed of his alter ego.

What kind of reality is this? It calls for a suspension of disbelief that is not so much willing as involuntary and intuitive. For the sense of reality on which the poem depends is one in which there is an incessant interplay, interpenetration, and interdependence of the subjective and objective worlds. It is also a multifaceted reality, in which the projections of an invented dream can effectively pinpoint and transform present realities (the death of Blanche, the grief of John of Gaunt); and one in which thought, emotion, and imagination are as significant as the mere presentation of facts and objects. 'Multifaceted' might also describe the debate on reality that engaged philosophers and theologians throughout the fourteenth century.[17] William of Ockham (*c.*1285–1349) developed a body of thought, which came to be known as nominalism, in which he argued that God and his truth are ultimately unknowable. The concepts that human beings might extrapolate from their experience (love, for example) might or might not be part of a higher reality. However, their primary mode of existence was as signs or names (hence 'nominalism') with an intrinsic and contingent, not absolute, value. Individuals thus have the ability to determine their own meanings, interpretations, and constructions of reality.

Bradwardine took Ockham to task, insofar as his ideas contradicted the notion of God's grace and foresight; but Wyclif was a much fiercer adversary.[18] If Ockham's was a tentative, 'bottom up', approach to knowledge of God, Wyclif's was an assertive 'top down' one. Reality, for Wyclif, exists in the mind of God. That is where the perfected idea or 'universal' of love, for instance, has its primary being. All of human knowledge is irradiated by the light of God's ultimate wisdom—an idea that derives from Augustine and, through him, from Plato. It is the task of human beings to discover God's truth in their own experience and especially, as Wyclif argued, through the reading and study of Scripture. The differences between nominalists and realists continued to drive scholastic controversy in the later fourteenth century. Mental images, dreams, optical illusions, and the effects of light shining through windows, became topics of debate as testing grounds for their rival theories.

CHAPTER 6

SCIENCE AND TECHNOLOGY

In the Squire's Tale, as King Cambyuskan (Genghis Khan) of Sarray
in the land of Tartarye sits feasting, there suddenly enters at the hall
door a stranger knight astride a steed of brass. In his hand he carries
a large, glass mirror; he wears a gold ring on his thumb; and has a
naked sword dangling at his waist. Horse, mirror, ring, and sword are
gifts, and each has miraculous powers.[1] The mirror, for instance, can
depict future threats to the kingdom, tell the king who is friend or
enemy, and reveal to any lady the treachery of her lover. It is the kind
of surveillance device that any self-respecting autocratic regime
would be glad to possess. The knight departs, and among the courtiers there ensues much ill-informed speculation on his gifts. Some
attribute their power to magic, others invent fantastical explanations,
just as ignorant people do (the Squire declares haughtily) about matters they do not understand. But when the debate rounds on the mirror, one courtier, at least, seems to have been reading more than
romances. The mirror's properties, he says, might well be explained

> Naturelly, by composiciouns
> Of anglis and of slye reflexiouns,   *complex*
> And seyde that in Rome was swich oon.
> They speken of Alocen, and Vitulon,   *Alhacen; Witelo*
> And Aristotle, that writen in hir lyves
> Of queynte mirours and of perspectives,   *ingenious*
> As knowen they that han hir bookes herd.
>   (SqT 229–35)

In other words, new technology, that might seem to be magical in
what it can do, may be accounted for in rational, scientific terms.

The above lines are Chaucer's own. There is nothing like them in
the known previous versions of the story, and they would seem to suggest, through the mouth of the Squire, a progressive or enlightened
attitude towards science and technology. Another of Chaucer's narrators has an opposite point of view—at least, when science is pursued

for its own ends. When the Canon and his Yeoman join the pilgrims en route at Boughton it is not long before the Canon flees in shame and guilt as the Yeoman reveals his master's practices. The Canon is an alchemist, an early form of chemist, ostensibly dedicated to the transmutation of base materials into gold, but he has lost his way. His science has become a secret obsession pursued on the fringes of society, where he lurks in the suburbs with robbers and thieves; alchemy has wasted his wealth and appearance and now he preys on others, gulling them for gold which he claims to be able to 'multiplye'. Such experiments as he conducts end in failure, explosion, and destruction, the ingredients obstinately refusing to be other than 'asshes, donge, pisse, and cley' (CYT 807). But science and technology do not have to be reductive, futile, and corrupting. In another instance they are treated with respect bordering on enthusiasm. Chaucer, writing for once *in propria persona*, or at least in the persona of a father, composed for his own son, 'Lyte Lowys' (little Lewis), a manual to accompany the gift of an astrolabe (*Astr* 1–3). Noting that the ten-year-old boy is keen on 'nombres and proporciouns', he proceeds to set out in plain language the various uses of the instrument. Its primary application is for observing the position of the stars, and thereby determining the calendar. Chaucer is, however, aware the astrolabe can be used for more nefarious purposes, to predict the future through astrological calculations. At this he draws the line: they are 'rytes of payens [pagan rites], in whiche my spirit hath no feith' (II. 4. 58–9).

From such examples it is possible to begin creating a map of Chaucer's account of science.[2] It has occult and unethical tendencies (as in the cases of astrology and alchemy); offers an alternative to magic, which, as with the mirror in the Squire's Tale, it can replace with its own esoteric mystique that is hardly more penetrable ('composiciouns | Of anglis and of slye reflexiouns'); and seems refreshingly progressive and rational if kept within acceptable bounds, as in Chaucer's treatise on the astrolabe. However, the map will remain sketchy and unreliable unless it incorporates two conventions unfamiliar to modern eyes. The first concerns the word *science* itself. In the later fourteenth century its primary meaning was simply 'knowledge'. It did not denote what is intended by the title of this chapter, namely the study of the laws of the material universe through the separate disciplines of chemistry, physics, mathematics, molecular biology, and so on. Even less did *science* describe a sphere of knowledge distinct from 'arts'. On the contrary, what we now call science and the arts went hand in glove. Chaucer was familiar with, and replicated, the practice of including scientific topics within literary works, such as occurs in Boethius and the *Romance of the Rose*. Second, Chaucer and his audience understood their universe and its laws according to principles radically different from those now accepted as true. The composition of matter from four elements; the explanation of human identity and behaviour, or *complexion*, according to four 'humours'; the influence of the stars (notwithstanding Chaucer's reservations); and the existence of the earth at the centre of a cosmos created by God—all of these are now regarded as 'pseudo-sciences'. A pseudo-science is a logically coherent system of explanation based on principles now held to be false. But unless we understand those principles, and the systems they supported, Chaucer's account of his world will remain deeply puzzling, as will the routes that lead from medieval to modern science.

The Universe

At the beginning of a psalter commissioned by Robert de Lisle (1288–1344) is a page headed 'Spera secundum fratrem J. de Pecham Archiepiscopum' (The Sphere according to brother J. Pecham, archbishop). John Pecham (d. 1292) was a Franciscan who became archbishop of Canterbury and he was the author of a number of works combining theology and science. In the psalter, part of the text of his treatise wraps around a coloured diagram made of concentric circles (Fig. 6).[3] It represents a cross-section through a model of the universe conceived as a nest of spheres. At the centre is earth (with 'Infernus' or hell within), surrounded in succession by the three other elements: water, air, and fire. Then there are the seven planets, each within its own sphere: the moon, Mercury, Venus, the sun, Mars, Jove or Jupiter, and Saturn. They are enclosed by the starry heaven (home of the zodiac), beyond which lies the sphere imparting movement to all the rest, sometimes called the 'first mover'. Finally there is the sphere of the unmoving empyrean, presided over by Christ, his hand raised in blessing.

Pecham's description contains some distinctive features but in general it is an accurate version of the universe known to Chaucer and his contemporaries.[4] The model derives from Ptolemy (AD *c*.90–*c*.168)

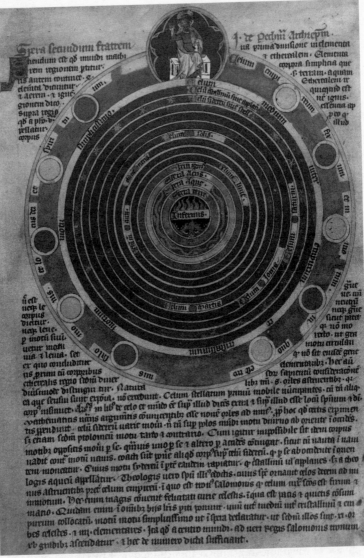

Fig. 6. A diagram of the universe (*c*.1308).

and it survived intact until Nicolaus Copernicus (1473–1543) proved that, in fact, the earth orbits the sun. Nevertheless, the medieval model is a faithful map of the natural phenomena then observable: to the naked eye, the earth is stable, the moon and other planets revolve around it, the sun rises and sets. According to this scheme, the planets move through their spheres at the same speed, but each takes a different length of time to complete a revolution according to its distance from the earth: the sun, a day; Saturn, the outermost planet, thirty days. At the same time, Pecham's diagram is full of qualitative, and not just quantitative, information. Its universe is hierarchical, the power of a planet greater the wider its arc. It incorporates a spiritual tension between its zenith, Christ, and its nadir, hell. It counterbalances movement with stability, and contrasts the sublime immobility of the empyrean with the wretched inertia of earth and the restlessness of hell. There is a corresponding opposition between the time-bound status of the earth, ruled by the planets, and the eternity of heaven. There is also a strong link between the two: God chose the form of man, depicted here as Christ, to enable humans to aspire from earth to heaven. Indeed the diagram is an aid to contemplation, a means of encouraging the spirit, as the text has it in its closing line, 'to ascend by stages from the centre of the world to the throne of Christ the true king Solomon' (*a centro mundi ad veri regis Salomonis tronum Cristi gradibus ascendatur*).

This is the universe, at once natural and theological, through which the spirit of Troilus ascends at the end of Chaucer's poem 'Up to the holughnesse [inner surface] of the eighthe spere'—presumably the starry heaven according to Pecham's scheme (*TCV.* 1807–20). To reach it he moves first from the earth through water, air, and fire, passing through the convex side of each sphere: 'In convers letyng [leaving] everich element'. Once ascended, his spirit discerns 'The erratik [wandering] sterres', or planets, and hears their harmonious melodies. Looking down, he sees how the earth is 'Embraced' by the sea—a term that might apply to the relationship of each sphere to the one or ones it contains. The Christian narrator urges his readers to look beyond a purely pagan, Ptolemaic notion of the spheres and recognize the supremacy of the figure who, at the end of *Troilus*, as in Pecham's treatise, governs the universe. It is as much an internal, visionary process as an external one: 'of youre herte up casteth the visage [face] | To thilke God that after his ymage | Yow made' (V. 1838–44).

The image is indeed immediately recognizable, and it embodies the power that informs all creation, prompting human beings to engage in the same force-field. The imperative is to 'loveth hym the which that right for love | Upon a crois, oure soules for to beye, | First starf [died], and roos, and sit in hevene above'. From his seat (or throne, as Pecham has it) Christ too embraces in love all that lies below: he is 'Uncircumscript, and al maist circumscrive' (V. 1865).

Chaucer knew this cosmology from a number of sources. It structures Dante's *Divina commedia* and especially its final section, the *Paradiso*, in which Dante ascends through the celestial spheres with Beatrice as his guide. The idea of a hero's spirit achieving transcendence after death Chaucer borrowed from Boccaccio's *Teseida*, where apotheosis is the fate of Arcita. In Chaucer's *House of Fame* it is the narrator himself, Geffrey, who explores the universe as he is borne aloft by a loquacious eagle sent by Jupiter. His charge is too 'astonyed and asweved' (astonished and dazed) to take it all in and he fears that he is about to die and be 'stellified', turned into a star (*HF* 549–87). The flight is a reward for faithful service to Venus. Jupiter wishes the eagle to show him a place where he will hear tidings of love, the House of Fame, whose palace stands 'in myddes [in the middle] of the weye | Betwixen hevene and erthe and see' (714–15). Geffrey gathers his wits enough to look down at the earth and see fields, plains, hills, mountains, valleys, forests, great beasts, rivers, cities, towns, huge trees, and ships sailing on the sea. Flying higher, they enter a 'large space' containing 'eyryssh bestes', perhaps the creatures of the zodiac (925–32). Beyond lies the Milky Way, created—according to the eagle—by the sun's own son, Phaeton. He was driving his father's chariot but, being inexperienced, he had little control of the horse. Frightened to death by the sight of the zodiac Scorpion he let slip the reins, the horse reared up, bolted, and raced up and down, scorching the earth and air until Jupiter intervened. Geffrey's interest in such matters soon wanes. Asked by the eagle if he does not want to know the stars' names and their signs, he replies abruptly 'No fors [way]' (1111–17). The eagle points out that it will help him understand the stories he reads of gods turning creatures and humans into stars: he will then be able to identify them in the sky. Geffrey is not persuaded. He believes his authors and feels no need for corroboration. When he reads it is as if he had seen the stars at first hand, 'As though I knew her places here'. Too much knowledge, or the wrong kind of knowledge, can be detrimental: the stars 'shynen here so bryghte, | Hit shulde shenden al my syghte [blind me] | To loke on hem'.

The *House of Fame* enacts a debate between the rival claims of two kinds of knowledge. One, represented by the eagle (who discourses on theories of sound as well as on the origins of stars), is empirical, objective, authoritative, rational, and, as we might say, scientific. The other, represented by Geffrey, is tentative, experiential, subjective, emotional, imaginative. The dialogue between authority and experience endured in various forms throughout Chaucer's poetic career. Here, one consequence is the depiction of a universe which, although structurally the same, seems quite different from the one inhabited by Troilus. There, the mood was solemn and reverential but here it is jocular. There the stars and spheres were an occasion for exhilaration at the sudden access of new knowledge, but here for trepidation and resistance in favour of the less threatening information culled from books. There the universe was subsumed in the Christian scheme of things, here the skies are animated by pagan mythology. There, the spheres and stars had an objective reality, here they are more like a literary resource. One explanation for the differences between Chaucer's universes (narrative priorities apart) is that one, in the *House of Fame*, dates from relatively early in his career and the other from relatively late. Although the earlier work plays with Dante's architectonics it does not take them seriously (although *Troilus* does) and Chaucer is more drawn to other authors. Among them—and Geffrey drops their names—is Macrobius, who in the fifth century wrote a commentary on the dream of Scipio, the closing portion of Cicero's *De re publica*. Cicero describes how Scipio had a dream in which his grandfather, Affricanus, appeared and took him on a conducted tour of the universe, in the course of which he predicted Scipio's future as the conqueror of Carthage. Thus the text is a product of a mind in a dream-state (Geffrey's condition in the *House of Fame*) and it provides an opportunity for a learned commentary by Macrobius (or his kindred spirit, the eagle).

Differences apart, Chaucer's sources of information on the universe agree on one thing: the littleness and insignificance of the earth in relation to the cosmos. From his standpoint close to the Milky Way, Scipio observes that the planets are much bigger than the earth, and that 'the earth appeared so small that I was ashamed of our [Roman] empire which is, so to speak, but a point on its surface'. It is a point on a point, for, as Macrobius writes, in comparison with the sun's orbit the earth itself 'occupies the space of a point'.[5] The idea is taken up by Lady Philosophy in Chaucer's *Boece*, who is herself something of a guide to the universe. She pours scorn on the idea of Fame when the places where men dwell on earth are a mere pinprick on a pinprick in relation to the skies: 'the leeste prykke of thilke prykke [i.e. the earth]' (*Bo* II, pr. 7. 43–4). Dante agreed: from the edge of that eighth heaven to which Troilus also journeys the earth is no more than a 'little threshing-floor, that makes us so fierce' (*Paradiso* XXII. 151).[6] Troilus describes it as a 'litel spot' (*TC* V. 1815), Geffrey as 'No more . . . than a prikke' (*HF* 907).

A map of observable phenomena, an aid to contemplation, a theological hierarchy stretching from hell to heaven, a source of literary inspiration, a means of putting the vanity of human endeavour into perspective—the medieval universe has many applications. It was also extremely useful as a time and orientation machine that the astrolabe was designed to read.[7] For instance, the stars were used to calculate the date of Easter. Easter Sunday, a 'movable feast', still falls on the first Sunday from the fourteenth day following the first full moon after the vernal equinox (21 March). Chaucer's pilgrim Shipman uses the moon for navigation: there was no mariner from Hull to Carthage who knew better how to reckon 'His herberwe [anchorage], and his moone' (*GP* 403). Before clocks became generally accessible (some towns in Europe, including London, had clocks in public places by the mid-fourteenth century) the skies were a common and practical way of telling the time of day or night.[8] At the beginning of the Man of Law's Tale, Harry Bailly, although not an educated man, being 'nat depe ystert [advanced] in loore [learning]', calculates first by the position of the sun that it is the eighteenth day of April (*MLT* I 4–14). Observing that the shadows of the trees are the same length as their height, he knows that the sun has moved forty-five degrees through its arc. Therefore 'for that day, as in that latitude, | It was ten of the clokke'. The Host would also have been able to tell from the sky what day of the week it was. Since the planets form different and distinctive patterns as they journey on their separate orbits, each day begins with a configuration in which one planet is dominant. The identity of a dominant planet is still embedded in the names of each weekday: Saturn's day, the sun's day, the moon's day, Mars's day (*mardi* in French), Mercury's day (*mercredi*), Jove's day (*jeudi*), Venus's day (*vendredi*).

In English, some of the days of the weeks are named instead after Norse gods with similar qualities (the war god Tiw for Tuesday, the traveller god Woden for Wednesday, the god of thunder, Thor, for Thursday, and the goddess Frigga for Friday).

The Science of Influence

If the universe is a timepiece then, carefully read, it holds the key to the future. Such an idea was not inimical to Christian thought. After all, the magi had correctly interpreted the stars as foretelling the birth of Christ. The skies, however, did not direct events on earth. As part of God's creation they acted as his handwriting, his description of what would come to pass, setting the parameters within which human beings might exercise their moral and spiritual choices. In the Man of Law's Tale Chaucer writes: 'in the sterres, clerer than is glas, | Is writen, God woot, whoso koude it rede, | The deeth of every man' (MLT 194–6). The calculation of future events from the scientific observation of the stars is practised by the Trojan Calkas, a 'gret devyn [diviner]' who is 'in science [arcane knowledge] so expert' that by his 'calkulynge', or plotting of the stars, he knows that Troy is doomed and therefore acts accordingly (*TC* I. 63–77). First he turns traitor and leaves the city for the Greek camp, and then he secures Criseyde's own departure. Such a person would be invaluable to a ruler seeking to plan policy on the basis of future developments. It is a marked feature of Richard II's governance that, as his grip on events grew increasingly weak, he depended more and more on the services of court astrologers.[9] Today, politicians divine the future with the help of economic advisers: a more prosaic device, but sometimes just as undependable.

To credit the stars with their own power would be tantamount to the astrological determinism practised by non-Christians, of the kind eschewed by Chaucer in his treatise on the astrolabe but represented in his pagan tale of *Troilus and Criseyde*. There, the planets are not merely celestial orbs circling through their spheres, but gods enacting the consequences of a back story that makes events on earth explicable. It is Phoebus's (the sun's) long-standing hostility towards Troy that so constrains human freedom of action and makes the fall of the city inevitable. In the Knight's Tale, set in ancient Athens, Venus and Mars squabble until their dispute is settled by Saturn, who favours his granddaughter, Venus. The implications of heavenly events are worked out in the death of Arcite and the marriage of his rival, Palamon, to Emelye. But the planets are not necessarily implicated in the grand sweep of ancient myth. They have, as it were, more mundane functions. As well as being linked to the days of the week they are tied to the hours of the day. While one planet sets the tone for the day after which it is named by governing its first hour, as the day progresses other planets in turn exert their own influences. Prior to the tournament at which his destiny will be decided, Arcite visits the temple of the planet-god he serves, Mars, and chooses an appropriate time at which to do so. Emelye having finished her devotions to Diana (goddess of the moon), Arcite begins his 'The nexte houre of Mars folwynge' (KnT 2367). So there are propitious moments at which to perform certain actions, moments when a particular planet-god is likely to be more receptive to individual needs. Pandarus knows as much as he searches for a time, a 'certeyn houre' (*TC* III. 532), to execute his plan to bring Troilus to Criseyde's bed. He chooses a night 'upon the chaungynge of the moone' (III. 549) when the world is dark and the weather likely to be rainy. The stars favour him:

> The bente moone with hire hornes pale,
> Saturne, and Jove, in Cancro joined were   *Cancer; in conjunction*
> That swych a reyn from heven gan avale   *come down*
> That every maner womman that was there
> Hadde of that smoky reyn a verray feere . . .

    (III. 624–8)

In the circumstances it is a relatively easy matter for Pandarus to persuade Criseyde and her retinue to stay overnight at his house, where they have come for a meal and where Troilus is already secreted.

    Pandarus's practices—at least as far as predicting the weather was concerned—would not have surprised Chaucer's audience.[10] In the Miller's Tale, set in their own world, the 'clerk of Oxenford', Nicholas, is similarly inclined. He is the proud possessor of an astrolabe which he uses for purposes for which it was not, in his culture, strictly intended, for 'al his fantasye | Was turned for to lerne astrologye' (MillT 3191–8). He claims to be able to determine by particular operations ('certeyn of conclusiouns') and calculations ('interrogaciouns') what the weather is going to do—'in certein houres | Whan that men sholde have droghte or elles shoures'—as well as what is likely to befall them. Such is Nicholas's reputation and panache that his land-lord, old John the carpenter, although a Christian, God-fearing man, is easily duped into believing that his lodger can foresee the future. Nicholas tells him that he has 'yfounde in myn astrologye' (3514–18), as he has studied the moon, that on 'Monday [the moon's day] next, at quarter night' a rain 'wilde and wood [frenzied]' will fall and inun-date the earth with a second Noah's flood. John's evasive action, sug-gested by Nicholas, is to hang three tubs in the rafters in which he, his beloved wife, and Nicholas can sleep until they float off on the rising waters. But of course the astrology and tub-building are elaborate and hilarious stratagems that enable Nicholas to fulfil his own destiny as the seducer of Alisoun.

Nicholas's chicanery and John's gullibility are sufficient indica-tions that the claims of astrology were treated with scepticism but also with credibility. Although stellified, the pagan gods had not entirely relinquished their identity and power to the Christian god. They directly influenced, in various ways, human experience, iden-tity, and behaviour. So much is clear from representations of the planets in medieval art, where they retain a number of traditional attributes. The planet Mars, for instance, appears as a knight in armour brandishing a sword and engaged in acts of violence and war. The planet-gods also appear with their 'children'—those engaged in the activities and experiences over which the planet exercises a par-ticularly strong influence. In the Knight's Tale, Saturn lays claim to drowning, imprisonment, strangling, hanging, rebellion, poisoning, the ruin of cities, and pestilence. Arcite is one of his victims, and he indicates as much when he declares to Palamon that their imprison-ment may be due to 'Some wikke [malign] aspect or disposicioun | Of Saturne, by some constellacioun' (KnT 1087–8). In other respects too his life (unlike Palamon's) develops in ways that suggests he is a 'child of Saturn', who, as a more powerful planet, overrides the influ-ence of Mars, Arcite's erstwhile deity. Having been released from prison and sent into exile, where he can no longer gaze upon Emelye, Arcite sinks into melancholy (a disorder Saturn controls). As a conse-quence, his appearance is so changed that he can return to Athens unrecognized, and in the guise of a 'povre laborer' whose role is to 'hewen wode [cut wood], and water bere [carry]'—an estate and activities frequently shown as part of Saturn's domain (1408–25). Finally, he dies a disgusting death, the symptoms of which recall Saturn's disease, the Black Death: internal clotting causing asphyxiation, futile remedies, every fibre of his body destroyed 'with venym and corrupcioun' (2754).

The twelve signs of the zodiac, no less than the seven planets, have their individual attributes and effects. Each is linked to that month of the year over which the sign exerts an especially strong influence. Insofar as each month is connected with seasonal activities, zodiac signs and labours of the month are familiar pairings in medieval calendar illustrations. Zodiac signs, like planets, also exert power over individuals. Someone under the influence of Scorpio, for example, will be 'light and unstable . . . and lesingmongere [a purveyor of lies]', according to a Latin encyclopedia, *De proprietatibus rerum* (On the properties of things) by Bartholomew the Englishman and translated into English by John Trevisa during Chaucer's lifetime.[11] It is appropriate, therefore, that the scorpion should be associated with Damyan, the squire in the Merchant's Tale who secretly seduces his lord's wife, May (albeit with encouragement from her). Ostensibly his lord, January, is seen by the narrator as a victim of Fortune, addressed as if the fickle goddess were a scorpion that 'flaterest with thyn heed whan thou wolt stynge' (MerchT 2057–67). But the instrument through which Fortune operates is Damyan, and the focus of the passage includes him, for he too 'so subtilly kanst [knows how to] peynt | Thy yiftes under hewe of stidefastnesse'. January has treated Damyan as a trusted friend; the narrator demands in an exasperated tone of voice, 'Why hastow Januarie thus deceived?' Part of the answer is that Damyan is a Scorpio. Significantly, the labour of the month paired with his zodiac sign is that of sowing seed. As in the cases of January and May themselves, human behaviour is to some extent conditioned by seasonal urges orchestrated by the stars.

The planets and the zodiac do not act separately, but in concert. The planets move through the zodiac signs in ever-changing configurations. Some planets are stronger in some signs than in others, and each has its own zodiac home or 'house' in which it is particularly effective (Capricorn and Aquarius for Saturn, for instance). As a planet leaves a sign its powers relative to that sign decline. In the Franklin's Tale the turning of the year, when the sun is weak, is described in such terms:

Phebus wax old, and hewed lyk laton,   *coloured; lead*
That in his hoote declynacioun
Shoon as the burned gold with stremes brighte;
But now in Capricorn adoun he lighte,
Where as he shoon ful pale, I dar wel seyn.

 (FrankT 1245–9)

Sometimes, two planets conjoin within a sign, as in the case of Saturn and Jupiter combining forces within Cancer to produce the weather conditions that Pandarus needed.

Whether through the hours of the day, the days of the week, the months, the seasons, or the weather, the influence of the planets and the zodiac was experienced at a personal level. Bartholomew likens the relationship to that between iron and a magnet: 'so everyche [every] creature uppon erthe hath a maner inclinacioun be [by] the meovinge of planetis'.[12] The basis of the attraction is twofold. First, human beings are subject to the changing effects of the stars because they live below the sphere of the moon. There, all creation is caught up in a process of growth and decay, whereas beyond the moon matter is incorruptible. Second, human beings, as part of the universe, are composed of the same ingredients as the stars themselves: earth, air, fire, and water. The elements are the building blocks of the universe, but they are mixed in different proportions from planet to planet and from person to person. Thus individual response to stellar influence varies according to personal constitution. Now each element has two of four possible qualities: hot, dry, cold, or moist. Earth is cold and dry; fire, dry and hot; air, hot and moist; water, cold and moist. Planets and zodiac signs have the same qualities. Saturn is cold and dry, Mars hot and dry, Venus hot and moist and Gemini likewise; Taurus cold and dry; and so on. The same applies to human beings, who possess four humours (body fluids) that mix the four qualities in different ways. The humour of black bile is cold and dry, like earth; that of yellow bile hot and dry, like fire; blood is hot and moist, like air; and phlegm is cold and moist, like water. The dominance of a particular humour in turn determines a person's predisposition to the influence of certain planets, what was known as an individual's 'complexion'. Black bile produces a melancholic person and, since it is cold and dry, it is governed by Saturn. Yellow bile yields a choleric complexion, governed by Mars; blood a sanguine one in which Jupiter and Venus hold sway; and phlegm a phlegmatic complexion, affected by the moon.

Some of the terms just used are still current as descriptors of personal traits. ('Is she in a good humour?' 'He adopted a phlegmatic approach to the ups and downs of life.') In the Middle Ages, the language of humours and complexions was a fundamental way of categorizing identity, a shorthand for a wide range of possible characteristics. Thus when Chaucer sketches the Reeve as a 'sclendre *colerik* man' (GP 587) he is indicating a complexion and therefore a particular kind of personality (grasping, self-serving). Similarly, the line in the Franklin's portrait, 'Of his complexioun he was sangwyn' (333), is not primarily about skin tone; instead, it speaks volumes abut the man's propensity for generosity and good living. Since the complexions and humours link back through their qualities to the planets and zodiac, a person's identity is connected in intimate ways to the stars. The connection has other layers of complexity. As the Wife of Bath acknowledged, the position of the planets at the time of birth is a key to personal predilections. Furthermore, the stars influence personal appearance. A sanguine person, like the Franklin, is governed by Jupiter and does, after all, have a healthy facial complexion as well as good teeth and fair hair, according to Bartholomew.

The connections between the human body and the cosmos are close, manifold, and problematic. The nature of its rapport is caught in the idea of the microcosm—that the human body is not only part and parcel of the universe, being composed of the selfsame elements, but a small-scale model of it, subject to the same celestial influences. The notion underlies images of 'zodiac man' in which parts of the body are allocated to those signs which rule them. Chaucer alludes to the idea in his *Treatise on the Astrolabe*: 'And everich of thise 12 signes hath respect to a certeyne parcel [part] of the body of a man, and hath it in governaunce; as Aries hath thin heved [head], and Taurus thy nekke and thy throte, Gemini thin armholes and thin armes, and so furth' (*Astr* I. 70–5). Appropriately enough, given Damian's behaviour, Scorpio rules the genitals. Such knowledge was critical to medical practice. Before treating a patient, doctors would make elaborate calculations which would factor in the zodiac sign holding sway over the affected part of the body, the patient's birth sign; and the time propitious for administering a cure.[13] Chaucer's Doctor of Physik is adept at this order of expertise. He is 'grounded in astronomye', able to identify a favourable ascendant planet—'Wel koude he fortunen the ascendent'—suitable to his patient's treatment, and knows the elemental and humoural constituents of every malady, 'Were it of hoot, or coold, or moyste, or drye . . . and of what humour' (GP 411–21). Indicated here is the complicating factor of the effect of the planets on the disease itself. As in the case of Saturn and plague, stellar configurations could influence the spread of disease on earth—an idea buried in the modern use of the term 'influenza'. The physician's task is to restore an appropriate balance among the humours. Their imbalance can of course be the outcome of events less dramatic than the intervention of a planet-god. Dame Pertelote, the knowledgeable hen of the Nun's Priest's Tale, pours scorn on her husband's terrifying dream of a threatening, hound-like beast, reddish in colour with black-tipped tail and ears. It is merely a product, she says, of indigestion, of 'compleccioun, | Whan humours been to habundant' (NPT 2923–66). The redness indicates a 'superfluytee | Of youre rede colera', just as excess of melancholy causes dreams of black bears, bulls, or devils. Since he dreamed of redness tinged with black, Chauntecleer should purge himself of both choleric and melancholic complexions in order to restore their balance within his body. His wife prescribes a henyard regimen: 'digestyves | Of wormes, er ye take youre laxatyves, | Of lawriol [laurel], centaure [centaury], and fumetere [fumitory]'.

The Mind

From an astrological viewpoint the human body seems passive, a case for treatment, but of course it was active, too, as it engaged with the physical world, interpreted it, and responded in thought, speech, and action. The way an individual did this, no less than the ways in which the stars exerted their influence, was subject to 'scientific' theorizing. From his translation of Boethius, Chaucer was aware that there were four faculties whereby an individual might know the world: wit, imagination, reason, and intelligence. Wit corresponds to the five senses of sight, touch, hearing, taste, and smell. It is a faculty that depends on contact with the external world and is shared even with crustaceans, 'as oistres and muscles and oothir swich schellefyssche of the see that clyven [cleave] and ben norissched to roches' (*Bo* V, pr. 5. 29–32). Imagination, on the other hand, acts in a detached manner.

It creates impressions or pictures of what the wit has apprehended, 'the figure withoute the matere' (V, pr. 4. 158–9). Human beings share this faculty, as well as that of wit, with 'remuable bestis [moving animals], that semen to han talent [inclination] to fleen or to desiren any thing' (V, pr. 5. 33–5). Reason, however, sets humans apart from animals, being exclusive 'oonly to the lynage [lineage] of mankynde'. It is a faculty that gives access to a more abstract variety of knowledge than that available to the imagination. By dint of comparison and generalizing, reason apprehends not just the thing itself but the idea or concept which gives rise to it—not a particular chair but the kind of object known as 'chair': it 'comprehendith by an universel lokynge [consideration] the comune spece [species] that is in the singuler peces [particular examples]' (V, pr. 4. 160–90). Finally, the faculty or 'eighe' (eye) of intelligence is strictly speaking God's province, though it is partially available to human beings through grace and spiritual intuition. Intelligence comprehends the idea of human creation itself, 'thilke same simple forme of man that is perdurablely [for ever] in the devyne thought', and apprehends all things and all other forms of knowing instantaneously, 'by o strook [one stroke] of thought'.

Wit, imagination, reason, and intelligence exist in a hierarchy. Intelligence subsumes the other faculties: 'it knoweth the universite of resoun, and the figure of ymaginacioun, and the sensible material conceyved by wit' (*Bo* V, pr. 4. 170–207). Reason in turn has access to imagination and wit but is excluded from intelligence, for 'the lower strengthe ne ariseth nat in no manere to the heyere strengthe', and so on. There is also a hierarchy within creation itself, running downwards from God though humankind to beasts and shellfish, which depends on the faculty or faculties enjoyed by a particular order of creation; and another that moves from the abundant and tangible variety of the sensory world to the abstract unity of the divine intelligence. At the same time, there is plenty of interaction between one faculty and those below. Reason uses the evidence accumulated by wit and imagination to come to the general conclusion that 'man is a resonable two-foted beast'—a thought that, of itself, is not available to the lower faculties. Similarly, imagination behaves in a constructive manner with the data provided by the senses (wit), encompassing 'alle thingis sensible' through its own innate power. That power, in the case of imagination, is creative in the modern meaning of the word. Sense perceptions, 'excitynge and moevynge the strengthes of the thought', stimulate 'semblable moevyngis' stored within the imagination, as for example when 'cleernesse smyteth the eyen [eyes] and moeveth hem to seen' (V, met. 4. 46–60). The imagination notes correspondences and so forms a new, composite image: 'medleth [mixes] the ymagis of thinges withoute-forth to the fourmes ihidd withynne hymself'.

The imagination is thus the engine of new image-making, sifting impressions from the senses, as well as being a storehouse of remembered images.[14] Later writers elaborated the functioning of the imagination in order to account for the complexity of its behaviour. Thus Bartholomew, whose encyclopedia is a useful summation of ideas current in the later fourteenth century, identifies three interlinked processes or 'cells' within the brain. The first he terms *ymaginativa* and it is essentially an assembly-room where 'thingis that the uttir [outer] witte apprehendith withoute beth iordeyned [are ordered] and iput togedres withinne'. The middle chamber is called *logica* and is governed by the 'vertue estimative' [power of discrimination], an instinctive response that judges one image attractive and another repellent. The third cell is *memorativa*, which 'holdith and kepith in the tresour [treasury] of mynde thingis that beth apprehended and iknowen bi the ymaginatif'.[15] The images stored in the memory were of particular value to scholars and authors working in circumstances where lengthy sermons, judicial speeches, or narrative poems might be delivered orally and without a script. Complex content could, however, be remembered if divided into linked sections and associated with a memorable image within an overarching schema. Geoffrey of Vinsauf, to whom Chaucer refers in the Nun's Priest's Tale, advises in his book of rhetoric or *Poetria nova*: 'fashion signs for yourself, whatever kind your own inclination suggests'.[16] The inclination of many involved in the oral publication of their work tended towards architecture. The interlinked parts of their discourse were recalled through the mnemonic of a building's façade, housing niches that contained distinctive figures with particular attributes.

Chaucer had a particular interest in the image-making activities of the mind and its three cells—what in the Second Nun's Tale he refers to as 'Memorie, engyn, and intellect' (SNT 339). Troilus, returning to the privacy of his bedchamber from the temple of Palladion and his first sight of Criseyde, makes 'a mirour of his mynde' (*TC* I. 365) in which he imagines her figure before composing a song and praying to the god of Love. January, somewhat less devout, is more engaged by the 'Heigh fantasye' of beautiful women in general (which May happens to fit) than by a particular individual. Night after night he visualizes 'Many fair shap and many a fair visage' in a process of reflection quite the reverse of Troilus's: 'As whoso tooke a mirour, polisshed bryght, | And sette it in a commune market-place' (MerchT 1580–3). Chaucer's recurrent use of the dream vision, with its key device of enigmatic images produced by the mind of a sleeping narrator, is a further case in point. The *House of Fame*, which retells the story of Dido and Aeneas, does so by describing a temple of glass in which their story is written on a table of brass. But, as he reads, the dreamer imagines the episodes and their retelling is more like an account of a series of pictures: 'First sawgh [saw] I the destruction | Of Troye . . . next that sawgh I how Venus . . . Doun fro the heven gan descende . . . And I saugh nexte, in al thys fere [fear] | How Creusa, daun Eneas wif . . . Fledden [fled] eke with drery chere [sorrowful expression]' (*HF* 151–79).

In the *House of Fame*, Chaucer is doing more than describing the activity of the mental faculty, imagination.[17] He is also representing the way in which text, no less than direct experience, creates images in the mind's eye. He himself, as a narrative poet in his own right, was especially adept at fashioning vivid descriptions. This feature of his writing was noted from the outset. William Caxton, Chaucer's first printer, in his *Boke of Cortasye* (1477) claims that Chaucer's language is 'so fayr and pertynente it semeth unto mannys [man's] heerynge not only the worde but verily the thynge'. Francis Beaumont, in a letter included in Speght's 1598 edition of Chaucer's work (the text Shakespeare knew), thought that Chaucer's capacity to make his readers visualize was exceptional: 'one gifte hee hath above other Authours, and that is, by the excellencie of his descriptions to possesse his Readers with a stronger imagination of seeing that done before their eyes, which they reade, than any other that ever writ in any tongue'.[18] Chaucer put his talent to strategic use. Knowing from faculty psychology that images are stored in the memory, he deployed many of his vivid narrative images as 'keys of remembraunce', mnemonics whereby his audience might remember the story and its underlying themes. Since his audience was chiefly of the listening, rather than the reading, variety, Chaucer could not afford to be too novel or ingenious in the memory images he devised. Rather, he worked with familiar motifs from, say, the *Romance of the Rose* or the *Consolation of Philosophy*, summoning up images already stored in the imaginations of his listeners from their knowledge of other books. These he combined to create new, composite images with multi-layered possibilities of interpretation relevant to his own narrative.

An example will illustrate the process. In the previous chapter an incident in the Knight's Tale, when Palamon and Arcite see and fall in love with Emelye, showed how each knight constructed his own version of reality. Of particular interest for the present discussion is the setting of that episode, a prison. How does Chaucer make it vivid and memorable? How does he invest it with meaning relevant to the story as a whole? A comparison with his source material in Boccaccio's *Teseida* reveals the considerable extent to which he has transformed the Italian version. There, Palemone and Arcita live in relative comfort within the palace of their captor, Teseo, enjoying some freedom of movement. The garden in which Emilia appears is adjacent to one room and on the same level. In the course of her repeated visits they hear her sing, exchange glances with her (Emilia is somewhat flirtatious), and discuss her manifold attractions. Chaucer, however, makes the incarceration of his protagonists extremely harsh. It is a lifelong sentence, without any possibility of ransom, in 'The grete tour, that was so thikke and stroong, | Which of the castel was the chief dongeoun' (KnT 1030–57). The tower rises high above the rest of the castle and the city, and the knights' captivity is a miserable experience, one of 'angwissh and . . . wo'. So Chaucer's stress is on misery, isolation, physical and psychological suffering, and on the contrast between the dark, restricting interior and the bright world outside, seen through iron bars, in which Emelye roams. Palamon and Arcite, like their Italian counterparts, might sight Emelye in the palace garden, but it is too far distant for them to hear her song and, at this stage of the story, she has no knowledge of their existence.

It is as if Chaucer has drawn in the margin of his manuscript a *nota bene* hand with the index finger extended and pointing at the passage which describes the life-changing morning on which Palamon and Arcite see Emelye and are devastated. For it is both a significant turning-point in the story and an encapsulation of its meaning. Once an audience or reader has taken the hint, the *idea* of imprisonment emerges as fundamental to an understanding of the story. It is an idea with various ramifications, and it is one that is carefully implanted throughout the narrative. Arcite, as already noted, attributes their imprisonment to Saturn, who, as he later reveals, is the god of prisons: 'Myn is the prison in the derke cote [cell]' (KnT 2457). So the imprisoning effects on human life of the planet-gods is one idea in play. Arcite also suggests that 'Fortune hath yeven [given] us this adversitee' (1086), and repeated references to 'cas' or chance associate her too with constraint. The association would have been made all the more readily by members of Chaucer's audience because they were familiar with representations of the blind goddess in which she turns her wheel within a tumbledown castle. Another imprisoning power is that of love itself. Arcite, released from gaol, declares, 'Now is my prisoun worse than biforn' because he can no longer see Emelye (1224). Those familiar with the *Romance of the Rose* would be familiar with an episode, frequently illustrated, when Love locks the heart of the lover with a key. The same text also pictures (literally, in its illuminated versions) a central locale, the closely guarded castle of Jalousie. Jealousy is what Palamon feels once Arcite has been released and so has the freedom to try and win Emelye—'the fyr of jalousie up sterte | Withinne his brest'—and with that consuming emotion Palamon's sense of imprisonment becomes more acute: the tower resounds to his 'youling' (howling) and the fetters around his shins are wet with bitter, salty tears (1277–300). Not all of the associations of imprisonment are negative. Lady Philosophy in Chaucer's *Boece* (another prison narrative) talks of the tower of reason, in which it is possible and desirable to seek shelter in order to escape the vicissitudes of life. To the extent that Palamon and Arcite engage in a rational philosophical discourse, deriving from Boethius, in which they attempt to reconcile themselves to their plight, the tower of reason, too, is incorporated in Chaucer's idea of imprisonment. The prison tower of the Knight's Tale is thus a symbolic locale as well as a literal one: made vivid by attention to detail, it articulates ideas of imprisonment already familiar to his audience and available to them in the memory bank of images stored in their imaginations. His new, complex image of imprisonment invited them to reflect on the differences between his tower and its precursors, to use their discriminative power but also their faculty of reason in arriving at an interpretation of the poem as a whole, to think in terms of the idea, not merely the thing.

The Sense of Sight

The Ptolemaic universe, astrology, and faculty psychology thoroughly inform Chaucer's writings. They represent ways of understanding the human body and its place in the world that were as valid in the fourteenth century as the concepts of relativity, genes, and psycho-analysis are today. As explanatory systems they were long-lived but are now thoroughly discredited by Western scientific thinking. The same is not true, however, of all medieval science. In some cases its principles and practices are recognizably like modern ones, and the transition from medieval to later periods is marked by progressive evolution and continuity rather than the abandonment of defunct conceptual models. Such is the case with the medieval science of sight, or optics, which covered visual perception, the psychology of sight including the causes of error, reflection, and refraction. It is a science which, by various routes, captured Chaucer's interest.

Chaucer's fascination for the experience of looking, seeing, inter-preting, and responding can be partially explained in terms of his predilections as a 'visual' poet; and by reference to faculty psychol-ogy, where the input of sense data is the first and fundamental step in the operation of imagination and reason. Yet his accounts of visual experience go far beyond what is strictly necessary in the faculty scheme of things.[19] The Knight's Tale episode just cited illustrates the point. True, the moment of vision is sudden, brief, and stunning, and described as if it were the traditional Cupid's arrow hitting the lover's eye and lodging in his heart: 'therwithal he bleynte [turned pale] and cride, "A!" | As though he stongen were unto the herte' (KnT 1066–79). However, prior to this moment there is steady and close attention to the psychological and perceptual circumstances in which love at first sight becomes credible. As already noted, the inter-ior and exterior scenes are contrasted in various ways. The enclosed monochrome gloom, misery, and restrictiveness of the prison are set against openness, light, colour, joy, and freedom as Emelye roams in the palace garden. The knights see her far below through a thickly barred window, 'thikke of many a barre | Of iren greet and square as any sparre', which accentuates a further contrast, between foreground and distance. Before Palamon does so his eye has been scanning with-out particular focus the generalized scene until it begins to narrow to one locale: 'he al the noble citee seigh [saw], | And eek the gardyn, ful of braunches grene'. There, his eye is caught initially not by Emelye as such, but by something bright, 'fressh Emelye the shene'—her sheen or brightness being a recurrent motif. Only subsequently does he recognize her for what (according to his particular predispositions) she is—Venus—an interpretation that strikes Arcite as a significant error of judgement.

Such an example could be multiplied from other passages in Chaucer's writings. It might reasonably be argued that he is doing no more than record his own observations of how the eye works. Yet he was doing so within a culture where the scientific study of sight enjoyed high intellectual prestige, so it is also reasonable to argue that his accounts of visual perception were affected by current ideas. Certainly two writers whose works Chaucer knew well, Dante and Jean de Meun (the second author of the *Roman de la Rose*), made extensive use of the science of optics, providing Chaucer with precedent as well as channels of influence. He was probably also aware of optical ideas from encyclopedic writers such as Vincent of Beauvais, whom he is known to have used and who incorporated lengthy summaries on the topic. If he did not read the specialized Latin scientific treatises themselves, he was at least aware of the existence of some of the key authors and the fact that they were studied at university. So much is evident from the Squire's lines quoted at the beginning of this chapter. The courtiers talk of 'perspectives', the Middle English equivalent of the Latin term, *perspectiva*, for the science of optics, and they mention three of the key authors. Aristotle's works on natural science, the *libri naturales*, were initially banned at the Sorbonne when translations from Arabic and Greek reached Paris in the early thirteenth century. Among them was *De sensu* (On the senses) which includes a lengthy account of visual perception. Alhacen (d. 1000), an Arab scientist from Basra, wrote an influential and compendious work on vision, *De aspectibus* (On seeing) combining Aristotelian theory and Euclidean theory. Witelo was a Silesian scholar responsible in the thirteenth century for an extended version of Alhacen's magnum opus. The line in the Squire's Tale that follows these allusions, 'As knowen they that han hir bokes *herd*' (SqT 235), refers to the circumstances, when Chaucer wrote, within which such works would be studied—as part of a university lecture (literally, a 'reading') in which the key texts, or sections thereof, were dictated with commentary so that students could acquire their own copies. Surviving medieval curricula from Oxford include Witelo and Alhacen as authors who might substitute for Euclid within the geometry section of the quadrivium. Their names, and those of other authors who wrote on *perspectiva*, are also found in the library catalogue of Merton College in the later fourteenth century. Merton had something of a reputation as a centre for scientific ideas and it was a college with which Chaucer's friend Ralph Strode had links.

To look at Alhacen's *De aspectibus*, or at Witelo's *Perspectiva*, is to experience some surprising shocks of recognition. Their account of light rays when reflected or refracted, according to Euclidean precepts, is familiar from modern elementary physics. Again, their treatises are full of observational data: the relative size of mountains in relation to clouds, the difficulty of accurate perception in a misty atmosphere, and so on. Moreover, such phenomena are subjected to rigorous empirical analysis which involves experiments designed to test and verify a particular proposition. One experiment concerns the ways in which bright light, entering a darkened room through a small hole, projects an image of the external scene on to a facing wall. It describes the same principle as that used in pinhole cameras of the nineteenth century. Other sections provide analogies for events in Theseus's prison tower. For instance, Alhacen indicates how preconceptions, of the sort to which Palamon is prone, can lead to errors of interpretation: 'vision that depends on previous knowledge, or defining features, or minimal visual scrutiny is not truly determinate. For perception of a visible object through previous knowledge or through defining features only involves the object as a whole according to its general nature.'[20] Thus Palamon sees a woman, quickly subsumed to his idea of Venus, rather than Emelye herself. And distance only lends enchantment to his eye, especially where universals such as Venus are involved:

. . . it is in the nature of recognition to assimilate an object that is currently in view to an object that has been seen before according to an acquired form, and from this assimilation sight apprehends what any thing is. Moreover, recognition is differentiated according to recognition of the individual, or of the universal, or of both, so every error in recognition will occur in either or both of these categories . . . For instance, there will be an error of recognition in the case of distance. If a known person is seen from a great distance, he may appear to be another person known to the viewer so that when he sees Peter the viewer sometimes assumes he has seen Martin, since it is unquestionable that both are known to him.[21]

How is it that a product of Islamic science occupied such an influential position at the heart of Christian culture, at a time when Arabic countries were subject to crusade? One explanation is the absence of any religious dimension to Alhacen's work: it appears to be ideologically neutral and therefore presents no problems of assimilation to Christian thought. The second and more significant explanation is indicated by the preface to Witelo's text in which he, a member of the papal curia, extols light as a manifestation of God's creative power and presence in the world. Thus to study optics is to grasp a fuller understanding of the workings of God. The ground for this rationale was laid by the first chancellor of Oxford University, Robert Grosseteste, notably in his treatise on light, *De luce* (1232).[22] He notes that light was made by God on the first day of creation and became the informing essence of the universe and of all forms within it. The study of light rays, according to geometrical principles, is therefore a devout practice. Archbishop Pecham, the author of the treatise on the sphere previously cited, certainly thought so. He composed an introduction to optical theory, *Perspectiva communis*, in which he wrote: 'perspective, in which demonstrations are devised through the use of radiant lines and in which glory is found physically as well as mathematically so that perspective is adorned by the flowers of both, is properly preferred to all the traditional teachings of mankind'.[23]

The texts of Alhacen and Witelo enjoyed a long and productive afterlife. There exists a manuscript of *De aspectibus* with annotations by Leonardo da Vinci. Leonardo was particularly interested in Alhacen's notion of the visual pyramid—the idea that clustered light rays from a perceived object or scene travel in the form of a cone and have their apex in the eye of the observer. Leonardo found that, if he placed a gridded 'window' to intersect the rays of the visual pyramid between object and eye, and then copied accurately the forms on the grid, the result was a picture of the object done with attention to all the visual cues (overlap, foreshortening) that prompt the eye to see in three dimensions. Thus was born vanishing-point perspective, or *perspectiva artificialis* as it was then known, to distinguish it from the natural variety, *perspectiva naturalis*, that was the subject of Alhacen's work. Leonardo's schema bears a striking resemblance to the scene in the Knight's Tale where the light from Emily (the base of the visual pyramid) is intersected by the frame of a barred window before it apexes (somewhat painfully) in Palamon's eye. This is not to say that Chaucer anticipated Leonardo; rather that both men, working within the same intellectual heritage, came to similar conclusions, albeit in different media. The late sixteenth-century printed edition of the combined works of Alhacen and Witelo, *Opticae thesaurus* (Treasury of optics), includes a frontispiece in which a range of the optical phenomena described within are incorporated in an engraving which adheres faithfully to Leonardo's discovery. Scientifically speaking, Witelo's ideas were taken up and developed by Kepler, Kepler's by Newton, and Newton's by modern researchers.[24] It is hardly surprising that Chaucer's account of visual experience can still strike present-day readers as unusually modern and immediate.

CHAPTER 7

NEW CONTEXTS

CHAUCER seems modern and accessible to each generation of readers, but the features of his work that speak with immediacy and relevance change with the prevailing winds of cultural value.[1] The first chapter indicated how his contemporaries saw him as predominantly a love-poet and translator. Then, under the Lancastrians, he became an icon of Englishness (a reputation he still enjoys) for a nation in the process of formation. In the sixteenth century he was appropriated by Catholics under Mary as a champion of the true faith; and praised by Protestants as a harbinger of the Reformation. The seventeenth century hailed him as a gentleman who upheld chivalric traditions through narratives such as the Knight's Tale and *Troilus and Criseyde*. Eighteenth-century literati established him for better or worse as the progenitor of English literature (the history of which was under construction), in Dryden's phrase the 'father of English poetry'.[2] Scholars of the following century, such as F. J. Furnivall and W. W. Skeat, subjected Chaucer's writings to systematic investigation, established the canon of his works, and installed him in the school and university curricula where he remains to this day. But if each generation of readers has its own 'Chaucer', it also has its own blind spots. The earthy Chaucer of the fabliaux was not something a seventeenth-century gentleman wished to consider. His metrics were a source of perplexity to the Augustan poets, and Chaucer's renown survived mainly by dint of translation. Today, it is perhaps the pervasiveness of Christian modes of thinking that is off the radar of many readers.[3]

As a writer whose texts are taught at university, and as a subject of literary scholarship, Chaucer has survived many attempts at appropriation by the proselytizers of particular critical sects which, at the same time, have enormously enhanced our understanding of the reach of his writings. The practice of close reading favoured in the 1950s produced an urbane and witty Chaucer, steeped in irony. Nothing he wrote was quite as it seemed—a condition highly favourable to the professional interpreters of his writings. Rumours of the death of the author, as circulated by Roland Barthes and others in the sixties, proved to be premature but helped to focus attention on the cultural contexts within which works of literature are produced. One influential attempt to 'historicize' Chaucer, that of D. W. Robertson Jr., cast him in the image of an Augustinian preacher whose message was *caritas* or charity. That message was heard by those giving privileged place to the writings of the Church Fathers, not texts that Chaucer himself (or most Chaucerians) widely consulted. There have been many subsequent attempts to inform critical interpretation with contexts that are both interesting in themselves (e.g. labour relations, manuscript production, the role of women, heresy) and also capable of shedding light on diverse features of Chaucer's writing.[4] Other critical movements have produced their own Chaucers. Postcolonial Chaucer theorizes an author caught up in processes of cultural conflict, as between Christianity and Islam.[5] Queer Chaucer focuses on such matters as the homoerotic tendencies of male bonding in the chivalric tradition.[6]

Chaucer's adaptability to new readings, and resistance to their reductive tendencies, is in part explained by the wide range of his writings, which can absorb many different approaches, and in part by his refusal to be authoritative. He leaves a generous space for interpretation, giving his readers room to stamp their own authority on a particular text (and enough rope with which to hang themselves). Alongside the various Chaucers propagated by academic institutions, and celebrated every two years at the international congress of the New Chaucer Society, there exists the Chaucer of popular tradition. He is rather less protean than his institutional counterpart, and his salient features have proved remarkably constant over five centuries. There are essentially three: sex, character, and plot. Bawdiness has long been associated with Chaucer's name. By the 1500s 'a Canterbury tale' was a byword for a filthy story or a trivial one, or both. The kind of story itself—graphic, fast-moving, scandalous—was therefore linked to Chaucer as his characteristic output, usually in ignorance of the actual details of those tales that might justify such a reputation, and certainly without knowledge of those other writings by Chaucer which far outreach the fabliaux in extent and significance. With a name for saucy plots came a name for 'larger than life' characters. Here, the Miller and Wife of Bath are prominent: their reputations preceded them while their stories remained largely unread.

The Chaucer of academia and the Chaucer of popular imagination are products of textual traditions. The advent of new media in the twentieth century meant that the two traditions could not remain polarized: popular Chaucer gained some substance by being referred back to the narratives that had given rise to his notoriety; academic or thoughtful Chaucer made inroads into versions of his tales that had mass appeal. Chaucer, as ever, proved amenable to these processes. It is precisely his interest in the visual (sharply described people, scenes, objects, events) that is one of his most appealing features to a director. And his aptitude for visual process (scanning, focusing, zooming in) means that his work, superficially at least, is easily adapted to the lens. Nevertheless, many difficulties lie in the path of the would-be updater of Chaucer's works for general consumption. There is a balance to be struck between what is immediately accessible to modern audiences (sex, plot, character) and what might generally be called the medieval otherness of Chaucer. That otherness may well be one of the most intriguing aspects of Chaucer for a present-day viewer jaded by the conventions of realist drama. The wheel of Fortune, the figure of death, the prison of jealousy, are all fascinating points of entry into Chaucer's thought-world. But they are commercially risky since they might alienate the viewer. Then there is the problem of religion. The reference points for so much of Chaucer's meaning and humour are to be found in what for his own society was the small change of Christian culture, in which saints, liturgy, prayer, were part and parcel of everyday life. Oddly, modern secular mentalities react with faux piety to Chaucer's mocking of his own ideology. The idea that, in the Miller's Tale, 'hende' Nicholas's grabbing of Alisoun's crotch could be a deliberate parody of Gabriel's annunciation to the Virgin Mary is greeted with wide-eyed shock. There are fissures of sensibility here that are not easily bridged.

The Problem of Realism

Chaucer's realism is highly functional. In the fabliaux, with which his realism is chiefly associated, information about objects, settings, and appearances is included not merely for its own sake but to serve the interests of the plot and its themes. It is an extremely economical form of story-telling, in which each detail has a job or more to do. For instance, Absolon in the Miller's Tale is, among his other attributes, a barber: 'Wel koude he [He knew well how to] . . . clippe and shave' (MillT 3326). Being a barber is one of the ways in which this most gregarious of individuals maintains his social networks. But the occupation also provides him with a high degree of sensitivity to facial hair. When, one dark night, he inadvertently but 'Ful savourly' kisses Alisoun's naked arse at the infamous shot-window, his first inkling that something is 'amis' relates back to his day job, and so increases the hilarity of the moment: 'For wel he wiste a womman hath no berd. | He felte a thing al rough and long yherd' (3734–7). Similarly, the baldness of the miller, Symkyn, in the Reeve's Tale, may seem no more than a way of delineating his apish foolishness ('As piled as an ape was his skulle') and his propensity for the strong drink that makes his head sweaty ('wel hath this millere vernysshed his heed') and his mind less alert than it usually is (RT 3935 and 4149). But his possession of this kind of cranium is crucial to the credibility of the final scene. In a gloomy light, with the moon reflecting off shiny objects, his wife mistakes her husband's white head for the nightcap of an errant student, and brings a stout staff crashing down on top of it.

By and large, the nature of Chaucer's realism goes unobserved by his modern adapters. His attention to detail is instead seen as a godsend by those who work in media that are voracious of realistic trivia. They take it as a cue to create the warp and weft of medieval life to an extent never imagined by Chaucer himself. The emphasis therefore falls on a curiously antiquarian authenticity, and on vicarious participation, on the part of the viewer, in 'medieval life'. Such tendencies are taken to extremes in the ersatz visitor attraction, the 'Canterbury Tales', located within the deconsecrated medieval church of St Margaret's, Canterbury.[7] There, tourists are provided with the virtual experience of journeying from Southwark to Canterbury in the space of twenty minutes. While the exhibit was under construction the present author, as a local 'Chaucer expert', was telephoned and asked whether or not the Wife of Bath would have worn make-up: an interesting question in the history of cosmetics, but hardly relevant to her portrait in the General Prologue. The end result is a hyper-realism, bordering on caricature, of the people, sounds, buildings, streets, objects, of late medieval English town life. Along the way, five of Chaucer's tales, in highly abbreviated versions, come to life by means of animatronics and mechanical tableaux. The stories are told by celebrity narrators heard through earphones, although the pace of the recording and the timing of the mechanized events tend to get out of sync, with unintentionally hilarious results. So the Canterbury Tales Visitor Attraction is in every sense a distraction, and after twenty years of operation a somewhat tawdry one at that. In its attempt to simulate the real it alienates the latter-day pilgrim visitor, who emerges into the daylight, or rather the souvenir shop, with at best a hazy sense of popular Chaucer: what characters! what bawdiness! what plots! The idea that Chaucer's narratives contain symbolic images, ones that might be truly exciting windows on to his world; or that his characters are constructed according to rather different categories of identity than present-day ones, is nowhere entertained.

A visit to the 'Canterbury Tales' is a depressing experience because the attraction fails to look beyond the surface of what is tangible; reduces the otherness of Chaucer's world to a cosy but claustrophobic set of familiar features; and does little to stimulate the imagination: the imaging is done by others, the visitor made into a passive consumer. Another modern version of popular Chaucer, the film *A Knight's Tale* (2001), directed by Brian Helgeland, is more cavalier with its use of historical and literary detail but manages to create an exuberance all of its own by engaging inventively with its material, using postmodern panache.[8] The final, lengthy scene of the world jousting championship, *c.*1370, is a thoroughly absorbing and exciting episode. Lances splinter, helmets are knocked from their riders' heads. It captures some of the vitality of Chaucer's bravura description of the tournament between Palamon and Arcite in the Knight's Tale—'Ther shyveren shaftes upon sheeldes thikke . . . The helmes they tohewen and toshrede' (KnT 2605–9)—as well as the enthusiasm for tournaments in the last decades of the fourteenth century. But it is salutary to remember just how artificial realism (whether filmic or literary) is. The impressively shivering shafts of *A Knight's Tale* were created using tips of balsa wood hollowed out and filled with balsa chips, uncooked linguine, and sawdust. (Reality also intervened in the form of accidents on set.) Helgeland was conscious of the unattainability of the world he was seeking artificially to recreate, and used deliberate anachronism: an airborne helmet is caught by the crowd as if it were a football; the crowd stamps on the wooden flooring of their seating to the beat of the rock band Queen's 'We Will Rock You'. The effect of such devices is to represent the past with a degree of irony, although the director's stated intention was more prosaic: to bring the Middle Ages to the audience rather than force the audience into the Middle Ages.

What version of the Middle Ages is being brought to the audience?[9] One of the consequences of taking too much liberty with the historical past is to create a travesty that undermines the credibility (though not, perhaps, the commercial viability) of the entire enterprise. That is the case with the Chaucer figure (Paul Bettany), who plays a major part. In general his role is that of go-between and enabler. Chaucer mediates between the inarticulate peasant hero, William Thatcher (Heath Ledger), and his desire to become a tournament champion, which is normally the preserve of the nobility. 'Chaucer', not unlike Pandarus in *Troilus and Criseyde*, orchestrates Thatcher's aspirations as knight-lover and mediates between groups of different social status by virtue of his superior eloquence, native wit, and winning ways. So the role, broadly speaking ('Chaucer' as Heath Ledger's publicity agent), is plausible; and the story (poor boy makes good and wins the—aristocratic—girl by proving he has a noble spirit) not unknown in the realms of medieval romance, even if this version comes via Walter Scott and Hollywood 'rom com'. Along the way, William encounters some historical figures such as the Black Prince, and adopts the soubriquet of Ulrich von Liechtenstein—in point of historical fact a knight of the previous century, although the film leaves this complicating detail out of the plot.

In other respects, however, the figure of Chaucer is distorted beyond belief in an effort to make him seem accessible to a modern audience. What was he like? What did he do? How did he speak? Uncannily like Paul Bettany: he was young, attractive, outgoing, energetic, eloquent, inventive, prone to mishap, a ne'er-do-well in the picaresque vein, and frequently naked. Chaucer, apparently, had a gambling habit and was prone to wager every last stitch of clothing on bad hunches. The gambling idea may have some tenuous connection with the Pardoner's Tale, and the losing of money with Chaucer's documented experiences of being mugged three times in quick succession in September 1390—the worst incident being the first, at 'le fowle ok', when he lost his horse, other possessions, and £20 6s 8d of the king's money. The nakedness, though, is director's licence and a way of boosting box-office revenue with the not unattractive sight of Paul Bettany *au naturel*. Bettany's success in portraying Chaucer, in spite of all the distortions and inaccuracies, is not helped by a script that resorts to cliché and *double entendre*. When the curvaceous lady Jocelyn (Shannyn Sossamon) first encounters William in his new, knightly role, and before she is persuaded of his charms, her line is from a *Carry On* farce: 'You're just a silly boy with a horse and a stick.' This is not the kind of line even 'Chaucer'—who declares at the end of the film that he must write the story down—would have penned. What is worse, his allegedly astonishing, crowd-captivating rhetoric turns out to be the tired alliteration of a chat-show compère. Introducing his hero to the assembled company, he declares: 'I have the pride, the privilege, nay the pleasure . . .' Was this the father of English poetry?

Allusions and Analogues

The Canterbury Tales Visitor Attraction and *A Knight's Tale* represent two extremes when it comes to repositioning Chaucer for present-day consumption. Too excessive a fidelity to the medieval past kills Chaucer's symbolic content and obscures his own highly selective and functional approach to realism. Too uncontrolled a response to his work and to his historical identity distorts them almost beyond recognition. Both labour under the necessity of making their versions of Chaucer commercially successful, to which end the immediate appeal of realism is an attractive option. But there are other ways, beyond those of imitation or resuscitation, in which modern media have established new contexts for Chaucer and his writings. The three examples discussed in the present section work by means of allusion and analogue. They have an oblique, rather than a direct, relationship with Chaucer and his narratives. They sidestep the whole issue of realism because adaptation itself is not their primary intention. Yet their very indirection invites reflection back on the Chaucerian bases of their inspiration. None attempts a medieval pastiche; each engages inventively and thoughtfully with different aspects of Chaucer and his writings. In the process they provide readings of Chaucer relevant to their own audiences.

The film *A Canterbury Tale* (1944), directed by Michael Powell and Emeric Pressburger, begins with a shot of the bells in Bell Harry Tower, the central tower of Canterbury cathedral (unbuilt in Chaucer's lifetime).[10] The peal becomes a single note, as if insistently summoning the faithful. Then a voice over (Esmond Knight) begins reading a modernized version of the opening lines of the General Prologue.

On screen is the relevant page from a private press edition such as circulated in the 1930s and 1940s, which fades to a map of the pilgrim routes to Canterbury from Winchester and London. The reading ends with a significant alteration to the text: pilgrims go to Canterbury 'the holy blissful martyr for to seek | That hem hath holpen when that they were *weak*'. There is then a pageant-like sequence of Chaucer's pilgrims riding in cavalcade through rolling countryside. They are recognizable from their appearance and attributes as described by Chaucer and illustrated in the Ellesmere manuscript. They behave true to form: for example, the Cook with his flesh-hook tumbles from his horse (helped on his way by a chortling Wife of Bath). There is much merriment, chatter, music, vitality, and an over-riding sense of carefree purpose. The Squire carries a peregrine and at the sight of a bird overhead he releases it. As the falcon dives and wheels it becomes a lone Spitfire executing a manoeuvre (powered by an engine, with its distinctive sound, named after another falcon, the merlin). When we next see the Squire's face it is that of a Tommy, framed by his helmet and with his bayonet at the ready. The voice over now makes some rhymed comparisons between past and present as the scene changes to a shot of the wider landscape: 'the Pilgrims' Way still winds above the Weald | Through hill and brake and many a fertile field' but another kind of pilgrim now travels the route. Armoured vehicles suddenly intrude on the pastoral idyll and a steam train appears in the valley. The commentary laments the passing of the genial Host, the ring of hooves, the creak of wheels, and adds: '*our* journey's just begun'.

Making connections with the Chaucerian past, especially through the motif of pilgrimage to Canterbury, is one of the film's preoccupations. It is particularly prominent in a scene midway through the action when Thomas Colpeper (Eric Portman), a local magistrate and amateur historian, delivers a lecture to some soldiers. He tells them that, just as in civilian life they might be clerks, cooks, and merchants, so six hundred years before their counterparts also passed along 'the old road' on their way to Canterbury to ask for a blessing or do penance. 'You, I hope,' says Colpeper, 'are on your way to secure blessings for the future.' The pilgrim route, the contours of the landscape it follows, are what connects present with past, deepening the sense of identity that the living share with the dead. Walking in their footsteps brings to mind 'the old England', for they too climbed 'Chillingbourne

Hill', sweated, paused for breath, saw bluebells, wild thyme, broom, and heather. Colpeper, so he would have his listeners believe, when lying on his back in that landscape and looking at the clouds, can hear 'the other pilgrims'—the sound of their horses, wheels, laughter, talk, music. At a bend in the road where the towers of Canterbury cathedral are visible he has only to turn his head to see Chaucer's pilgrims on the road behind him. Later, the sounds he described, along with bridle bells that recall the opening scene, are heard by a Land Girl, Alison Smith (Sheila Sim), as she climbs the Downs for a view of the cathedral. Colpeper, who, unknown to her, has chosen the same spot to daydream, explains: 'Those sounds come from inside not outside— only when you're concentrating, when you believe strongly in something' (Fig. 7). Alison does indeed believe strongly in that particular spot, for it is where she spent 'thirteen perfect days' with her fiancé, a geologist, before he went to war as a pilot. He has been unheard of since. 'If there is such a thing as a soul,' she declares, 'it must be here somewhere.'

Sensing Alison's experience of loss, isolation, and yearning, Colpeper encourages her to believe that her planned visit to Canterbury, for the banal reason of attending a meeting of the Agricultural Committee, might result in a miracle or a blessing. And so it transpires. While making a pilgrimage to a personal relic—her mothballed caravan—she receives news that her boyfriend is alive and well in Gibraltar. So Colpeper acts as an agent of connection, a geologist of the fossilized human spirit, at the personal as well as the historical level. He does so in two other cases, again by encouraging belief in miracle and blessing. Bob Johnson, a United States sergeant (John Sweet), has not heard from his girlfriend for many months and fears he has lost her. But on arrival in Canterbury he meets an army friend who hands over a whole cache of delayed letters. Again, a British sergeant, Peter Gibbs (Dennis Price), is in civilian life a well-paid cinema organist. He appears to be content with his lot but actually longs to play the church music for which his training has prepared him. In the cathedral he picks up a stray sheet of music, returns it to the regular organist, tells his story, and is invited to play. Although Colpeper does not mention the healing function of traditional pilgrimage, each of these characters has an epiphany and is made whole as a result of their arrival in Canterbury. They are reconnected with themselves and with others as part of a larger process of establishing

Fig. 7. Chaucer is the land: Sheila Sim as Alison and Eric Portman as Colpeper, in *A Canterbury Tale* (1944).

Fig. 8. A modern Miller's Tale: James Nesbitt as Nicholas and Billie Piper as Alison (2004).

connections and continuity between the personal present and the historical past, as well as between Englishness and Americanness. Adhesion, or bonding, is something of an obsession for Colpeper. In the course of the plot he is unmasked as 'the glueman'—a mysterious figure who has been putting glue in the hair of local girls at night. His motives, however, are relatively harmless: he wants to deter girls from the village so that the servicemen stationed nearby will not be distracted and thus free to attend his all-important lectures.

The key element in Colpeper's scheme of things is the land. He invokes a mysticism of the land, a sense of ancient spiritual values, that gradually suffuses all the key characters. The film accentuates its mystical moments with the strategic use of light and the haunting sounds of horses, wheels, bells, and music. These moments run counter to its otherwise realistic portrayal of a country at war, but they also transport the idea of Chaucer to another plane. What explains his transfiguration? Certainly he is being co-opted as an icon of national identity, of what it means to be English, much as Shakespeare was co-opted in the Laurence Olivier film of *Henry V* (also 1944). The impetus for doing so is to some extent explained by the content of the film itself, which suggests two main propaganda functions: to secure from Britain's American allies a greater understanding of the war effort; and to boost morale at a crucial moment in the conflict with Germany. The devastation wrought on medieval Canterbury by the Luftwaffe's Beidecker raids of April and June 1942 is made clear in the course of Alison's visit to the city, when she loses her sense of direction among the piles of rubble. Signs indicating the sites of shops and services, and their new addresses, are reminders of the loss suffered and the determination to continue and make the best of a bad job. As one local resident cheerily remarks, the demolition of so many buildings in the heart of the city improves the view of the cathedral. Now, however, the impetus of war has changed and the film witnesses to the build-up of Allied troops before the D-Day landings of June 1944 (the film was shown to the trade in early May). So the spirit of Chaucer, and through him the land, is requisitioned to help these new pilgrims—or Christian soldiers, as the climactic cathedral hymn, accompanied by Sergeant Gibbs, has it. They are making their way through Canterbury to the channel ports of Kent in preparation for the invasion of Europe, some strengthened by a visit to a city able through its cathedral, rising yet above the rubble, and its historical tradition of Chaucerian pilgrimage, to help and sustain the latter-day travellers 'whan that they were *weak*'. This order of propaganda is in turn related to one particular category identified by Lord Macmillan as Minister of Information in his memorandum of 1940 on themes appropriate to feature films: 'what Britain was fighting for'. The topic was eagerly adapted by Powell in his description of *A Canterbury Tale* as an account of 'why we fight'.

How is it that pilgrimage and Chaucer were so readily identified with the essence of England, its land and its countryside?[11] Some influential preparatory work had been done by Hilaire Belloc, whose book *The Old Road*, first published in 1904 but reprinted many times up to 1943, describes in rhapsodic terms the pilgrim route from Winchester to Canterbury. More apposite for the present case is a book on Chaucer by Belloc's friend, G. K. Chesterton, which appeared just seven years before the outbreak of the Second World War.[12] In its chapter on 'Chaucer as an Englishman' Chesterton identifies those traits emergent in Chaucer's writing, and especially in his persona, that were later recognized as quintessentially English: a modest, unassuming manner; a natural ability that enabled him to rise through social ranks (itself a peculiarly English possibility); geniality; self-effacing sociability; acceptance of the status quo; a belief in freedom and fraternity; tolerance; a sense of humour. Towards the end of the chapter Chesterton, via a discussion of pilgrimage, identifies what is absolutely irreducible about this Chaucerian, 'English' identity: 'there is, it seems, something primitive about this poet, because he is as large as the land and as old as the nation'. Moreover, he has a transcendental quality: 'it is impossible not to feel something mystical about his magnitude as an emblem of England'. He is an archetype, but at the same time lends something personal to the idea of England, for the land is Chaucer and Chaucer is the land. He is 'made out of the very elements of the land' and is embedded in it, if we could but see his 'titanic outlines . . . with our native hills for his bones and our native forests for his beard'. Then we might discern 'a single figure outlined against the sea and a great face staring at the sky'. This is just the kind of book Colpeper must have had in his library.

For the second example of allusion it is not necessary to dig so deep in order to establish its animating context, nor is the allusion to Chaucer's writing mystified in any way. Caryl Churchill's *Top Girls*, a stage play first produced in 1982 at the Royal Court Theatre in

London and directed by Max Stafford-Clarke, wears its sources and cultural reference-points on its sleeve.[13] The first act takes the form of a sequence of interlaced dialogues between historical and fictional women. Each has a life-story to tell, one that articulates their experiences and predicaments as women. By cross-cutting the dialogue to create interruptions and non-sequiturs Churchill paints a complex, hilarious, poignant, and surprising picture of the oppression suffered by women at the hands of men and their attempts, sometimes successful, to overcome it. The device of using characters from different cultures and periods of history, and of making them simultaneously present, creates a rich backcloth for the contemporary drama that follows in the second and third acts, which is anchored in an employment agency for secretaries.

The figure who links the acts is Marlene, a feisty woman who has forsaken her home roots, and who shuns domesticity in favour of her career as an up-and-coming manager in the process of ousting her male rival for promotion at the secretarial agency. In the first act she plays hostess at a dinner party for the figures who represent stages in the history of that female emancipation that has made her own experiences possible. Her guests are Joan, who, dressed as a man, was pope from 854 to 856; Lady Nijo (b. 1258), a courtesan of the Emperor of Japan and subsequently a Buddhist nun; Dull Gret, otherwise known as Mad Meg, who features in a painting of that name by Pieter Brueghel the Elder (1562), where she wears an apron and armour as she leads an army of women through hell, fighting with the devils; and Isabella Bird (1831–1904), an inveterate traveller. The meal is well under way, and the conversation already rich in aperçus, when the final guest arrives, for whom they have been waiting. Ironically, she is patient Griselda, tagged by Churchill as 'the obedient wife whose story is told by Chaucer in The Clerk's Tale of *The Canterbury Tales*'. Typically, and according to the stage direction, she '*arrives unnoticed*' and proceeds to tell her story in a self-effacing and apologetic manner. The much more assertive Marlene urges her to eat but Griselda, not wanting to put anyone to any trouble, refuses. Thus Griselda, in this multi-temporal and multi-cultural setting, is introduced as a comic and ridiculous figure, her life-story, as described by Marlene, a fairy-story in reverse: 'it starts with marrying the prince'. But Griselda, like Churchill's other characters, continues to live in her historical moment, her opinions and attitudes unchanged. As her story emerges it elicits a sympathetic, if sometimes incredulous, hearing. Her insistence on loving and obeying her husband challenges Marlene's sense of independence but chimes in with Lady Nijo's knowledge of gender relations at the Japanese court. Even Joan, who, as pope, might be thought to uphold the system of marital authority practised by Griselda's husband, Walter, is aghast at the lengths he appears to go to in order to test his wife: 'He killed his children to see if you loved him enough?' So Griselda achieves a measure of solidarity with her fellow guests. Her story, like theirs, is sufficiently different to command the others' interest and respect, sufficiently similar for them to recognize a common bond.

Chaucer is the transmitter of the story rather than a topic in his own right, as he was for Powell and Pressburger. As Marlene notes, the story of Griselda is one also told by his literary precursors, Petrarch and Boccaccio, from whom Chaucer borrowed his narrative. Nevertheless, the resituating of his version of the story in a radically different context does shed some retroactive light on it: it becomes part of a coherent master-narrative about the struggle of women to negotiate and overcome male dominance; and thereby it gains relevance to the contemporary circumstances to which Churchill is responding, those of Margaret Thatcher's Britain in the early 1980s. To those she has a deeply ambiguous attitude, captured in the dialogue of the final act between Marlene and her sister, Joyce. Joyce has stayed at home to care for the illegitimate daughter that Marlene had before leaving for the bright lights. Her emancipation depends to some extent on Joyce's traditional domesticity. It is a society that embraces, and needs, both female roles, however contradictory and conflicted they might seem. Similarly, the figure of Margaret Thatcher is at once inspiring—a woman in a man's role—and deeply depressing: her policies attack fundamental liberties, she is a man in woman's clothing, a 'Hitlerina' according to Joyce. In this kind of society Griselda does and does not have a place. Insofar as she represents the nurturing, supportive, and loving aspects of women's roles, then she is crucial to the upbringing of children and their future happiness and stability; insofar as she is submissive, unassertive, and deferential to male authority, she has no future. A woman called Louise, who comes into the secretarial agency looking for work, explains how she has dedicated her time to serving the company, at the expense of her social life. Her sexuality is also in abeyance for she has avoided office affairs and has had little time to meet men elsewhere. Successful to a degree, she has built up a department and spent twenty years in middle management, but is now stuck. Meanwhile, young men she has trained have gone on to better things. Quite deliberately, she has preferred not to attract attention. Like Griselda on entering the stage, she is utterly supportive and dedicated, but remains unnoticed: 'Nobody notices me, I don't expect it, I don't attract attention.'

The immediate future might belong not to Griselda figures but to the likes of Marlene and Margaret Thatcher (prime minister from 1975 to 1990). 'She's a tough lady, Maggie. I'd give her a job . . . Monetarism is not stupid.' But the headlong pursuit of wealth and success comes at a price. The kind of toll it exacts is encapsulated in Danny Boyle's 1994 film, *Shallow Grave*.[14] Its three main characters enjoy high levels of material prosperity. Alex (Ewan McGregor) is a journalist, David (Christopher Eccleston) an accountant, and Juliet (Kerry Fox) a doctor. They share an opulent flat in Edinburgh and are ostensibly close friends, but their friendship is corrupted, and eventually destroyed, by self-interest, greed, jealousy, and the desire to possess both people and things. In the dénouement they attack each other in a frenzy of violence and hatred. It is tempting to see them as Thatcher's children, and to invoke her often-quoted declaration, made in an interview for *Woman's Own* (31 October 1987), that 'there's no such thing as society'. Although she went on to laud the virtues of individualism, she concluded: 'It is our duty to look after ourselves and then, also, to look after our neighbours.' Alex, David, and Juliet are out only for themselves.

In order to orchestrate their self-seeking interactions the scriptwriter, John Hodge, turned to the Pardoner's Tale. Just as the Pardoner repeatedly uses a biblical text, *Radix malorum est cupiditas* (Greed is the root of evil), which his tale then illustrates, so Alex's voice over begins and ends the film with 'If you can't trust your friends, what then?' The answer is that human relations disintegrate to bestial levels. It is as if Hodge has taken Thatcher's remark about society as a prompt to consider an even worse scenario, but one that lies in the logic of there being 'no such thing'. In *Shallow Grave* there is no such thing as family, neighbour, or friend, merely the individual, out to win. The incipient cruelty of self-interest is evident in the opening sequence, when the three flatmates interview a series of applicants for a vacant room. They use the interviews for their own amusement as occasions to humiliate and insult their unsuspecting victims by probing for weak spots and exposing them to merciless mockery. One is ridiculed for her religious beliefs; an older man is brought to tears when accused of being lonely and unloved. The Chaucerian parallel is with the three rioters of the Pardoner's Tale, who, in the course of their search for death, encounter an old man at a stile. For no good reason other than their own boorishness they insult and abuse him and blaspheme, even though he has the potential to tell them what they need to know. The old man nevertheless greets them courteously, but they in turn pillory his clothing and decrepit appearance. Having reminded them of biblical injunctions to respect the elderly he directs them down a 'croked way' where, thanks to their own avarice, they do indeed find death 'in that grove . . . | Under a tree' (PardT 762–3). They discover hidden treasure, fight over it, and kill each other. Similarly, the Edinburgh flatmates do their level best to kill each other (David does die) over a suitcase full of cash which they find in the room of their eventual and soon deceased lodger, Hugo (Keith Allen). The killings in the Pardoner's Tale seem civilized by comparison.

Chaucer's degenerate trio seek death because they mistakenly believe it to be a person, something outside of themselves which they can kill in revenge for his killing of one of their fellows in an outbreak of the plague. Their mode of apprehending the world is entirely literal; they have no perception of the figurative, of abstract concepts, or spiritual values. Their world is reduced to its material presence and they can imagine nothing better. The one person who did overcome death, Christ, is meaningful to them only as a rich source of curses and amusement. Their blasphemous oaths are so extreme, so 'dampnable', that it is as if they are crucifying Christ a second time, ripping his body apart: 'Oure blissed Lordes body they totere [tear]— | Hem thoughte that Jewes rente [tore] hym noght ynough— | And ech of hem at otheres synne lough [laughs]' (PardT 474–6). In a comparable way, the Edinburgh trio wilfully violate the ideas of friendship and respect and find hilarity in doing so. Having betrayed Alex by sleeping with Hugo, Juliet leaves by Alex's bed a set of plastic letters spelling the word 'love', and smiles winningly as she does so. Their world, too, is borne down by the sheer weight of materialism—not merely by the moral torpor it produces, but also by the problems of dealing with a case full of banknotes and other weighty objects. As Alex remarks: 'We took the money: it was a material calculation.' They wrap Hugo's body, stiff and heavy, in a bin bag, and bind it with parcel tape, then take it downstairs at the dead of night. The episode turns comic as the corpse gets stuck on the winding staircase, they stagger under the load, and Juliet drops her torch. They take Hugo to a wood for burial, digging under a tree like Chaucer's rioters, but first dismember the body. The sound of a hacksaw on bone, and the sight of David's vomiting as he performs the task, emphasize the irredeemably corporal nature of their horizons. What the film does not have access to, unlike the medieval version, is a range of Christian reference-points that deepen the significance of the plot. The Pardoner, for all his failings, can invoke a landscape with religious and spiritual resonance, within which the actions of the rioters seem only the more heinous. As they gamble for their newly found gold beneath a tree they seem to re-enact a scene at the foot of the Cross (a tree where Christ found death, only to overcome it) when the soldiers who crucified him diced for his garments, failing to realize the larger import of the event, the sublime comedy of his rising from the dead.

Adaptation

Chaucer would have recognized the nature of the interplay between his narratives and subsequent versions because he engaged in similar processes of allusion and imitation. For instance, he borrowed the story of *Troilus and Criseyde* from Boccaccio's *Il Filostrato* (without acknowledgement) but altered the plot to ensure Troilus's survival, or at least the survival of his spirit. Similarly, Hodge changes the ending of the plot he borrowed from the Pardoner's Tale since both Alex and Juliet survive—Alex to become the narrator. Chaucer himself modelled the Pardoner's Tale on a folk narrative. Again, he might have appreciated the changes in register wrought by transposing a plot from one genre to another. The ending of the Merchant's Tale, for instance, teases out the fabliau tendencies in the romance that precedes it, and allows them full and scandalous play. In a comparable way, a reading of the Pardoner's Tale by a modern screenwriter brings out its deep cynicism as promising material for a *film noir* treatment.[15]

No such transposition seems to have occurred to Pier Paolo Pasolini for his version of the Pardoner's Tale in *I racconti di Canterbury* (1972). At the end of the film, with the director himself in the role of Chaucer, he writes: 'Here end the Canterbury Tales told for the mere pleasure of the telling. Amen.' The story of the three rioters appears to be a case in point. Pasolini films it with careful attention to Chaucer's details, economy, and pace, and faithfully follows the sequence of scenes: tavern, search for death, encounter with the old man, discovery of treasure, visit to apothecary, death of rioters. Their violent end, as in Chaucer's version, is the inevitable outcome of their obdurate attention to the world of appearances—a world which film is particularly well suited to represent. Some of the details of Chaucer's narrative are enhanced by the medium. The sound of the passing bell stops the three young men in mid-carouse, and switches attention to the scene outside, where the corpse of their friend is being borne on a bier. As the serving boy tells them, he was suddenly killed while doing exactly what they are doing: sitting on a bench, drinking. An atmosphere of menace and foreboding builds ominously. Memorable by any standards is the encounter between the old man and the rioters. No matter that it is shot on Romney Marsh in Kent, with a church for a backdrop and sheep wandering, and that the old man with his crook is unmistakably a shepherd-pastor—all of these reworkings add value to Chaucer's mysterious figure and suggest new possibilities of interpretation. The wide open sky and flat, directionless terrain are particularly well suited to the rioters' loss of moral compass. And the low bridge over a waterway, substituting for the stile of Chaucer's version, is an eloquent marker of transition and threshold as the rioters, faced with a choice (the possibility of amending their behaviour), soon pass beyond the point of no return.

Although the Italian rioters roundly abuse the old man, and he rebukes them for their trouble, Pasolini does not exploit this aspect of Chaucer's dialogue, as Hodge does for *Shallow Grave*. Instead, he focuses on another feature of Chaucer's text, the disparity between youth and age, death and life, transcribing verbatim the words from the Pardoner's Tale. The old man says:

I've wandered even as far as India and found no one who would exchange their youth for my old age. Poor wretch, I go about the world and morning and night beat the earth with my staff and I ask my Mother Earth 'O Mother, do let me in. When will my bones have their eternal rest? Mother, I'd give all I have for that shroud that envelops you beneath the ground.' But still she will not grant me this grace.[16]

The rioters, like many a critic after them, register blank incomprehension, and return to their headlong pursuit of death, but in this exchange we may detect something of the larger agenda that lies behind Chaucer-Pasolini's disingenuous avowal that he is merely telling such tales for the pleasure of it. *I racconti di Canterbury* is the second of three related films later to be called by Pasolini his *Trilogia della vita* (Trilogy of Life). All are based on framed collections of stories: the first, in 1970, was Boccaccio's *Il Decamerone* (The Decameron), and the third, in 1974, *Il fiore delle mille e una notte* (A Thousand and One Nights). One of the avowed aims of the trilogy was to combat the old, the dead, the bourgeois, the cynical, the staid, the hypocritical, with the young, the vibrant, the energetic, the innocent. A dominant mode of doing so, throughout these films, is by celebrating the beauty and vitality of the human body, especially but not exclusively through depictions of nudity and sexual behaviour, what Pasolini called 'that fight for the democratization of the "right to self-expression" and for sexual liberalization, which were two fundamental elements in the struggle for progress in the fifties and sixties'.[17] His challenge to authority and convention was initially successful: *I racconti di Canterbury* was judged obscene by Italian courts and its release delayed.

The encounter between age and youth, death and life, in the Pardoner's Tale has a particular resonance, and its application to Pasolini's immediate concerns is suggested in the appearance of the rioters. Although they wear medieval costumes and inhabit a medieval world, their hairstyles (complete with sideburns) are pure 1970s. On the other hand, the Pardoner's Tale does not sit comfortably with Pasolini's avowed intentions, for in it the wisdom of innocence belongs to old age, and the cynicism of experience to youth. The point is emphasized in a prolonged sequence that prefaces the tale proper and which, while uncanonical, is an exposé of the rioters' mentalities. Each is shown in a brothel engaging in various kinds of sexual practice, including fellatio and flagellation, but with little sense of joy, and considerable tedium, for those involved. One rioter, called Rufus, then pisses a prodigious amount of urine from a balcony on to the inn's clientèle below, lecturing them the while on the evils of lechery and gambling in the manner of the Pardoner. Pasolini evidently discovered in Chaucer a darker vein, a more complex account of the shifting relationships between innocence, sexuality, experience, and self-interest. It was one that came to dominate his thinking. Dismayed by the commercial exploitation of sexuality in the media, by 1975 he had abjured his

Trilogia, much as Chaucer retracted the *Canterbury Tales*, although it was too late to do so. His work had already spawned a thriving sub-genre of pornographic films based on 'medieval' narratives.

Whatever else Pasolini's *Canterbury Tales* might be, they are an adaptation for a particular era and audience.[18] While staying faithful to Chaucer's plot and characters, he emphasizes certain elements of the stories so that they become a stalking-horse for his own preoccupations. That is not to say that Chaucer's narratives are demeaned or traduced, rather that they become the product of a dialogue between present and past, and between one artistic medium and another, such as lies at the core of all adaptations. In being made accessible to their 1970 Italian audience Chaucer's tales reveal some of the mainsprings of their continuing vitality and relevance. Pasolini adapted eight—those of the Merchant, Friar, Cook, Miller, Wife of Bath, Reeve, Pardoner, and Summoner—leaving out of account the business of pilgrimage except to provide an inn setting for the initial gathering of a miscellaneous collection of people from different walks of life. Instead, the linking device is that of the author-director, Pasolini in the guise of Chaucer, perhaps to indicate that, beneath the insouciance, there is a good deal of mischievous authorial intention.

Insouciance is also the prevailing mode of the animated *Canterbury Tales* of 1998, intended for a young audience, made by various directors with a screenplay by Jonathan Myerson, the executive director. Chaucer, of course, makes great play with his *faux naif* narrative persona and he does so, as Pasolini after him, to smuggle in weightier matters. The Myerson script and its animated Chaucer, all crinkly eyes and winks, goes to considerable lengths to suggest an experienced author who knows much more than he lets on, but exactly what those undisclosed matters might be never becomes clear. Instead of his famous self-effacement he is afforded a major role as the only begetter of the pilgrimage (helped by the Host), the *animateur* of the pilgrims, commentator on their traits and behaviour, and authoritative intervenor when their quarrels get out of hand. By contrast with Pasolini, Myerson foregrounds the pilgrimage (directed by Aida Zyablikova) as a garrulous and contumacious affair during which the idiosyncrasies of the participants are fully on display (the 'posh' Prioress, mouthing French whenever she can, is a joy). As well as providing Chaucer with a central role, it also enables the director to change the atmosphere (menace in the inn yard when the Pardoner begins his tale, piety as the pilgrims kneel before the sight of a distant Canterbury cathedral), and articulate those occasions which drive particular pilgrims to tell their tales: goading by the Host, rivalry, drunkenness. So connection between pilgrimage and tale-telling is organic: one gives rise to the other. Here, the tales of the Squire, Canon's Servant (Yeoman), Miller, Reeve, Nun's Priest, Knight, Wife of Bath, Merchant, Pardoner, and Franklin get an airing.

All of this innovation is authentic in the sense that it has a strong basis in the original: the artistic licence has a constructive relationship with Chaucer's text—although Myerson stretches a point by including a return journey from Canterbury to London. What suffers is meaningful cultural context. It is as if the figurines of the Canterbury Tales Visitor Attraction have been at once brought to life and at the same time held in their artificial world, devoid of any application to present-day realities. From the animated pilgrimage it is a short step to the further animations (in different styles, using different techniques) of the tales themselves, but in one case the relationship of pilgrimage to tale threatens to be not so much a frame as a sledge-hammer. The seething quarrel between Miller and Reeve becomes an excuse to intercut their narratives, so that the telling of one story is repeatedly interrupted by the complaints of the other, who presents a fragment of his own story until he, too, is interrupted. Granted that the quarrel is a valid motif, and that the plots are similar (as a split screen eventually demonstrates), the effect is to emphasize the staginess of the stories, their core fabliau insistence on action and things, and to create a further level of unreality and fantasy: that of an absurd fairy-tale, entertaining in itself but resistant to any thematic depth medieval or modern.

As already noted, Chaucer's fabliau plots are themselves economical to a fault. Each detail is there for a purpose. So to strip down the narrative yet further runs the risk of removing component parts vital to the proper functioning of the narrative. For instance, when Myerson's Absolon kisses Alisoun's arse at the window he reacts in an authentic manner by recoiling and saying: 'Women don't have beards!' Although humorous in itself, the point of the remark is lost because there is no previous reference to Absolon's work as a barber. A rather different set of issues arises from the BBC's dramatized version of the Miller's Tale, part of their 2004 retelling of six Canterbury tales in a modern idiom (the others were the tales of the Wife of Bath, Knight,

Sea Captain (Shipman), Pardoner, and Man of Law). Whereas the Miller's Tale and Reeve's Tale combined last for ten minutes in Myerson's version, the BBC version, with a script by Peter Bowker, extends to sixty. The main problem of adaptation was therefore to find ways of expanding the storyline without straying too far from Chaucer's text.

There are some brilliant and audacious innovations. The setting is moved entirely from a university town and transposed to a large Kent village somewhere on the road between London and Canterbury, a community that is just as inward-looking as its Oxford counterpart. Here, the focus of male attention is Alison (Billie Piper), transmogrified as the glamorous aspiring singer and young wife of a seedy old pub landlord (Dennis Waterman). To this pub comes Nick (James Nesbitt) in the guise of a pop music manager but in practice an inveterate confidence trickster (Fig. 8). Seeing an opportunity, he inveigles his way into John and Alison's household by promising Alison success beyond her wildest dreams and John—Chaucer's 'riche gnof'—untold wealth. The updating of Chaucer's tale is made entirely credible as a parable of small-town aspiration in the age of celebrity culture, *Heat* magazine, and the pop impresario.

In order to flesh out this world, Bowker takes a number of cues from Chaucer, expanding and developing them to suit his own purposes. Music certainly plays a significant part in the Miller's Tale, whether through Nicholas's version of 'Angelus ad virginem' (a fourteenth-century 'hit'), or Absolon's crooning outside the shot-window. In the BBC film, popular music is central to the culture of the people involved, especially through the karaoke stage at John's pub. That is where Nick first spies Alison, performing with the enamoured Dannie Absolon (Kenny Doghty) an execrable rendition of Elton John and Kiki Dee's 'Don't Go Breaking My Heart'. Later Dannie, persuaded by Nick that 'he's got music as his weapon' in wooing Alison, serenades her at her window with a tuneless 'Till There Was You'. Dannie's daytime existence as a lisping, narcissistic hairdresser, preening himself and using spray mouthwash before a hoped-for tryst, makes him a worthy successor to Chaucer's Absolon. John, too, is a convincing update of his precursor, and demonstrates regular fits of anger, jealousy, and possessiveness. As Nick arrives at the pub John is forcibly ejecting a customer for merely looking at his wife. And the encounter between medieval and modern produces some flashes of inspiration. One of the medieval Absolon's pet names for Alisoun is 'my sweete cynamome' (MillT 3699). When Dannie addresses Alison in the same terms she retorts: 'You make me sound like a Danish pastry!'

Chaucer's plot, however wittily adapted, is not sufficient to sustain an hour of viewing time, so various invented sub-plots run alongside. Nick, in tandem with his duping of Alison and John over his credentials in the music industry, runs three other scams. He charges an inordinate volume of expenses to John's credit card; wins the trust of a local news-agent and then cleans out his stock; and devises a plan to relieve an old lady of her savings. While carefully interwoven with the Chaucerian narrative these other strands distract attention from it so that the exhil-arating pace of Chaucer's finale is lost. Oddly, no use is made of Dannie's knowledge of hair during the window scene, where he feebly remarks to Alison: 'How could you? You dirty . . . !' John's superstitious piety, crucial to his gullibility, is replaced with a marijuana-induced stupor in which he mumbles about world religions; the love-making of Nick and Alison, while John slumbers, loses its urgency; and Dannie resorts to a plumber's blowtorch and metal pipe, found by chance, to replace Absolon's blacksmith and red-hot 'coulter'.

Tomorrow

Chaucer's hold on various levels and kinds of audience seems secure. The curriculum of any university English department worthy of its name at least acknowledges his existence. At the same time the tri-umph of English as a world language means that curiosity about the origins of that phenomenon continue to include accounts of Chaucer as one of its main progenitors. Once levels of interest in the English language and its literature reach a certain level, translations of Chaucer follow. The first translations of the *Canterbury Tales* into Chinese got under way several decades ago. In whichever culture he is encountered, Chaucer's narratives seem to be accessible and to pro-vide mirrors for his readers that make him feel 'modern'. In the age of iPads the interactive availability of text, image, and film is a milieu in which his writing, so well attuned to the visual world, will continue to find new enthusiasts.

For Chaucer is a most adaptable writer. He provides academic the-orists with ample food for thought but also fits in with modern idioms of storytelling and representation. He thereby has a ticket to the twenty-first century. Since many of his works are highly performable—a feature rooted in their original mode of publication—they will continue to exert a grip on the popular imagination as well as on academic scholarship. At the same time it is noticeable that the range of narratives given a modern make-over is increasing. Unusually for a stage performance, the recent production of the *Canterbury Tales* by the Royal Shakespeare Company included many stories tending more towards 'sentence' than 'solaas'. So while the Miller's Tale and Nun's Priest's Tale proved again that they are inherently theatrical, it was surprising to witness the extent to which a sombre story such as the Clerk's Tale held the audience spellbound.[19] For a secular society, Chaucer's insistence on the multiple interconnections of the material and the spiritual holds its own kind of fascination. Perhaps he knew something that we have forgotten.

NOTES

CHAPTER 1. The Life of Geoffrey Chaucer

1. M. M. Crow and C. C. Olson (eds.), *Chaucer Life-Records* (Oxford: Clarendon Press, 1966), 14.
2. C. Cannon, '*Raptus* in the Chaumpaigne Release and a Newly Discovered Document Concerning the Life of Geoffrey Chaucer', *Speculum* 68 (1993), 74–94.
3. Crow and Olson (eds.), *Chaucer Life-Records*, 478.
4. References to Chaucer's writings throughout this book are from *The Riverside Chaucer*, gen. ed. L. D. Benson (Oxford: Oxford University Press, 1988).
5. P. L. Allen, 'Reading Chaucer's Good Women', *ChauR* 21 (1987), 419–34; S. Delany, *The Naked Text: Chaucer's 'Legend of Good Women'* (Berkeley: University of California Press, 1994), ch. 1; J. M. Gellrich, *The Idea of the Book in the Middle Ages: Language Theory, Mythology, and Fiction* (Ithaca: Cornell University Press, 1985), ch. 6; J. Simpson, 'Ethics and Interpretation: Reading Wills in Chaucer's *Legend of Good Women*', *SAC* 20 (1998), 73–100.
6. J. C. Fumo, 'The God of Love and Love of God: Palinodic Exchange in the Prologue of the *Legend of Good Women* and the "Retraction"', in C. Collette (ed.), *The 'Legend of Good Women': Context and Reception*, Chaucer Studies, 36 (Cambridge: Brewer, 2006), 157–75.
7. A. J. Minnis, *Medieval Theory of Authorship: Scholastic Literary Attitudes in the Later Middle Ages* (London: Scolar Press, 1984), ch. 5; R. F. Yeager, 'Books and Authority', in C. Saunders (ed.), *A Concise Companion to Chaucer* (Oxford: Blackwell, 2006), 51–67.
8. S. Trigg, *Congenial Souls: Reading Chaucer from Medieval to Postmodern*, Medieval Cultures, 30 (Minneapolis: University of Minnesota Press, 2002), ch. 3.
9. D. Brewer (ed.), *Chaucer: The Critical Heritage*, 2 vols. (London: Routledge & Kegan Paul, 1978), i. 40.
10. Ibid. 43.
11. Ibid. 43–4.
12. Ibid. 40.
13. Ibid. 45–8.
14. Ibid. 50–7.
15. T. Hoccleve, *The Regiment of Princes*, ed. C. R. Blyth (Kalamazoo, Mich.: Medieval Institute Publications for TEAMS, 1999); N. Perkins, *Hoccleve's 'Regiment of Princes': Counsel and Constraint* (Cambridge: Brewer, 2001); E. Knapp, *The Bureaucratic Muse: Thomas Hoccleve and the Literature of Late Medieval England* (University Park: Pennsylvania State University Press, 2001), ch. 4.

16. D. Pearsall, 'Hoccleve's *Regement of Princes*: The Poetics of Royal Self-Representation', *Speculum* 69 (1994), 386–410.
17. Brewer (ed.), *Chaucer: The Critical Heritage*, i. 107–9.
18. C. F. E. Spurgeon, *Five Hundred Years of Chaucer Criticism* (Cambridge: Cambridge University Press, 1925), i, pp. xix–xxi and 83–6; L. Georgianna, 'The Protestant Chaucer', in C. D. Benson and E. Robertson (eds.), *Chaucer's Religious Tales*, Chaucer Studies, 15 (Cambridge: Brewer, 1990), 55–69; A. Gillespie, *Print Culture and the Medieval Author: Chaucer, Lydgate, and Their Books 1473–1557* (Oxford: Oxford University Press, 2006), ch. 5.
19. D. Pearsall, 'Chaucer's Tomb: The Politics of Reburial', *Medium Aevum* 64 (1995), 51–73; H. Cooper, 'Chaucerian Representation', in R. G. Benson and S. J. Ridyard (eds.), *New Readings of Chaucer's Poetry*, Chaucer Studies, 31 (Cambridge: Brewer, 2003), 7–29.
20. J. Gardner, *The Life and Times of Chaucer* (London: Paladin, 1979), 242.
21. Terry Jones et al., *Who Murdered Chaucer? A Medieval Mystery* (London: Methuen, 2003); reviewed by G. Olson in *Speculum* 80 (2005), 900–1.
22. P. Strohm, *Social Chaucer* (Cambridge, Mass.: Harvard University Press, 1989), ch. 2; K. Robertson, 'Laboring in the God of Love's Garden: Chaucer's Prologue to *The Legend of Good Women*', *SAC* 24 (2002), 115–47.
23. P. Hardman, 'The *Book of the Duchess* as a Memorial Monument', *ChauR* 28 (1994), 205–15; J. J. N. Palmer, 'The Historical Context of the *Book of the Duchess*: A Revision', *ChauR* 8 (1974), 253–61.
24. For general critical commentary see A. J. Minnis et al., *The Shorter Poems*, Oxford Guides to Chaucer (Oxford: Clarendon Press, 1995), 73–160.
25. A. Goodman, *John of Gaunt: The Exercise of Princely Power in Fourteenth-Century Europe* (Harlow: Longman, 1992), ch. 15.
26. A. W. Bahr, 'The Rhetorical Construction of Narrator and Narrative in Chaucer's the *Book of the Duchess*', *ChauR* 35 (2000), 43–59.

CHAPTER 2. The Social Body

1. S. H. Rigby, 'England: Literature and Society', in Rigby (ed.), *Companion to Britain in the Later Middle Ages* (Oxford: Blackwell with The Historical Association, 2003), 499–508; his *English Society in the Later Middle Ages: Class, Status and Gender* (Houndmills: Macmillan, 1995), 25–6; R. N. Swanson, 'Social Structures', in P. Brown (ed.), *A Companion to Chaucer* (Oxford: Blackwell, 2000), 399–401.
2. Sr M. A. Devlin (ed.), *The Sermons of Thomas Brinton, Bishop of Rochester (1373–1389)*, 2 vols., Camden Society 3rd Ser. 85 and 86 (London: Royal Historical Society, 1954), i. 111; Rigby, *English Society*, 308–10.
3. Strohm, *Social Chaucer*, 2–6; G. Duby, *The Three Orders: Feudal Society Imagined*, trans. A. Goldhammer (Chicago: University of Chicago Press, 1980), 263–8; G. Constable, *Three Studies in Medieval Religious and Social Thought: The Interpretation of Mary and Martha; The Idea of the Imitation of Christ; The Orders of Society* (Cambridge: Cambridge University Press, 1995), 324–41.

4. S. H. Rigby, 'Society and Politics', in S. Ellis (ed.), *Chaucer: An Oxford Guide* (Oxford: Oxford University Press, 2005), 26–7; his *English Society*, chs. 5 and 6.

5. John Gower, *Vox clamantis*, in E. W. Stockton (trans.), *The Major Latin Works of John Gower: The Voice of One Crying and the Tripartite Chronicle* (Seattle: University of Washington Press, 1962), 282–3; see also a sermon of *c.*1388 by Thomas Wimbledon, *Wimbledon's Sermon 'Redde Rationem Villicationis Tue': A Middle English Sermon of the Fourteenth Century*, ed. I. K. Knight, Duquesne Studies, Philological Series, 9 (Pittsburgh: Duquesne University Press, 1967), 61–8, excerpted in G. Chaucer, *The Canterbury Tales: Fifteen Tales and the General Prologue*, 2nd edn., ed. V. A. Kolve and G. Olson (New York: Norton, 2005), 333–5.

6. Gower, *Vox clamantis*, trans. Stockton, 221.

7. Ibid. 259.

8. F. E. Baldwin, *Sumptuary Legislation and Personal Regulation in England*, Johns Hopkins University Studies in Historical and Political Science, series 42, no. 1 (Baltimore: Johns Hopkins, 1926), 46–55.

9. R. B. Dobson (ed.), *The Peasants' Revolt of 1381*, 2nd edn. (London and Basingstoke: Macmillan, 1983), 105–11; Strohm, *Social Chaucer*, 6–10.

10. May McKisack, *The Fourteenth Century 1307–1399*, The Oxford History of England, 5 (Oxford: Clarendon Press, 1959), 529.

11. A. J. Johnston, *Clerks and Courtiers: Chaucer, Late Middle English Literature and the State Formation Process*, Anglistische Forschungen, 302 (Heidelberg: Winter 2001), ch. 2.

12. L. Patterson, *Chaucer and the Subject of History* (London: Routledge, 1991), 32–9 (p. 39); Strohm, *Social Chaucer*, 10–13; N. Saul, *Knights and Esquires: The Gloucestershire Gentry in the Fourteenth Century* (Oxford: Clarendon Press, 1981), 6–29.

13. S. H. Rigby, *Chaucer in Context: Society, Allegory and Gender* (Manchester: Manchester University Press, 1996), 7–17; but see P. A. Olson, *The Canterbury Tales and the Good Society* (Princeton: Princeton University Press, 1986), ch. 1.

14. Swanson, 'Social Structures', 399–401.

15. J. Mann, *Chaucer and Medieval Estates Satire: The Literature of Social Classes and the General Prologue to the Canterbury Tales* (Cambridge: Cambridge University Press, 1973); Patterson, *Chaucer and the Subject of History*, 27–32; Rigby, 'Society and Politics', 27–9.

16. Gower, *Vox clamantis*, trans. Stockton, 165–83.

17. J. P. Hermann, 'A Monk Ther Was, a Fair for the Maistrie', in L. C. Lambdin and R. T. Lambdin (eds.), *Chaucer's Pilgrims: An Historical Guide to the Pilgrims in 'The Canterbury Tales'* (Westport, Conn.: Greenwood Press, 1996), 69–79; L. F. Hodges, *Chaucer and Clothing: Clerical and Academic Costume in the General Prologue to 'The Canterbury Tales'*, Chaucer Studies, 34 (Cambridge: Brewer, 2005), ch. 4.

18. D. F. Pigg, '"With Hym Ther Was a Plowman, Was His Brother"', in Lambdin and Lambdin (eds.), *Chaucer's Pilgrims*, 263–70.

19. H. Crocker, 'Affective Politics in Chaucer's *Reeve's Tale*: "Cherl" Masculinity after 1381', *SAC* 29 (2007), 225–58.

20. R. Horrox (ed. and trans.), *The Black Death* (Manchester: Manchester University Press, 1994), 4–8.

21. Ibid. 66.

22. Ibid. 141.

23. Ibid. 124.

24. Ibid. 24.

25. Ibid. 159.

26. Ibid. 66.

27. Ibid. 70.

28. Ibid. 307.

29. Rigby, *English Society*, 80–7.

30. Minnis et al., *Shorter Poems*, 147–9; G. Olson, *Literature as Recreation in the Later Middle Ages* (Ithaca: Cornell University Press, 1982), ch. 5.

31. G. Boccaccio, *The Decameron*, trans. G. H. McWilliam, 2nd edn. (Harmondsworth: Penguin, 1972), 11–12.

32. G. de Machaut, *The Judgment of the King of Navarre*, trans. R. B. Palmer (New York and London: Garland, 1988).

33. C. M. Lewis, 'Framing Fiction with Death: Chaucer's *Canterbury Tales* and the Plague', in Benson and Ridyard (eds.), *New Readings*, 139–64; D. V. Smith, 'Plague, Panic Space, and the Tragic Medieval Household', *South Atlantic Quarterly* 98 (1999), 367–414.

34. A. Butterfield, 'Nationhood', in Ellis (ed.), *Chaucer: An Oxford Guide*, 52–5.

35. Genealogy in McKisack, *Fourteenth Century*, 106.

36. M. H. Keen, *England in the Later Middle Ages: A Political History*, 2nd edn. (London: Routledge, 2003), 90–7.

37. Crow and Olson (eds.), *Chaucer Life-Records*, 370.

38. See the map in C. J. Rogers (ed.), *The Wars of Edward III: Sources and Interpretations* (Woodbridge: Boydell Press, 1999), p. xxvii.

39. Crow and Olson (eds.), *Chaucer Life-Records*, 370.

40. Ibid. 42–53.

41. J. Froissart, *Chronicles*, trans. Geoffrey Brereton, rev. edn. (Harmondsworth: Penguin, 1978), 194.

42. Ibid. 146–55.

43. J. M. Bowers, 'Chaucer after Retters: The Wartime Origins of English Literature', in D. N. Baker (ed.), *Inscribing the Hundred Years' War in French and English Cultures* (Albany: State University of New York Press, 2000), 91–125; S. Meecham-Jones, 'The Invisible Siege—The Depiction of Warfare in the Poetry of Chaucer', in C. Saunders, F. Le Saux, and N. Thomas (eds.), *Writing War: Medieval Literary Responses to Warfare* (Cambridge: Brewer, 2004) 147–67; J. H. Pratt, *Chaucer and War* (Lanham, Md.: University Press of America, 2000); K. J. Thompson, 'Chaucer's Warrior-Bowman: The Roles and Equipment of the Knight's Yeoman', *ChauR* 40 (2006), 386–415.

44. Crow and Olson (eds.), *Chaucer Life-Records*, 64–6; B. F. Taggie, 'Chaucer in Spain: The Historical Context', in B. F. Taggie, R. W. Clement, and

J. E. Caraway (eds.), *Spain and the Mediterranean* (Kirksville, Mo.: Thomas Jefferson University Press, 1992), 35–44.

45. Dobson (ed.), *Peasants' Revolt*, 63–72; R. Hilton, *Bond Men Made Free: Medieval Peasant Movements and the English Rising of 1381* (London: Methuen, 1977), 154–5.

46. Dobson (ed.), *Peasants' Revolt*, 135.

47. Hilton, *Bond Men*, 16, 171, 207–13; and see his ch. 7 on the social composition of the rebels.

48. Dobson (ed.), *Peasants' Revolt*, 125.

49. Hilton, *Bond Men*, ch. 6, on the geography of the revolt.

50. Dobson (ed.), *Peasants' Revolt*, 133–4.

51. Ibid. 128.

52. Hilton, *Bond Men*, 218.

53. Ibid. 156, ch. 9; Dobson (ed.), *Peasants' Revolt*, 342–3, 370.

54. Dobson (ed.), *Peasants' Revolt*, 177.

55. Ibid. 374.

56. For a detailed chronology of the events of the rising see ibid. 36–44.

57. Ibid. 169–70.

58. Ibid. 161.

59. Gower, *Vox clamantis*, trans. Stockton, 57.

60. Ibid. 77.

61. W. Langland, *Piers Plowman: A New Annotated Edition of the C-Text*, rev. edn., ed. D. Pearsall (Exeter: University of Exeter Press, 2008). All subsequent references are to this edition.

62. Dobson (ed.), *Peasants' Revolt*, 381.

63. Ibid. 173.

64. Ibid. 185, 368.

65. Patterson, *Chaucer and the Subject of History*, ch. 5; Olson, *Canterbury Tales*, ch. 5; A. Blamires, 'Chaucer the Reactionary: Ideology and the General Prologue to *The Canterbury Tales*', *Review of English Studies*, NS 51 (2000), 523–39.

66. H. Barr, *Socioliterary Practice in Late Medieval England* (Oxford: Oxford University Press, 2001), ch. 4; D. Gordon, L. Monnas, and C. Elam (eds.), *The Regal Image of Richard II and the Wilton Diptych* (London: Harvey Miller, 1997).

67. Crow and Olson (eds.), *Chaucer Life-Records*, 402, 514.

68. R. R. Edwards, 'Ricardian Dreamwork: Chaucer, Cupid and Loyal Lovers', in Collette (ed.), *'Legend of Good Women'*, 59–82.

CHAPTER 3. The Literary Scene

1. For a colour reproduction of the frontispiece and a discussion of its significance see *Troilus and Criseyde: A Facsimile of Corpus Christi College Cambridge MS 61*, introd. M. B. Parkes and E. Salter (Cambridge: Brewer, 1978); for recent interpretations A. Helmbold, 'Chaucer Appropriated: The *Troilus* Frontispiece as Lancastrian Propaganda', *SAC* 30 (2008), 205–34.

2. A. Butterfield, 'Chaucerian Vernaculars', *SAC* 31 (2009), 25–51.

3. P. Strohm, *Hochon's Arrow: The Social Imagination of Fourteenth-Century Texts* (Princeton: Princeton University Press, 1992), ch. 4.

4. Crow and Olson (eds.), *Chaucer Life-Records*, 524–5.

5. N. Saul, *Richard II* (New Haven: Yale University Press, 1997), 357–65; M. J. Bennett, 'The Court of Richard II and the Promotion of Literature', in B. A. Hanawalt (ed.), *Chaucer's England, Literature in Historical Context*, Medieval Studies at Minnesota 4 (Minneapolis: University of Minnesota Press, 1992), 3–20; P. J. Eberle, 'Richard II and the Literary Arts', in A. Goodman and J. Gillespie (eds.), *Richard II: The Art of Kingship* (Oxford: Clarendon Press, 1999), 231–53; R. F. Green, *Poets and Princepleasers: Literature and the English Court in the Late Middle Ages* (Toronto: University of Toronto Press, 1980), ch. 4; Minnis et al., *Shorter Poems*, 9–35; V. J. Scattergood, 'Literary Culture at the Court of Richard II', in V. J. Scattergood and J. W. Sherborne (eds.), *English Court Culture in the Later Middle Ages* (London: Duckworth, 1983), 29–43.

6. Saul, *Richard II*, 117–20, 141–2, 157–6; J. Coleman, '"A bok for king Richardes sake": Royal Patronage, the *Confessio*, and the *Legend of Good Women*', in R. F. Yeager (ed.), *On John Gower: Essays at the Millennium*, Studies in Medieval Culture, 46 (Kalamazoo: Medieval Institute Publications, 2007), 104–23; Patterson, *Chaucer and the Subject of History*, 47–61; B. Windeatt, 'Courtly Writing', in Saunders (ed.), *Concise Companion*, 90–109.

7. Crow and Olson (eds.), *Chaucer Life-Records*, 268–9, 369.

8. S. H. Rigby, *Wisdom and Chivalry: Chaucer's Knight's Tale and Medieval Political Theory*, Medieval and Renaissance Authors and Texts, 4 (Leiden: Brill, 2009).

9. Saul, *Richard II*, 339–58.

10. Ibid. 351–2; S. Lindenbaum, 'The Smithfield Tournament of 1390', *Journal of Medieval and Renaissance Studies*, 20 (1990), 1–20; L. M. Clopper, 'The Engaged Spectator: Langland and Chaucer on Civic Spectacle and the *Theatrum*', *SAC* 22 (2000), 115–39.

11. Crow and Olson (eds.), *Chaucer Life-Records*, 472–3.

12. Saul, *Richard II*, 22–3 for the funeral arrangements for Edward III in London.

13. Ibid. 337, 339–40, 343–4, 353–4, 461; G. Kipling, *Enter the King: Theatre, Liturgy, and Ritual in the Medieval Civic Triumph* (Oxford: Clarendon Press, 1998), 11–21.

14. Saul, *Richard II*, 455. Cf. 132–3.

15. J. Ferster, *Fictions of Advice: The Literature and Politics of Counsel in Late Medieval England* (Philadelphia: University of Pennsylvania Press, 1996); Green, *Poets and Princepleasers*, chs. 5 and 6; L. Staley, 'Gower, Richard II, Henry of Derby, and the Business of Making Culture', *Speculum* 75 (2000), 68–96.

16. Saul, *Richard II*, and see 248–50.

17. The section on 'Peace' in Chapter 4, below, discusses another tale which draws on the 'mirrors for princes' tradition.

18. Strohm, *Social Chaucer*, chs. 2 and 3.

19. Strohm, *Hochon's Arrow*, ch. 3; D. Pearsall, 'The *Canterbury Tales* and London Club Culture', in A. Butterfield (ed.), *Chaucer and the City*, Chaucer Studies, 37 (Cambridge: Brewer, 2006), 95–108.

20. D. Pearsall, *The Life of Geoffrey Chaucer: A Critical Biography* (Oxford: Blackwell, 1992), 130–1.

21. Text and translation in Brewer, *Chaucer: The Critical Heritage*, i. 40–2; W. Calin, 'Deschamps's "Ballade to Chaucer" Again, or the Dangers of Intertextual Medieval Comparatism', in D. Sinnreich-Levi (ed.), *Eustache Deschamps, French Courtier-Poet: His Work and his World*, AMS Studies in the Middle Ages, 22 (New York: AMS Press, 1998), 73–83; D. Wallace, 'Chaucer and Deschamps, Translation and the Hundred Years' War', in R. Voaden, R. Tixier, T. Sanchez Roura, and J. R. Rytting (eds.), *The Medieval Translator/Traduire au Moyen Age*, The Theory and Practice of Translation in the Middle Ages, 8 (Turnhout: Brepols, 2003), 179–88.

22. Pearsall, *Chaucer*, 71.

23. Green, *Poets and Princepleasers*, ch. 2; C. Given-Wilson, *The Royal Household and the King's Affinity: Service, Politics and Finance in England 1360–1413* (New Haven: Yale University Press, 1986), 160–74.

24. On Strode see the note to *Troilus* V. 1856–9 in the *Riverside Chaucer*, 1058; J. A. W. Bennett, *Chaucer at Oxford and at Cambridge* (Oxford: Clarendon Press, 1974), 63–5; Pearsall, *Chaucer*, 133–4.

25. Crow and Olson (eds.), *Chaucer Life-Records*, 282–3.

26. Ibid. 54, 60.

27. Saul, *Richard II*, 436–7; K. Olsson, 'Composing the King, 1390–1391: Gower's Ricardian Rhetoric', *SAC* 31 (2009), 141–73; J. H. Fisher, *John Gower: Moral Philosopher and Friend of Chaucer* (New York: New York University Press, 1964), ch. 5.

28. Brewer (ed.), *Chaucer: The Critical Heritage*, i. 43.

29. Strohm, *Social Chaucer*, 72–3.

30. Crow and Olson (eds.), *Chaucer Life-Records*, 500–3.

31. Pearsall, *Chaucer*, 167–8; Strohm, *Social Chaucer*, 73–4, 76–8.

32. Pearsall, *Chaucer*, 166–7.

33. Strohm, *Social Chaucer*, 97.

34. Pearsall, *Chaucer*, 129–30, 225; Crow and Olson (eds.), *Chaucer Life-Records*, 104, 506, 508.

35. For further details see *The Works of Sir John Clanvowe*, ed. J. Scattergood (Cambridge: Brewer, 1965), 25–7.

36. Crow and Olson (eds.), *Chaucer Life-Records*, 104, 343, 347; Pearsall, *Chaucer*, 10.

37. On the nature and extent of Clanvowe's borrowing, see Strohm, *Social Chaucer*, 78–82.

38. Saul, *Richard II*, 411–13, 424–5.

39. P. Strohm, 'Politics and Poetics: Usk and Chaucer in the 1380s', in L. Patterson (ed.), *Literary Practice and Social Change in Britain, 1380–1530* (Berkeley: University of California Press, 1990), 83–112; M. Turner,

'"Certaynly his Noble Seyenges Can I Not Amende": Thomas Usk and *Troilus and Criseyde*', *ChauR* 37 (2002), 26–39; for editions of the *Testament of Love* see those by G. W. Shawver and J. F. Leyerle, Toronto Medieval Texts and Translations, 13 (Toronto: University of Toronto Press, 2002) and R. A. Shoaf (Kalamazoo: Medieval Institute Publications for TEAMS, 1998).

40. Minnis et al., *Shorter Poems*, 443–54; F. Percival, *Chaucer's Legendary Good Women*, Cambridge Studies in Medieval Literature, 38 (Cambridge: Cambridge University Press, 1998), ch. 15; D. Wallace, *Chaucerian Polity: Absolutist Lineages and Associational Forms in England and Italy* (Stanford: Stanford University Press, 1997), 357–76; A. Taylor, 'Anne of Bohemia and the Making of Chaucer', *SAC* 19 (1997), 95–119; Strohm, *Hochon's Arrow*, ch. 5; N. F. McDonald, 'Chaucer's *Legend of Good Women*, Ladies at Court and the Female Reader', *ChauR* 35 (2000), 22–42; her 'Games Medieval Women Play', in Collette (ed.), '*Legend of Good Women*', 176–97; J. Coleman, 'The Flower, the Leaf, and Philippa of Lancaster', ibid. 33–58; C. P. Collette, 'Joan of Kent and Noble Women's Roles in Chaucer's World', *ChauR* 33 (1999), 350–62.

41. C. D. Benson, *Chaucer's Drama of Style: Poetic Variety and Contrast in the 'Canterbury Tales'* (Chapel Hill: University of North Carolina Press, 1986), chs. 4 and 5.

42. J. Coleman, *Public Reading and the Reading Public in Late Medieval England and France*, Cambridge Studies in Medieval Literature, 26 (Cambridge: Cambridge University Press, 1996), ch. 6; W. A. Quinn, *Chaucer's 'Rehersynges': The Performability of the 'Legend of Good Women'* (Washington: Catholic University of America Press, 1994), ch. 1; his 'The *Legend of Good Women*: Performance, Performativity, and Presentation', in Collette (ed.), '*Legend of Good Women*', 1–32.

43. A. C. Spearing, *Criticism and Medieval Poetry*, 2nd edn. (London: Arnold, 1972), 16–27; J. A. Burrow, *Medieval Writers and Their Work: Middle English Literature and Its Background 1100–1500* (Oxford: Oxford University Press, 1982), 47–55.

44. S. Kruger, 'Dialogue, Debate, and Dream Vision', in L. Scanlon (ed.), *The Cambridge Companion to Medieval English Literature 1100–1500* (Cambridge: Cambridge University Press, 2009), 71–82; R. P. McGerr, *Chaucer's Open Books: Resistance to Closure in Medieval Discourse* (Gainesville: University Press of Florida, 1998).

45. For commentary on all aspects of *Troilus* see B. Windeatt, *Troilus and Criseyde*, Oxford Guides to Chaucer (Oxford: Clarendon Press, 1992). His edition, *Troilus and Criseyde: 'The Book of Troilus'*, ed. B. A. Windeatt (London: Longman, 1984), prints the text alongside that of Chaucer's sources.

46. H. Cooper, 'The Classical Background', in Ellis (ed.), *Chaucer: An Oxford Guide*, 255–71; C. Baswell, 'England's Antiquities: Middle English Literature and the Classical Past', in P. Brown (ed.), *Companion to Medieval English Literature, and Culture c.1350–c.1500* (Oxford: Blackwell, 2007), 231–46. See also the section on 'Paganism' in Chapter 5, below.

47. S. Federico, *New Troy: Fantasies of Empire in the Late Middle Ages*, Medieval Cultures, 36 (Minneapolis: University of Minnesota Press, 2003); M. Turner, *Chaucerian Conflict: Languages of Antagonism in Late Fourteenth-Century London* (Oxford: Clarendon Press, 2007), chs. 2 and 3; S. N. Brody, 'Making a Play for Criseyde: The Staging of Pandarus's House in Chaucer's *Troilus and Criseyde*', *Speculum* 73 (1998), 115–40.

48. R. Ellis, 'Translation', in Brown (ed.), *Companion to Chaucer*, 443–58; T. W. Machan, 'Chaucer as Translator', in R. Ellis (ed.), *The Medieval Translator: The Theory and Practice of Translation in the Middle Ages* (Cambridge: Brewer, 1989), 55–67.

49. N. Havely, 'The Italian Background', in Ellis (ed.), *Chaucer: An Oxford Guide*, 313–31; D. Wallace, 'Italy', in Brown (ed.), *Companion to Chaucer*, 218–34; his 'Chaucer's Italian Inheritance', in P. Boitani and J. Mann (eds.), *The Cambridge Companion to Chaucer*, 2nd edn. (Cambridge: Cambridge University Press, 2003), 36–57; R. R. Edwards, *Chaucer and Boccaccio: Antiquity and Modernity* (Basingstoke: Palgrave, 2002).

50. C. D. Eckhardt, 'Genre', in Brown (ed.), *Companion to Chaucer*, 180–94; J. Ferster, 'Genre in and of the *Canterbury Tales*', in Saunders (ed.), *Concise Companion*, 179–98.

51. A. Lynch, 'Love in Wartime: *Troilus and Criseyde* as Trojan History', in Saunders (ed.), *Concise Companion*, 113–33; D. Wallace, *Chaucer and the Early Writings of Boccaccio*, Chaucer Studies, 12 (Cambridge: Brewer, 1985), ch. 6.

52. N. Havely, *Chaucer's Boccaccio: Sources of 'Troilus' and the Knight's and Franklin's Tales*, Chaucer Studies, 3 (Cambridge: Brewer, 1980), 49–50.

53. D. R. Carlson, *Chaucer's Jobs* (Houndmills: Palgrave Macmillan, 2004), 44–54; and see the section on 'Love' in Chapter 5.

54. J. Boffey, 'From Manuscript to Modern Text', in Brown (ed.), *Companion to Medieval English Literature*, 107–22; A. S. G. Edwards, 'Manuscripts and Readers', ibid. 93–106; A. S. G. Edwards and D. Pearsall, 'The Manuscripts of the Major English Poetic Texts', in J. Griffiths and D. Pearsall (eds.), *Book Production and Publishing in Britain 1375–1475* (Cambridge: Cambridge University Press, 1989), 257–78; R. F. Green, 'Textual Production and Textual Communities', in Scanlon (ed.), *Cambridge Companion*, 25–36.

55. B. A. Shailor, *The Medieval Book: Illustrated from the Beinecke Rare Book and Manuscript Library*, Medieval Academy Reprints for Teaching, 28 (Toronto: University of Toronto Press in association with the Medieval Academy of America, 1991); C. de Hamel, *Scribes and Illuminators* (London: British Library, 1992).

56. A. Taylor, 'Authors, Scribes, Patrons and Books', in J. Wogan-Browne, N. Watson, A. Taylor, and R. Evans (eds.), *The Idea of the Vernacular: An Anthology of Middle English Literary Theory, 1280–1520* (University Park: Pennsylvania State University Press, 1999), 353–65.

57. J. Boffey and A. S. G. Edwards, 'Manuscripts and Audience', in Saunders (ed.), *Concise Companion*, 34–50.

58. L. R. Mooney, 'Chaucer's Scribe', *Speculum* 81 (2006), 97–138; A. I. Doyle and M. B. Parkes, 'The Production of Copies of the *Canterbury Tales* and the *Confessio Amantis*', in M. B. Parkes and A. G. Watson (eds.), *Medieval Scribes, Manuscripts and Libraries: Essays Presented to Neil Ker* (London: Scolar Press, 1978), 163–210; S. Horobin, 'Adam Pinkhurst, Geoffrey Chaucer, and the Hengwrt Manuscript of the *Canterbury Tales*', *ChauR* 44 (2010), 351–67; A. Gillespie, 'Books', in P. Strohm (ed.), *Middle English*, Oxford Twenty-First Century Approaches to Literature, 1 (Oxford: Oxford University Press, 2007), 86–103.

59. C. P. Christianson, 'Evidence for the Study of London's Late Medieval Manuscript-Book Trade', in Griffiths and Pearsall (eds.), *Book Production*, 87–108.

60. On the development of the stationers' role, see Pearsall, 'Introduction', ibid. 3–5.

61. R. Hanna, *Pursuing History: Middle English Manuscripts and their Texts* (Stanford: Stanford University Press, 1996), ch. 1.

62. J. Boffey and J. J. Thompson, 'Anthologies and Miscellanies: Production and Choice of Text', in Griffiths and Pearsall (eds.), *Book Production*, 279–315; A. S. G. Edwards, 'Manuscripts and Readers', in Brown (ed.), *Companion to Medieval English Literature*, 93–106; J. Boffey, 'From Manuscript to Modern Text', ibid. 107–22.

63. D. Raybin and L. T. Holley (eds.), *Closure in the 'Canterbury Tales': The Role of the Parson's Tale*, Studies in Medieval Culture, 41 (Kalamazoo: Western Michigan University, 2000).

64. R. Hanna, *London Literature, 1300–1380*, Cambridge Studies in Medieval Literature, 57 (Cambridge: Cambridge University Press, 2005); S. Lindenbaum, 'London Texts and Literate Practice', in Wallace (ed.), *Cambridge History*, 284–309; M. Turner, 'Conflict', in Strohm (ed.), *Middle English*, 258–73.

65. D. Pearsall, 'The Alliterative Revival: Origins and Social Backgrounds', in D. Lawton (ed.), *Middle English Alliterative Poetry and Its Literary Background* (Cambridge: Brewer, 1982), 34–53; T. Turville-Petre, *The Alliterative Revival* (Cambridge: Brewer, 1977).

66. M. J. Bennett, in D. Brewer and J. Gibson (eds.), *A Companion to the 'Gawain'-Poet* (Cambridge: Brewer, 1997), 71–90; E. Salter, *Fourteenth-Century English Poetry: Contexts and Readings* (Oxford: Clarendon Press, 1983), ch. 3.

67. J. J. Anderson (ed.), *Sir Gawain and the Green Knight, Pearl, Cleanness, Patience* (London: Dent, 1996); S. Armitage (trans.), *Sir Gawain and the Green Knight* (London: Faber, 2007).

68. C. M. Barron, 'William Langland: A London Poet', in Hanawalt (ed.), *Chaucer's England*, 91–109; D. Pearsall, 'Langland's London', in S. Justice and K. Kerby-Fulton (eds.), *Written Work: Langland, Labor, and Authorship* (Philadelphia: University of Pennsylvania Press, 1997), 185–207; C. E. Bertolet, 'Fraud, Division, and Lies: John Gower and London', in Yeager (ed.), *On John Gower*, 43–70.

69. C. D. Benson, 'London', in Ellis (ed.), *Chaucer: An Oxford Guide*, 66–80; his 'Literary Contests and London Records in the *Canterbury Tales*', in Butterfield (ed.), *Chaucer and the City*, 129–44; H. Fulton, 'Cheapside in the Age of Chaucer', in R. Evans, H. Fulton, and D. Matthews (eds.), *Medieval Cultural Studies: Essays in Honour of Stephen Knight* (Cardiff: University of Wales Press, 2006), 138–51; M. Hanrahan, 'London', in Brown (ed.), *Companion to Chaucer*, 266–80; M. Turner, 'Politics and London Life', in Saunders (ed.), *Concise Companion*, 13–33; her 'Greater London', in Butterfield (ed.), *Chaucer and the City*, 25–40; D. Wallace, 'Chaucer and the Absent City', in Hanawalt (ed.), *Chaucer's England*, 59–90.

70. M. B. Parkes, 'The Literacy of the Laity', in D. Daiches and A. Thorlby (eds.), *Literature and Western Civilization*, vol. 2: *The Medieval World* (London: Aldus, 1973), 555–77; S. Penn, 'Literacy and Literary Production', in Ellis (ed.), *Chaucer: An Oxford Guide*, 113–29; D. Burnley, 'Language', in Brown (ed.), *Companion to Chaucer*, 235–50; C. Cannon, *The Making of Chaucer's English: A Study of Words*, Cambridge Studies in Medieval Literature, 39 (Cambridge: Cambridge University Press, 1998); T. W. Machan, *English in the Middle Ages* (Oxford: Oxford University Press, 2003), chs. 3 and 4; W. Rothwell, 'The Trilingual England of Geoffrey Chaucer', *SAC* 16 (1994), 45–67; W. Scase, 'Re-inventing the Vernacular: Middle English Language and Its Literature', in Scanlon (ed.), *Cambridge Companion*, 11–23; L. Wright, 'The Languages of Medieval Britain', in Brown (ed.), *Companion to Medieval Literature*, 143–58.

71. Hanna, *London Literature*, 15–24.

72. Turville-Petre, *Alliterative Revival*, 1–6 and ch. 2; S. Trigg (ed.), *Wynnere and Wastoure*, EETS OS 297 (1990).

73. Hanna, *London Literature*, ch. 1; R. Beadle, 'Prolegomena to a Literary Geography of Later Medieval Norfolk', in F. Riddy (ed.), *Regionalism in Late Medieval Manuscripts and Texts: Essays Celebrating the Publication of 'A Linguistic Atlas of Late Mediaeval English'*, York Manuscripts Conferences: Proceedings Series, 2 (Cambridge: Brewer, 1991), 89–108; W. Scase, 'The English Background', in Ellis (ed.), *Chaucer: An Oxford Guide*, 272–91; D. V. Smith, 'Chaucer as an English Writer', in S. Lerer (ed.), *The Yale Companion to Chaucer* (New Haven and London: Yale University Press, 2006), 87–121.

74. Hanna, *London Literature*, 9.

CHAPTER 4. Society and Politics

1. A. D. Brown, *Popular Piety in Late Medieval England: The Diocese of Salisbury 1250–1550* (Oxford: Clarendon Press, 1995), chs. 6 and 7.

2. C. Phythian-Adams, *Desolation of a City: Coventry and the Urban Crisis of the Late Middle Ages* (Cambridge: Cambridge University Press, 1979), ch. 7.

3. Pearsall, *Life*, 21–2; Hanna, *London Literature*, 35–6; C. M. Barron, *London in the Later Middle Ages: Government and People 1200–1500*

(Oxford: Oxford University Press, 2004), ch. 9; her 'The Parish Fraternities of Medieval London', in C. M. Barron and C. Harper-Bill (eds.), *The Church in Pre-Reformation Society: Essays in Honour of F. R. H. du Boulay* (Woodbridge: Boydell Press, 1985), 13–37.

4. B. A. Hanawalt and B. R. McCree, 'The Guilds of *Homo Prudens* in Late Medieval England', *Continuity and Change* 7.2 (1992), 163–79.

5. M. Rubin, 'Small Groups: Identity and Solidarity in the Late Middle Ages', in J. Kermode (ed.), *Enterprise and Individuals in Fifteenth-Century England* (Stroud: Sutton, 1991), 132–50.

6. Wallace, *Chaucerian Polity*, chs. 2 and 3; H. Cooper, 'London and Southwark Poetic Companies: "Si tost c'amis" and the *Canterbury Tales*', in Butterfield (ed.), *Chaucer and the City*, 109–25; A. Blamires, *Chaucer, Ethics, and Gender* (Oxford: Oxford University Press, 2006), ch. 1; Turner, *Chaucerian Conflict*, ch. 5.

7. J. M. Ganim, 'Identity and Subjecthood', in Ellis (ed.), *Chaucer: An Oxford Guide*, 224–38; L. Staley, 'Personal Identity', in Brown (ed.), *Companion to Chaucer*, 360–77; Saul, *Richard II*, ch. 17.

8. W. Ginsberg, *The Cast of Character: The Representation of Personality in Ancient and Medieval Literature* (Toronto: University of Toronto Press, 1983), ch. 5; H. M. Leicester, *The Disenchanted Self: Representing the Subject in the 'Canterbury Tales'* (Berkeley: University of California Press, 1990); K. C. Little, *Confession and Resistance: Defining the Self in Late Medieval England* (Notre Dame: University of Notre Dame Press, 2006).

9. L. F. Hodges, *Chaucer and Costume: The Secular Pilgrims in the General Prologue*, Chaucer Studies, 26 (Cambridge: Brewer, 2000), ch. 4; Mann, *Chaucer and Medieval Estates Satire*, 99–103.

10. Patterson, *Chaucer and the Subject of History*, ch. 7.

11. A. Galloway, 'Authority', in Brown (ed.), *Companion to Chaucer*, 23–39.

12. T. Williams, '"T'assaye in thee thy wommanheede": Griselda Chosen, Translated, and Tried', *Studies in the Age of Chaucer* 27 (2005), 93–127.

13. Saul, *Richard II*, 248–56 and ch. 15.

14. Wallace, *Chaucerian Polity*, ch. 10.

15. See the section on 'Social Structures' in Chapter 2, above.

16. N. Saul, 'Chaucer and Gentility', in Hanawalt (ed.), *Chaucer's England*, 41–55; C. Given-Wilson, *The English Nobility in the Late Middle Ages: The Fourteenth-Century Political Community* (London: Routledge & Kegan Paul, 1987), ch. 3.

17. Strohm, *Social Chaucer*, 10–13.

18. E. M. Sembler, 'A Frankeleyn Was In His Compaignye', in Lambdin and Lambdin (eds.), *Chaucer's Pilgrims*, 135–44.

19. S. Shahar, *The Fourth Estate: A History of Women in the Middle Ages*, trans. C. Galai (London: Methuen, 1983); J. M. Bennett, 'England: Women and Gender', in Rigby (ed.), *Companion to Britain*, 87–106; C. M. Meale, 'Women's Voices and Roles', in Brown (ed.), *Companion to Medieval English Literature*, 74–90.

20. Saul, *Richard II*, 333; C. M. Barron, 'The "Golden Age" of Women in Medieval London', *Reading Medieval Studies* 15: *Medieval Women in Southern England* (1989), 35–58.
21. Cf. CIT 836.
22. A. Blamires with K. Pratt and C. W. Marx (eds.), *Woman Defamed and Woman Defended: An Anthology of Medieval Texts* (Oxford: Clarendon Press, 1992); A. Blamires, *The Case for Women in Medieval Culture* (Oxford: Clarendon Press, 1997).
23. R. Evans and L. Johnson (eds.), *Feminist Readings in Middle English Literature: The Wife of Bath and All Her Sect* (London: Methuen, 1994); A. Blamires, 'Sexuality', in Ellis (ed.), *Chaucer: An Oxford Guide*, 208–23; N. Hallett, 'Women', in Brown (ed.), *Companion to Chaucer*, 480–94; Rigby, *Chaucer in Context*, ch. 4; J. Mann, *Feminizing Chaucer*, 2nd edn., Chaucer Studies, 30 (Cambridge: Brewer, 2002); A. J. Weisl, *Conquering the Reign of Femeny: Gender and Genre in Chaucer's Romance*, Chaucer Studies, 22 (Cambridge: Brewer, 1995).
24. Patterson, *Chaucer and the Subject of History*, ch. 6; E. Scala, 'Desire in the *Canterbury Tales*: Sovereignty and Mastery Between the Wife and the Clerk', *SAC* 31 (2009), 81–124.
25. R. W. Kaeuper and M. Bohna, 'War and Chivalry', in Brown (ed.), *Companion to Medieval English Literature*, 273–91.
26. P. Coss, *The Knight in Medieval England 1000–1400* (Stroud: Sutton, 1993); J. L. Gillespie, 'Richard II: Chivalry and Kingship', in J. L. Gillespie (ed.), *The Age of Richard II* (Stroud: Sutton, 1997), 115–38; M. H. Keen, *Chivalry* (New Haven: Yale University Press, 1984); his 'Chivalry and the Aristocracy', in M. Jones (ed.), *The New Cambridge Medieval History*, vol. 6: *c.1300–c.1415* (Cambridge: Cambridge University Press, 2000), 209–21; McKisack, *Fourteenth Century*, ch. 9; J. Vale, *Edward III and Chivalry: Chivalric Society and Its Context 1270–1350* (Woodbridge: Boydell Press, 1982).
27. M. Sherman, 'Chivalry', in Ellis (ed.), *Chaucer: An Oxford Guide*, 97–112; D. Brewer, 'Chivalry', in Brown (ed.), *Companion to Chaucer*, 58–74; M. H. Keen, 'Chaucer and Chivalry Re-visited', in M. Strickland (ed.), *Armies, Chivalry and Warfare in Medieval Britain and France: Proceedings of the 1995 Harlaxton Symposium*, Harlaxton Medieval Studies, NS 7 (Stamford: Watkins, 1998), 1–12; Patterson, *Chaucer and the Subject of History*, ch. 3.
28. Froissart, *Chronicles*, trans. Brereton, 131–2, 143–4, 167–9.
29. Clanvowe, *Works*, ed. Scattergood.
30. Keen, *Chivalry*, 233–7.
31. Olson, *Canterbury Tales and the Good Society*, 57–9; Saul, *Richard II*, 305–6.
32. Ibid. 14–15.
33. Ibid. 112–17.
34. Ibid. 208–9, 253.
35. Ibid. 112, 129–30, 133, 158.
36. Ibid. 356–8.
37. J. Barnie, *War in Medieval Society: Social Values and the Hundred Years War 1337–99* (London: Weidenfeld & Nicolson, 1974), ch. 5; L. S. Johnson,

'Inverse Counsel: Contexts for the *Melibee*', *Studies in Philology* 87 (1990), 137–55; L. Staley, 'Chaucer and the Postures of Sanctity', in D. Aers and L. Staley, *The Powers of the Holy: Religion, Politics, and Gender in Late Medieval English Culture* (University Park: Pennsylvania State University Press, 1996), 179–259; Turner, *Chaucerian Conflict*, ch. 6; R. F. Yeager, '*Pax Poetica*: On the Pacifism of Chaucer and Gower', *SAC* 9 (1987), 97–121; J. Ferster, 'Chaucer's Tale of Melibee: Contradictions and Context', in Baker (ed.), *Inscribing the Hundred Years' War*, 73–89. On mirrors for princes see the section on that topic in Chapter 3, above.

38. Saul, *Richard II*, ch. 10, on the search for peace.
39. S. Crane, *The Performance of Self: Ritual, Clothing, and Identity During the Hundred Years War* (Philadelphia: University of Pennsylvania Press, 2002), ch. 1.

CHAPTER 5. Intellectual Ideas

1. G. Shepherd, 'Religion and Philosophy in Chaucer', in D. Brewer (ed.), *Geoffrey Chaucer*, Writers and their Background (London: Bell, 1974), 262–89; G. Leff, *Medieval Thought: St Augustine to Ockham* (Harmondsworth: Penguin, 1958).
2. Wyclif, *De veritate sacre scripture*, quoted by Shepherd, 'Religion and Philosophy', 286.
3. Introduction to A. Hudson (ed.), *Selections from English Wycliffite Writings* (Cambridge: Cambridge University Press, 1978) and her *The Premature Reformation: Wycliffite Texts and Lollard History* (Oxford: Clarendon Press, 1988).
4. Keen, *England*, ch. 10; Saul, *Richard II*, ch. 13.
5. S. Justice, 'Lollardy', in Wallace (ed.), *Cambridge History*, 662–89; M. Aston, *Lollards and Reformers: Images and Literacy in Late Medieval Religion* (London: Hambledon Press, 1984).
6. Hudson (ed.), *Selections*, 24–9.
7. Little, *Confession and Resistance*, ch. 5.
8. A. Blamires, 'The Wife of Bath and Lollardy', *Medium Aevum* 58 (1989), 224–42; A. J. Fletcher, 'Chaucer the Heretic', *SAC* 25 (2003), 53–121; W. Kamowski, 'Chaucer and Wyclif: God's Miracles Against the Clergy's Magic', *ChauR* 37 (2002), 5–25; P. Knapp, 'The Words of the Parson's "Vertuous Sentence"', in Raybin and Holley (eds.), *Closure in the 'Canterbury Tales*', 95–113; F. McCormack, *Chaucer and the Culture of Dissent: The Lollard Context and Subtext of the Parson's Tale* (Dublin: Four Courts Press, 2007); A. J. Minnis, *Fallible Authors: Chaucer's Pardoner and Wife of Bath* (Philadelphia: University of Pennsylvania Press, 2008); N. Pattwell, '"The Venym of Symony": The Debate on the Eucharist in the Late Fourteenth Century and the Pardoner's Prologue and Tale', in K. Cawsey, K. and J. Harris (eds.), *Transmission and Transformation in the Middle Ages: Texts and Contexts* (Dublin: Four Courts Press, 2007), 115–30; H. Phillips, 'Register, Politics, and the *Legend of Good Women*', *ChauR* 37 (2002),

101–28; D. G. Pitard, 'Sowing Difficulty: *The Parson's Tale*, Vernacular Commentary, and the Nature of Chaucerian Dissent', *SAC* 26 (2004), 299–330; P. Strohm, *Theory and the Premodern Text*, Medieval Cultures, 26 (Minneapolis: University of Minnesota Press, 2000), ch. 11.

9. S. A. Legassie, 'Chaucer's Pardoner and Host—On the Road, in the Alehouse', *ChauR* 29 (2007), 183–223; Minnis, *Fallible Authors*, ch. 2; C. M. Waters, *Angels and Earthly Creatures: Preaching, Performance, and Gender in the Later Middle Ages* (Philadelphia: University of Pennsylvania Press, 2004), ch. 2.
10. Brewer (ed.), *Chaucer: The Critical Heritage*, i. 40–4.
11. B. O'Donoghue, 'Love and Marriage', in Ellis (ed.), *Chaucer: An Oxford Guide*, 239–52; H. Phillips, 'Love', in Brown (ed.), *Companion to Chaucer*, 281–95; C. Saunders, 'Love and the Making of the Self: *Troilus and Criseyde*', in Saunders (ed.), *Concise Companion*, 134–55.
12. R. Boase, *The Origin and Meaning of Courtly Love: A Critical Study of European Scholarship* (Manchester: Manchester University Press, 1977); S. Gilles, 'Love and Disease in Chaucer's *Troilus and Criseyde*', *SAC* 25 (2003), 157–97; M. F. Wack, *Lovesickness in the Middle Ages: The 'Viaticum' and Its Commentaries* (Philadelphia: University of Pennsylvania Press, 1990).
13. M. Miller, *Philosophical Chaucer: Love, Sex, and Agency in the 'Canterbury Tales'* (Cambridge: Cambridge University Press, 2004); B. Windeatt, 'Love', in Brown (ed.), *Companion to Medieval English Literature*, 322–38.
14. J. Marenbon, *Boethius* (Oxford: Oxford University Press, 2003).
15. J. M. Fyler, 'Pagan Survivals', in Brown (ed.), *Companion to Chaucer*, 349–59; J. P. McCall, *Chaucer among the Gods: The Poetics of Classical Myth* (University Park: Pennsylvania State University Press, 1979); A. J. Minnis, *Chaucer and Pagan Antiquity*, Chaucer Studies, 8 (Cambridge: Brewer, 1982).
16. J. A. Mitchell, *Ethics and Eventfulness in Middle English Literature* (New York: Palgrave Macmillan, 2009).
17. R. Utz, 'Philosophy', in Ellis (ed.), *Chaucer: An Oxford Guide*, 158–73; W. H. Watts, 'Chaucer's Clerks and the Value of Philosophy', in H. Keiper, C. Bode, and R. J. Utz (eds.), *Nominalism and Literary Discourse: New Perspectives*, Critical Studies, 10 (Amsterdam: Rotopi, 1997), 145–55.
18. E. W. Dolnikowski, *Thomas Bradwardine: A View of Time and a Vision of Eternity in Fourteenth-Century Thought*, Studies in the History of Christian Thought, 65 (Leiden: Brill, 1995); G. Leff, *Bradwardine and the Pelagians: A Study of His 'De Causa Dei' and Its Opponents*, Cambridge Studies in Medieval Life and Thought, NS 5 (Cambridge: Cambridge University Press, 1957).

CHAPTER 6. Science and Technology

1. P. C. Ingham, 'Litte Nothings: *The Squire's Tale* and the Ambition of Gadgets', *SAC* 31 (2009), 53–80; S. Lightsey, 'Chaucer's Secular Marvels and the Medieval Economy of Wonder', *SAC* 23 (2001), 289–316.
2. W. C. Curry, *Chaucer and the Mediaeval Sciences*, 2nd edn. (New York: Barnes & Noble, 1960); M. Manzalaoui, 'Chaucer and Science', in Brewer (ed.),

Geoffrey Chaucer, 224–61; I. Taavitsainen, 'Science', in Brown (ed.), *Companion to Chaucer*, 378–96; J. A. Tasioulas, 'Science', in Ellis (ed.), *Chaucer: An Oxford Guide*, 175–89; L. E. Voigts, 'Scientific and Medical Books', in Griffiths and Pearsall (eds.), *Book Production and Publishing*, 345–402.

3. L. F. Sandler, *The Psalter of Robert de Lisle in the British Library* (London: Harvey Miller with Oxford University Press, 1983), plate 2.

4. J. D. North, *Chaucer's Universe* (Oxford: Clarendon Press, 1988).

5. W. H. Stahl (trans.), *Macrobius: Commentary on the Dream of Scipio*, Records of Civilization, Sources and Studies, 48 (New York: Columbia University Press, 1952), 72, 154.

6. Dante Aligheri, *The Divine Comedy*, trans. J. D. Sinclair (Oxford: Oxford University Press, 1961), vol. 3: *Paradiso*.

7. G. Chaucer, *A Treatise on the Astrolabe*, ed. S. Eisner, *Variorum Edition of the Works of Geoffrey Chaucer*, vol. 6: *The Prose Treatises*, pt. 1 (Norman: University of Oklahoma Press, 2002); M. Osborn, *Time and the Astrolabe in 'The Canterbury Tales'*, Series for Science and Culture, 5 (Norman: University of Oklahoma Press, 2002).

8. C. Humphrey, 'Time and Urban Culture in Late Medieval England', in C. Humphrey and W. M. Ormrod (eds.), *Time in the Medieval World* (York: York Medieval Press, 2001), 105–17.

9. H. M. Carey, *Courting Disaster: Astrology at the English Court and University in the Later Middle Ages* (Houndmills: Macmillan, 1992), ch. 5.

10. L. R. Mooney, 'Chaucer and Interest in Astronomy at the Court of Richard II', in G. Lester (ed.), *Chaucer in Perspective: Middle English Essays in Honour of Norman Blake* (Sheffield: Sheffield Academic Press, 1999), 139–60.

11. M. C. Seymour et al. (eds.), *On the Properties of Things: John Trevisa's Translation of 'Bartholomaeus Anglicus De Proprietatibus Rerum'*, 3 vols. (Oxford: Clarendon Press, 1975–88), vol. 1, p. 470.

12. Ibid. 474. L. E. Voigts, 'Bodies', in Brown (ed.), *Companion to Chaucer*, 40–57; S. Macdougall, 'Health, Diet, Medicine and the Plague', in C. Given-Wilson (ed.), *An Illustrated History of Late Medieval England* (Manchester: Manchester University Press, 1996), 82–99.

13. R. French, 'Astrology in Medieval Practice', in L. García-Ballester, R. French, J. Arrizabalaga, and A. Cunningham (eds.), *Practical Medicine from Salerno to the Black Death* (Cambridge: Cambridge University Press, 1994), 30–59; F. Getz, *Medicine in the English Middle Ages* (Princeton: Princeton University Press, 1998); N. Siraisi, *Medieval and Early Renaissance Medicine: An Introduction to Knowledge and Practice* (Chicago: University of Chicago Press, 1990).

14. V. A. Kolve, *Chaucer and the Imagery of Narrative: The First Five Canterbury Tales* (London: Arnold, 1984), ch. 1; M. W. Bundy, *The Theory of Imagination in Classical and Mediaeval Thought*, University of Illinois Studies in Literature and Language, 12 (Urbana: University of Illinois, 1928; rpt. 1978); E. R. Harvey, *The Inward Wits: Psychological Theory in the Middle Ages and the Renaissance*, Warburg Institute Surveys, 6 (London: Warburg Institute, 1975).

15. Seymour et al. (eds.), *On the Properties of Things*, vol. 1, p. 98.

16. Geoffrey of Vinsauf, *Poetria Nova*, trans. N. F. Nims (Toronto: Pontifical Institute of Medieval Studies, 1967), 89.

17. M. Carruthers, *The Book of Memory: A Study of Memory in Medieval Culture*, Cambridge Studies in Medieval Literature, 10 (Cambridge: Cambridge University Press, 1990); M. Carruthers and J. M. Ziolkowski (eds.), *The Medieval Craft of Memory: An Anthology of Texts and Pictures* (Philadelphia: University of Pennsylvania Press, 2002).

18. Brewer (ed.), *Chaucer: The Critical Heritage*, i. 138–9.

19. P. Brown, *Chaucer and the Making of Optical Space* (Oxford: Lang, 2007).

20. Alhacen, *Alhacen's Theory of Visual Perception: The First Three Books of Alhacen's De Aspectibus*, ed. and trans. A. M. Smith, 2 vols., Transactions of the American Philosophical Society, 91, pts. 4 and 5 (Philadelphia: American Philosophical Society, 2001), vol. 2, p. 526.

21. Ibid. 597.

22. A. C. Crombie, *Robert Grosseteste and the Origins of Experimental Science 1100–1700* (Oxford: Clarendon Press, 1953).

23. J. Pecham, *John Pecham and the Science of Optics: Perspectiva Communis*, ed. and trans. D. C. Lindberg (Madison: University of Wisconsin Press, 1970), 61.

24. D. C. Lindberg, *Theories of Vision from Al-Kindi to Kepler* (Chicago: University of Chicago Press, 1976).

CHAPTER 7. New Contexts

1. J. J. Thompson, 'Reception: Fifteenth to Seventeenth Centuries', in Ellis (ed.), *Chaucer: An Oxford Guide*, 497–511; D. Matthews, 'Reception: Eighteenth and Nineteenth Centuries', ibid. 512–27; E. Robertson, 'Modern Chaucer Criticism', ibid. 355–68; S. Trigg, 'Reception: Twentieth and Twenty-First Centuries', ibid. 528–43; her 'Chaucer's Influence and Reception', in Lerer (ed.), *Yale Companion*, 297–323.

2. S. Ellis, *Geoffrey Chaucer* (Plymouth: Northcote House with the British Council, 1996), 62–4.

3. S. Ellis, *Chaucer at Large*, Medieval Cultures, 24 (Minneapolis: University of Minnesota Press, 2000); S. Trigg, *Congenial Souls: Reading Chaucer from Medieval to Postmodern*, Medieval Cultures, 30 (Minneapolis: University of Minnesota Press, 2002).

4. G. Ashton, 'Feminisms', in Ellis (ed.), *Chaucer: An Oxford Guide*, 369–83; S. Federico, 'New Historicism', ibid. 16–31; P. C. Ingham, 'Psychoanalytic Criticism', ibid. 463–78; B. Windeatt, 'Postmodernism', ibid. 400–15.

5. J. J. Cohen, 'Postcolonialism', in Ellis (ed.), *Chaucer: An Oxford Guide*, 448–62; G. Heng, *Empire of Magic: Medieval Romance and the Politics of Cultural Fantasy* (New York: Columbia University Press, 2003).

6. G. Burger, 'Queer Theory', in Ellis (ed.), *Chaucer: An Oxford Guide*, 432–47; T. Pugh, 'Queer Pandarus? Silence and Sexual Ambiguity in Chaucer's *Troilus and Criseyde*', *Philological Quarterly* 80 (2001), 17–35;

R. E. Zeikowitz, *Homoeroticism and Chivalry: Discourses of Male Same-Sex Desire in the Fourteenth Century* (New York: Palgrave Macmillan, 2003).

7. S. Trigg, 'Walking through Cathedrals: Scholars, Pilgrims, and Medieval Tourists', *New Medieval Literatures* 7 (2005), 9–33.

8. H. Crocker, 'Chaucer's Man Show: Anachronistic Authority in Brian Helgeland's *A Knight's Tale*', in L. T. Ramey and T. Pugh (eds.), *Race, Class, and Gender in 'Medieval' Cinema* (New York: Palgrave Macmillan, 2007), 183–97; N. A. Haydock, *Movie Medievalism: The Imaginary Middle Ages* (Jefferson: McFarland, 2008), ch. 3.

9. Ibid., ch. 1; A. Bernau and B. Bildhauer (eds.), *Medieval Film* (Manchester: Manchester University Press, 2009); Ramey and Pugh (eds.), *Race, Class, and Gender*.

10. A. Aldgate and J. Richards, *Best of British: Cinema and Society from 1930 to the Present*, 2nd edn. (London: Tauris, 1999), ch. 4; I. Christie, ' "History is Now and England": *A Canterbury Tale* in Its Contexts', in I. Christie and A. Moor (eds.), *The Cinema of Michael Powell: International Perspectives on an English Film-Maker* (London: British Film Institute, 2005), 75–93; S. Freer, 'The Mythical Method: Eliot's "The Waste Land" and *A Canterbury Tale* (1944)', *Historical Journal of Film, Radio and Television* 27 (2007), 357–70; A. Moor, *Powell and Pressburger: A Cinema of Magic Spaces* (London: Tauris, 2005), ch. 3.

11. P. Tritton, *A Canterbury Tale: Memories of a Classic Wartime Movie*, 2nd edn. (Canterbury: Parkers, 2006).

12. G. K. Chesterton, *Chaucer*, 2nd edn. (London: Faber & Faber, 1949), 214–16.

13. C. Churchill, *Top Girls*, with commentary by B. Naismith and notes by N. Worrall (London: Methuen, 1991).

14. J. Hodge, *Shallow Grave* (London: Faber & Faber, 1996).

15. K. J. Harty, 'Chaucer in Performance', in Ellis (ed.), *Chaucer: An Oxford Guide*, 560–75.

16. My transcription. For the script see P. P. Pasolini, *Trilogia della Vita: Decameron, I Racconti di Canterbury, Il Fiore delle Mille e Una Notte*, ed. G. Gattei, Dal Soggetto al Film: Serie Retrospettiva, 4 (Bologna: Cappelli, 1975).

17. Quoted from Ellis, *Chaucer at Large*, 191 n. 10.

18. A. Blandeau, *Pasolini, Chaucer and Boccaccio: Two Medieval Texts and Their Translation to Film* (Jefferson: McFarland, 2006).

19. Review by P. J. Smith and G. Walker of a performance of *The Canterbury Tales*, adapted by Mike Poulton in two parts and directed by Gregory Doran, Rebecca Catward, and Jonathan Munby for the Royal Shakespeare Company, at The Swan Theatre, Stratford-upon-Avon, 19 and 21 December 2005, Centre Stalls, in *Cahiers Elisabéthains* 69 (2006), 53–7.

FURTHER READING

A. CRITICAL COMMENTARY

Boitani, P., and Mann, J. (eds.), *The Cambridge Companion to Chaucer*, 2nd edn. (Cambridge: Cambridge University Press, 2003).

Brewer, D., *A New Introduction to Chaucer*, 2nd edn. (London: Longman, 1998).

Brown, P. (ed.), *A Companion to Chaucer* (Oxford: Blackwell, 2000).

——— (ed.), *A Companion to Medieval English Literature and Culture c.1350–c.1500* (Oxford: Blackwell, 2007).

Cooper, H., *The Canterbury Tales*, Oxford Guides to Chaucer (Oxford: Clarendon Press, 1989).

Ellis, S. (ed.), *Chaucer: An Oxford Guide* (Oxford: Oxford University Press, 2005).

Gray, D. (ed.), *The Oxford Companion to Chaucer* (Oxford: Oxford University Press, 2003).

Lerer, S. (ed.), *The Yale Companion to Chaucer* (New Haven and London: Yale University Press, 2006).

Minnis, A. J., with Scattergood, V. J., and Smith, J. J., *The Shorter Poems*, Oxford Guides to Chaucer (Oxford: Clarendon Press, 1995).

Saunders, C. (ed.), *A Concise Companion to Chaucer* (Oxford: Blackwell, 2006).

Scanlon, L. (ed.), *The Cambridge Companion to Medieval English Literature 1100–1500* (Cambridge: Cambridge University Press, 2009).

Strohm, P. (ed.), *Middle English*, Oxford Twenty-First Century Approaches to Literature, 1 (Oxford: Oxford University Press, 2007).

Wallace, D. (ed.), *The Cambridge History of Medieval English Literature* (Cambridge: Cambridge University Press, 1999).

Windeatt, B., *Troilus and Criseyde*, Oxford Guides to Chaucer (Oxford: Clarendon Press, 1992).

B. BIOGRAPHY

Ackroyd, P., *Chaucer* (London: Chatto & Windus, 2004).

Boffey, J., 'Middle English Lives', in Wallace (ed.), *Cambridge History*, 610–34.

Cannon, C., 'The Lives of Geoffrey Chaucer', in Lerer (ed.), *Yale Companion*, 31–54.

Carlson, D. R., *Chaucer's Jobs* (Houndmills: Palgrave Macmillan, 2004).

Crow, M. M., and Olson, C. C. (eds.), *Chaucer Life-Records* (Oxford: Clarendon Press, 1966).

de Looze, L., *Pseudo-Autobiography in the Fourteenth Century: Juan Ruiz, Guillaume de Machaut, Jean Froissart, and Geoffrey Chaucer* (Gainesville: University of Florida Press, 1997).

Dillon, J., *Geoffrey Chaucer* (Houndmills: Macmillan, 1993).

—— 'Life Histories', in Brown (ed.), *Companion to Chaucer*, 251–65.

du Boulay, F. R. H., 'Historical Chaucer', in D. Brewer (ed.), *Geoffrey Chaucer*, Writers and Their Background (London: Bell, 1974), 33–57.

Evans, R., 'Chaucer's Life', in Ellis (ed.), *Chaucer: An Oxford Guide*, 9–25.

Pearsall, D., *The Life of Geoffrey Chaucer: A Critical Biography* (Oxford: Blackwell, 1992).

Strohm, P., *Social Chaucer* (Cambridge, Mass.: Harvard University Press, 1989).

C. HISTORICAL SOURCES AND STUDIES

Barber, R., *Edward, Prince of Wales and Aquitaine: A Biography of the Black Prince* (Woodbridge: Boydell Press, 1978).

—— (ed. and trans.), *The Life and Campaigns of the Black Prince: From Contemporary Letters, Diaries and Chronicles, including Chandos Herald's Life of the Black Prince*, repr. with new illus. (Woodbridge: Boydell Press, 1986).

Barnie, J., *War in Medieval Society: Social Values and the Hundred Years War 1337–99* (London: Weidenfeld & Nicolson, 1974).

Bennett, M. J., *Richard II and the Revolution of 1399* (Stroud: Sutton, 1999).

Brown, A. D., *Church and Society in England, 1000–1500* (Houndmills: Palgrave Macmillan, 2003).

—— *Popular Piety in Late Medieval England: The Diocese of Salisbury 1250–1550* (Oxford: Clarendon Press, 1995).

Dobson, R. B. (ed.), *The Peasants' Revolt of 1381*, 2nd edn. (London and Basingstoke: Macmillan, 1983).

du Boulay, F. R. H., and Barron, C. M. (eds.), *The Reign of Richard II: Essays in Honour of May McKisack* (London: University of London Athlone Press, 1971).

Froissart, J., *Chronicles*, trans. Geoffrey Brereton, rev. edn. (Harmondsworth: Penguin, 1978).

Given-Wilson, C. (ed. and trans.), *Chronicles of the Revolution 1397–1400: The Reign of Richard II* (Manchester: Manchester University Press, 1993).

—— (ed.), *An Illustrated History of Late Medieval England* (Manchester: Manchester University Press, 1996).

Goodman, A., *John of Gaunt: The Exercise of Princely Power in Fourteenth-Century Europe* (Harlow: Longman, 1992).

—— and Gillespie, J. (eds.), *Richard II: The Art of Kingship* (Oxford: Clarendon Press, 1999).

Green, D., *The Black Prince* (Stroud: History Press, 2001).

Grigsby, B. L., *Pestilence in Medieval and Early Modern English Literature*, Studies in Medieval History and Culture, 23 (London: Routledge, 2004).

Harvey, B., 'Introduction: The "Crisis" of the Early Fourteenth Century', in B. M. S. Campbell (ed.), *Before the Black Death: Studies in the 'Crisis' of the Early Fourteenth Century* (Manchester: Manchester University Press, 1991), 1–24.

Hatcher, J., 'England in the Aftermath of the Black Death', *Past and Present* 144 (1994), 3–35.

Hilton, R., *Bond Men Made Free: Medieval Peasant Movements and the English Rising of 1381* (London: Methuen, 1977).

—— and Aston, T. H. (eds.), *The English Rising of 1381* (Cambridge: Cambridge University Press, 1984).

Horrox, R. (ed. and trans.), *The Black Death* (Manchester and New York: Manchester University Press, 1994).

Hudson, A., *The Premature Reformation: Wycliffite Texts and Lollard History* (Oxford: Clarendon Press, 1988).

Keen, M. H., *England in the Later Middle Ages: A Political History*, 2nd edn. (London: Routledge, 2003).

Ormrod, W. M., *The Reign of Edward III: Crown and Political Society in England 1327–1377* (New Haven: Yale University Press, 1990).

Pantin, W. A., *The English Church in the Fourteenth Century* (Cambridge: Cambridge University Press, 1954).

Platt, C., *King Death: The Black Death and Its Aftermath in Late-Medieval England* (London: Routledge, 1996).

Rigby, S. H. (ed.), *A Companion to Britain in the Later Middle Ages* (Oxford: Blackwell with The Historical Association, 2003).

Rogers, C. J. (ed.), *The Wars of Edward III: Sources and Interpretations* (Woodbridge: Boydell Press, 1999).

Rubin, M., *The Hollow Crown: A History of Britain in the Late Middle Ages* (London: Penguin Books, 2005).

Saul, N., *Richard II* (New Haven: Yale University Press, 1997).

Shinners, J. (ed.), *Medieval Popular Religion, 1000–1500* (Peterborough, Ont.: Broadview Press, 1997).

—— and Dohar, W. J. (eds.), *Pastors and the Care of Souls in Medieval England*, Notre Dame Texts in Medieval Culture, 4 (Notre Dame: University of Notre Dame Press, 1998).

Sumption, J., *The Hundred Years War*, vol. 1: *Trial by Battle* (London: Faber, 1990), vol. 2: *Trial by Fire* (London: Faber, 1999), and vol. 3: *Divided Houses* (London: Faber, 2009).

Swanson, R. N. (trans.), *Catholic England: Faith, Religion and Observance before the Reformation* (Manchester: Manchester University Press, 1993).

—— *Church and Society in Late Medieval England* (Oxford: Blackwell, 1989).

D. LITERATURE IN CONTEXT

Aers, D., *Faith, Ethics and Church: Writing in England, 1360–1409* (Cambridge: Brewer, 2000).

—— 'Representations of the "Third Estate": Social Conflict and its Milieu around 1381', *Southern Review* 16 (1983), 335–49.

—— '*Vox Populi* and the Literature of 1381', in Wallace (ed.), *Cambridge History*, 432–53.

Barr, H., *Socioliterary Practice in Late Medieval England* (Oxford: Oxford University Press, 2001).

Baswell, C., 'Aeneas in 1381', *New Medieval Literatures* 5 (2002), 7–58.

Blamires, A., 'Crisis and Dissent', in Brown (ed.), *Companion to Chaucer*, 133–48.

Brown, P., and Butcher, A., *The Age of Saturn: Literature and History in the 'Canterbury Tales'* (Oxford: Blackwell, 1991).

Cole, A., *Literature and Heresy in the Age of Chaucer* (Cambridge: Cambridge University Press, 2008).

Crane, S., 'The Writing Lesson of 1381', in B. A. Hanawalt (ed.), *Chaucer's England: Literature in Historical Context*, Medieval Studies at Minnesota, 4 (Minneapolis: University of Minnesota Press, 1992), 201–21.

Giancarlo, M., *Parliament and Literature in Late Medieval England* (Cambridge: Cambridge University Press, 2007).

Hanawalt, B. A. (ed.), *Chaucer's England: Literature in Historical Context*, Medieval Studies at Minnesota, 4 (Minneapolis: University of Minnesota Press, 1992).

Hirsh, J. C., 'Christianity and the Church', in Saunders (ed.), *Concise Companion*, 241–60.

Hudson, A., '*Piers Plowman* and the Peasants' Revolt: A Problem Revisited', *Yearbook of Langland Studies* 8 (1994), 85–106.

Jewell, H., '*Piers Plowman*—A Poem of Crisis: An Analysis of Political Instability in Langland's England', in J. Taylor and W. Childs (eds.), *Politics and Crisis in Fourteenth-Century England* (Gloucester: Sutton, 1990), 59–80.

Justice, S., *Writing and Rebellion: England in 1381*, The New Historicism, 27 (Berkeley: University of California Press, 1994).

Muscatine, C., *Poetry and Crisis in the Age of Chaucer*, University of Notre Dame, Ward-Phillips Lectures in English Language and Literature, 4 (Notre Dame: University of Notre Dame Press, 1972), ch. 1.

Olson, P. A., *The Canterbury Tales and the Good Society* (Princeton: Princeton University Press, 1986).

Patterson, L., *Chaucer and the Subject of History* (London: Routledge, 1991).

Rhodes, J., 'Religion', in Ellis (ed.), *Chaucer: An Oxford Guide*, 81–96.

Rigby, S. H., *Chaucer in Context: Society, Allegory and Gender* (Manchester: Manchester University Press, 1996).

Salisbury, E., 'Violence and the Sacrificial Poet: Gower, the *Vox*, and the Critics', in R. F. Yeager (ed.), *On John Gower: Essays at the Millennium*, Studies in Medieval Culture, 46 (Kalamazoo: Medieval Institute Publications, 2007), 124–43.

Strohm, P., *Hochon's Arrow: The Social Imagination of Fourteenth-Century Texts* (Princeton: Princeton University Press, 1992).

Turner, M., *Chaucerian Conflict: Languages of Antagonism in Late Fourteenth-Century London* (Oxford: Clarendon Press, 2007).

Wallace, D., *Chaucerian Polity: Absolutist Lineages and Associational Forms in England and Italy* (Stanford: Stanford University Press, 1997).

Watson, N., 'Christian Ideologies', in Brown (ed.), *Companion to Chaucer*, 75–89.

WEBSITES

http://academics.vmi.edu/english/chaucer.html
   Baragona's Chaucer Page. Link-based annotated directory of useful sites bibliographical, literary, cultural, including online texts.
http://uchaucer.utsa.edu
   The Chaucer Bibliography Online. Searchable database of scholarly publications.
http://www.unc.edu/depts/chaucer
   The Chaucer MetaPage. A portal providing access to a wide range of sites and resources.
http://academics.vmi.edu/english/audio/Audio_Index.html
   The Criyng and the Soun. Audio files of selected readings.
http://www.courses.fas.harvard.edu/~chaucer
   The Harvard Chaucer Page. Includes sound files on Chaucer's pronunciation and surveys of contextual topics.

VERSIONS OF THE *CANTERBURY TALES* FOR FILM AND TELEVISION

The Canterbury Tales (TV series, 1969; directors M. Bakewell and R. Graham, writers M. Starkie and N. Coghill)

I racconti di Canterbury (feature film, director P. P. Pasolini, 1972)

Trinity Tales (TV series, 1975; directors T. de Vere Cole and Roger Tucker; writer Alan Plater)

The Canterbury Tales (TV series in animation, 1998; series director and writer J. Myerson)

The Canterbury Tales (TV series, 2003; directors J. McKay, A. de Emmony, M. Munden, J. Jarrold; writers T. Marchant, P. Bowker, T. Grounds, S. Wainwright, O. Hetreed, A. Luthra)

INDEX

MORE ABOUT | **OXFORD WORLD'S CLASSICS**

The Oxford World's Classics Website

www.oup.com/uk/worldsclassics

- Information about new titles
- Explore the full range of Oxford World's Classics
- Links to other literary sites and the main OUP webpage
- Imaginative competitions, with bookish prizes
- Articles by editors
- Extracts from Introductions
- Special information for teachers and lecturers

www.oup.com/uk/worldsclassics

American Literature

Authors in Context

British and Irish Literature

Children's Literature

Classics and Ancient Literature

Colonial Literature

Eastern Literature

European Literature

History

Medieval Literature

Oxford English Drama

Poetry

Philosophy

Politics

Religion

The Oxford Shakespeare

A complete list of Oxford World's Classics, including Authors in Context, Oxford English Drama, and the Oxford Shakespeare, is available in the UK from the Marketing Services Department, Oxford University Press, Great Clarendon Street, Oxford OX2 6DP, or visit the website at www.oup.com/uk/worldsclassics.

In the USA, visit www.oup.com/us/owc for a complete title list.

Oxford World's Classics are available from all good bookshops. In case of difficulty, customers in the UK should contact Oxford University Press Bookshop, 116 High Street, Oxford OX1 4BR.